THE GOSPEL-CENTERED EVANGELICALISM
OF ALEXANDER CARSON

The Gospel-Centered Evangelicalism
of Alexander Carson

JOHN GILL

foreword by Ian Hugh Clary

☙PICKWICK *Publications* · Eugene, Oregon

THE GOSPEL-CENTERED EVANGELICALISM OF ALEXANDER CARSON

Monographs in Baptist History 34

Copyright © 2025 John Gill. All rights reserved. Except for brief quotations in critical publications or reviews, no part of this book may be reproduced in any manner without prior written permission from the publisher. Write: Permissions, Wipf and Stock Publishers, 199 W. 8th Ave., Suite 3, Eugene, OR 97401.

Pickwick Publications
An Imprint of Wipf and Stock Publishers
199 W. 8th Ave., Suite 3
Eugene, OR 97401

www.wipfandstock.com

PAPERBACK ISBN: 979-8-3852-2684-9
HARDCOVER ISBN: 979-8-3852-2685-6
EBOOK ISBN: 979-8-3852-2686-3

Cataloguing-in-Publication data:

Names: Gill, John J., author. | Clary, Ian Hugh, foreword.

Title: The Gospel-centered evangelicalism of Alexander Carson / John Gill.

Description: Eugene, OR: Pickwick Publications, 2025 | Monographs in Baptist History 34 | Includes bibliographical references.

Identifiers: ISBN 979-8-3852-2684-9 (paperback) | ISBN 979-8-3852-2685-6 (hardcover) | ISBN 979-8-3852-2686-3 (ebook)

Subjects: LCSH: Carson, Alexander, 1776–1844. | Baptists—History.

Classification: BX6331.3 .G54 2025 (paperback) | BX6331.3 (ebook)

VERSION NUMBER 07/29/25

Scripture quotations are from the King James or Authorized Version.

To my wife and best friend
Jin Gill

Contents

Foreword: John Gill on Alexander Carson, by Ian Hugh Clary | ix

Preface | xi

List of Abbreviations | xiii

Introduction | xv

1 The Life of Alexander Carson | 1
2 Alexander Carson on the Bible | 23
3 Alexander Carson on the Cross | 65
4 Alexander Carson on Conversion | 92
5 Alexander Carson's Activism | 117
6 Conclusion | 142

Bibliography | 149

Foreword
John Gill on Alexander Carson

CHRISTIANITY FIRST TOOK ROOT in Ireland through the faithful witness of a man named Palladius (d. ca. 433) who had been sent there on mission from Rome in 431. His ministry was somewhat limited in terms of its effect, and unfortunately we know little of his life and work as his memory has been overshadowed by Patrick of Ireland (390–461). We know from ancient records that Palladius was sent to the "Scots" (Irish) to help the small number of Christians who were in Ireland at the time, and that he helped form a bulwark against Pelagian tendencies that were starting to make waves on Irish shores. Palladius and Patrick share a number of similarities, not least that they helped establish and spread Christianity in Ireland. Though Patrick is well remembered by people outside of Ireland and the church, both missionaries are clouded by mists of the past. Patrick, of course, is celebrated in many countries today with parades and green beer, yet those revelers have no idea that they are getting inebriated in the name of a man who brought the gospel of Christ to Irish barbarians. Were we to dive into ancient sources to find out who the real Patrick was, however, we discover that he is skewed by myth and hagiography. To know either early Irish evangelist requires painstaking historical scholarship, which has thankfully been performed in the last number of years.

Things haven't changed much for Irish Christians since the ancient church; even those who lived well into the modern period are little remembered. Alexander Carson (1776–1844) is a case in point. As you will learn in the pages of this important book, Carson had a significant impact on Evangelicalism in modern Ireland, and yet Christians today, whether Irish or not, know little about him—even those Christians called Baptists, of which he was one. Many thanks, then, are due to John Gill for this excellent

Foreword

study of Carson's Evangelicalism. Gill not only gives us a clearer portrait of this Irish saint that heretofore has not been provided, but he performs that painstaking scholarly task of cutting through mist and myth in order to help us set Carson in his times, evaluating his importance, and recommending him for use in the church today. This he does by placing Carson's Evangelicalism in light of the work of historian David Bebbington. Here we are treated to an examination of Carson's views on the cross of Christ, the need for conversion, the importance of biblical authority, and the need to bring the gospel to the nations.

I have spent many years reading and thinking about Carson, and each time I return to him the more impressed I am with his brilliance. His scholarship was largely polemical, engaged with the latest controversies of his own day, most famously with Roman Catholics, but more importantly with Unitarians and even fellow Evangelicals who were going soft on the doctrine of the Trinity. He also argued convincingly for the inspiration and authority of Scripture. Carson wrote with force and verve, and modeled what a true Christian controversialist should look like. Gill picks up on Carson's forceful irenicism and well communicates to readers not only what Carson's arguments were, but why they are compelling for the challenges Evangelicalism continues to face today, especially in regard to the inerrancy of the Bible and the classic doctrine of the Trinity. Of greatest personal interest to me is Gill's description of Carson's views on the nature of saving faith in light of the Sandemanianism that many Baptists were wrestling with in his day. I am thrilled that Gill's work is now published. Scholars interested in Irish church history, the history of the Baptists, and the nature of Evangelicalism will find this to be a helpful resource. And I am especially happy to commend this work of my friend and colleague.

IAN CLARY
Colorado Christian University
Labor Day, 2024

Preface

I WOULD NOT HAVE completed this book without the help and encouragement of numerous people. First, I thank my wife, Jin, for the sacrifices she made and the encouragements she gave, without which I would not have finished this project. I am also thankful to my young children who were understanding of their father's periodic absence. Gratitude also goes to both our parents for their prayers and the financial support that gave me the time to complete my writing. I thank Michael A. G. Haykin, my supervisor and mentor, whose direction, encouragement, and critique were timely and invaluable. Deep appreciation goes to Eric and Isabel Lindsay in Dromore and David and Carolyn Clark in Welwyn for their warm fellowship and generous hospitality during my research trips in Northern Ireland and London. I also thank Albert Wallace of Tobermore for taking the time out of his busy schedule to give me a tour of the Tobermore Baptist Church, Carson's home, and his grave. A special thanks goes to the librarians at the various libraries who kindly gave me access to materials I could not have accessed otherwise: David Kerry and Donald Garvie at Union Theological College's Gamble Library, the Special Collections staff at the McClay Library of Queen's University in Belfast, the Public Records Office of Northern Ireland, Maurice Dowling and others at the Irish Baptist College, Reverend Emma Walsh and Emily Burgoyne at the Angus Library of Regent's Park College in Oxford, Dr. Joanna Parker at the Library of Worcester College in Oxford, the staff of the British Library's St. Pancras reading rooms and copy services, and Ben Gantt at The Southern Baptist Theological Seminary's Boyce Library. Finally, I thank the Lord for the support, encouragement, and means to complete this work. I dedicate this work to him, because I want everything I do to be rooted in a desire to glorify him.

JOHN GILL

List of Abbreviations

ODNB   *Oxford Dictionary of National Biography: In Association with the British Academy; From the Earliest Times to the Year 2000; Index of Contributors.* Edited by H. C. G. Matthew and Brian Harrison. Oxford: Oxford University Press, 2004

Works   *The Works of the Rev. Alexander Carson, LL. D.* By Alexander Carson. 6 vols. Dublin: Carson, 1847–64

RGSU   *Records of the General Synod of Ulster, from 1691 to 1820.* By Presbyterian Church in Ireland. 3 vols. Belfast: Archer and Sons, Reid and Co., 1890–98

Introduction

CARSON'S GOSPEL-CENTERED EVANGELICALISM

Alexander Carson (ca. 1776–1844) is primarily known in the present day as an apologist for Baptist principles, due to his treatise *Baptism in Its Mode and Subjects Considered* (1831). As a Presbyterian, then Congregationalist, and finally Baptist minister in a small village in the northern part of Ireland, Carson's name was almost unknown to the general Christian community in Great Britain. It was not until his work on baptism was published that he became widely known as a champion for believer's baptism by immersion. As one reviewer of Carson's work noted,

> He was at that time but little known in England; but the intrinsic qualities of his book obtained for it a greater degree of attention than publications on baptism generally receive. It was evident that he was a man of great natural acuteness, a vigorous reasoner, and much in earnest in the pursuit of truth. It was apparent also that his acquaintance with Greek literature was very extensive, that he had studied the philosophy of language deeply, and that he was well versed in biblical criticism.[1]

While *Baptism in Its Mode and Subjects* was widely praised by Baptists throughout Great Britain and the United States, it also received criticism from pedobaptists in no small measure.[2] Yet, Carson was not unaccustomed to theological controversy. Though he began his ministry in the largest Presbyterian denomination in Ireland, Carson soon found much to be

---

1. *Baptist Magazine*, Unsigned review of *Baptism*, 185.
2. Some critiques of Carson's views include the following: Beecher, *Baptism: Import*; Beecher, *Baptism, with Reference*; Bickersteth, *Treatise on Baptism*; Munro, *Modern Immersion Directly Opposed*; *Presbyterian Review and Religious Journal*, Unsigned review of *Baptism*.

Introduction

dissatisfied with in this communion of churches and became a Congregationalist. In the wake of his departure, he produced numerous controversial works, most of them dealing primarily with ecclesiology, such as *Reasons for Separating from the General Synod of Ulster* (1805). His ecclesiological works have also been noted by present-day historians as a major facet of his theology.

While Carson's views on baptism and church order are admittedly important aspects of his theology, they are subordinate to his understanding of the gospel. Carson's own words are sufficient to come to this conclusion. Preaching at the fiftieth anniversary of the Baptist Missionary Society, he said, "Brethren, I yield to no man in zeal for baptism: but baptism is not my gospel. I love all who love Christ."[3] In *Reasons for Separating from the General Synod of Ulster*, in which he argued against the Presbyterian form of church government and order, he wrote,

> But I have other reasons for separating from the general synod, which still more pungently touch my conscience. One of these is the continual necessity I would be under, of prostituting the ordinances of Christ by promiscuous communion. . . . Though they are able to disprove all that I have said on the subject of church government, yet if I can convince them, of the sinfulness of admitting to communion, any but the credible disciples of Christ, and to persuade them to act up to their convictions, I will not have lost my labour.[4]

By "pure communion," Carson was referring to a regenerate church membership. He believed the prime test for church membership must be a conversion through faith in the gospel. The issue of the gospel and its effectiveness in the believer was more important than church polity per se.

The goal of this book is not to show that Carson's views on baptism and ecclesiology are unimportant. Rather, it is to examine more closely what Carson himself considered to be most important, namely, the gospel. Though Carson's views on the gospel could be approached in numerous ways, the four characteristics of Evangelicalism as set forth by David Bebbington in his now-classic *Evangelicalism in Modern Britain: A History from the 1730s to the 1980s* provide a helpful framework for detailing and analyzing Carson's understanding of the gospel. In this work Bebbington argued that British Evangelicalism has really only existed since the early eighteenth

---

3. Acworth and Carson, *Two Sermons*, 80; *Works* 152.
4. A. Carson, *Reasons for Separating* (1806), 87–88; *Works* 4:87–88.

Introduction

century and can be recognized by the following four distinctives: biblicism, a supreme regard for the Bible as the rule of life and faith; crucicentrism, a riveted focus on Christ's work on the cross; conversionism, the conviction that the gospel changes lives and that the true Christian is one who has had a personal conversion; and activism, which was "an expression of the gospel in effort" and entailed missions and various philanthropic enterprises.[5]

The decision to use Bebbington's quadrilateral as a working definition for Carson's Evangelicalism is primarily due to its ubiquitous presence in historical and theological studies on Evangelicalism. As Timothy Larson pointed out, "what immediately stands out as a truly remarkable achievement is the extraordinary way that [Bebbington's] definition of evangelicalism has become the standard one."[6] This is evidenced in multiple ways. Numerous reviews of Bebbington's *Evangelicalism in Modern Britain* were generally accepting of his quadrilateral. Robert G. Clouse's endorsement of Bebbington's work was especially strong, "This book should be required reading for all who are interested in Evangelicalism, whether adherents of the faith or students of history and religion."[7] John Wolffe similarly viewed *Evangelicalism in Modern Britain* as a work that any "serious student of evangelicalism" must read.[8] These recommendations came despite the acknowledgement of some controversy over aspects of Bebbington's work.

Though criticism of Bebbington's work was not limited to book reviews, the wide acceptance of his views and the breadth of his research have presented his critics with a difficult challenge. Larson described critics of the quadrilateral as approaching "their work as if they have taken on the Herculean task of vanquishing a hydra whose ugly heads reappear as fast as you can cut them off."[9] Yet, a number of cogent critiques of aspects of Bebbington's study have been produced. For example, *The Emergence of Evangelicalism: Exploring Historical Continuities* (2008), edited by Michael A. G. Haykin and Kenneth J. Stewart, offers a critique of the view that Evangelicalism was a novel movement beginning in the 1730s and characterized by four primary characteristics. While the numerous essays contained in this work show that Bebbington's characterization of Evangelicalism did not put an end to discussions on its definition, they can also be seen as

---

5. Bebbington, *Evangelicalism in Modern Britain*, 2–3.
6. Larson, "Reception Given," 25.
7. Clouse, Review of *Evangelicalism*, 166.
8. Wolffe, Review of *Evangelicalism*, 347.
9. Larson, "Reception Given," 26.

Introduction

proof of how influential and widespread Bebbington's views have become. Andrew Holmes, for example, felt the need to address the quadrilateral in a work on Ulster Presbyterianism even though Bebbington's own work explicitly did not deal with Evangelicalism in Ireland.[10]

Bebbington's definition of Evangelicalism did not gain widespread acceptance without merit though. In pointing out that the quadrilateral provided a useful working definition for those in need of a set of boundaries for their research, Larson also noted that even those dissatisfied with the quadrilateral made use of it.[11] Holmes, for example, recognized the usefulness of Bebbington's quadrilateral as a "framework for assessing the doctrinal characteristics of the movement," despite having reservations of limiting it to a new movement of the eighteenth century.[12] This admitted usefulness of the quadrilateral, its ubiquity, and the fact that this book does not require an examination of Carson in terms of continuity with previous theological perspectives make Bebbington's definition of Evangelicalism an effective and legitimate framework by which to examine Carson's Evangelicalism. This quadrilateral is effective in emphasizing Carson's views on the Bible as the divine source of the gospel, the cross of Christ as the center of the gospel, the influence of the gospel through conversion, and the evangelistic effort to spread the gospel. Carson would likely see these as simply being Christian characteristics. Yet, the reasons for calling this book a study of Carson's Evangelicalism are twofold. First, Carson considered himself an Evangelical, and the theological matters he discussed while identifying himself as such dealt with the gospel, and not baptism or ecclesiastical polity.[13] Second, due to the general ubiquity and acceptance of Bebbington's quadrilateral in evangelical studies, one is able to discern the focus of this study from the title.[14]

Therefore, considering Bebbington's quadrilateral to be a sound framework for understanding Carson's view of the gospel, the thesis of this study is that Carson's belief in the Bible as a verbally and completely inspired text provided him with an infallible source for his understanding of the gospel as being centered upon the atonement, effective through justification by faith alone, and the motivation for evangelism. Carson's theology

---

10. A. Holmes, *Ulster Presbyterian Belief*, 33–34.
11. Larson, "Reception Given," 26–27.
12. A. Holmes, *Ulster Presbyterian Belief*, 33.
13. For example, A. Carson, *Letters on "Evangelical Preaching"*; *Works* 1:308–59.
14. Atherstone, Review of *Emergence*.

Introduction

will be examined in each area through a study of his pertinent works, the works written by those with whom he interacted, the larger theological, social, economic, and political context surrounding those works. This will be preceded by a brief look at Carson's life.

Whenever possible, the latest British edition or imprint of Carson's works during his lifetime were used. For example, all citations from Carson's *Reasons for Separating from the General Synod of Ulster* were taken from the second edition published in 1806, rather than from the original 1805 edition. While most of his works did not undergo noticeable changes, some works did, such as his *Baptism in Its Mode and Subjects Considered* between the 1831 and 1844 editions, and *History of Providence as Unfolded in the Book of Esther* between the 1833 and 1835 editions.[15] Also, a number of his works were republished in the United States as individual or collated works, all of which were published after his name became widely known in 1831. These editions were not used unless to highlight a relevant alteration or Carson's significance in America. It should also be noted that some of Carson's writings were only published posthumously as part of a six-volume collection of his works. This was the case, for instance, with Carson's *The Doctrine of the Atonement* (1847). Citations of any of Carson's works that were republished in this collection will therefore include reference information from this collection as well as from the last edition Carson would have handled. This is done for the sake of accessibility for readers. As most of Carson's works were polemical in nature, this study required an examination of the works against which he wrote. In such cases, the edition of works to which he responded were used when available. Though Carson never noted which editions he responded to, the edition he used can be determined sometimes by his rare provision of a page reference. When the exact edition Carson used could not be determined, the latest edition prior to Carson's response was usually used, even if the only edition available was one published in the United States. Possible changes in style in an American edition were chosen over the common practice of "improving" later editions.

---

15. A. Carson, *History of Providence in Esther* (1833); *Works* 6:71–154.

1

The Life of Alexander Carson

ALEXANDER CARSON WAS BORN in 1776 in the small village of Annahone, near Stewartstown, County Tyrone, in Ulster.¹ Carson was of Scottish descent, and his family's religious affiliation reflected that in their Presbyterianism. Carson's father, William Carson, and mother raised him in the Presbyterian faith, being a part of the General Synod of Ulster.² Carson's

---

1. Annahone, now called Annaghone, was home of the Annahone colliery, which was active until the 1820s. Annahone was located approximately two miles northwest of Stewartstown.

Ulster is the name of the northern province of Ireland. Ireland was divided into five provinces, Ulster, Munster, Connacht, Leinster, and Meath, which was later incorporated into Leinster after the Norman invasion. The provinces were divided into counties in the thirteenth century by the Normans who invaded Ireland in the twelfth century. Present-day Northern Ireland is composed of six of the province's nine counties. The Ulster counties are Antrim, Armagh, Down, Fermanagh, Londonderry, Tyrone, Cavan, Donegal, Monaghan. The latter three counties are not a part of Northern Ireland.

2. There is very little data available on Carson's parents. For example, the name of Carson's mother was never given in his works or biographies. There are a number of reasons for the general lack of data in the eighteenth century. While the Synod of Ulster made resolutions for recordkeeping from the early eighteenth century, records were not consistently kept. For example, the Synod of Ulster passed a resolution for maintaining birth, baptism, and marriage records in 1819, which implies an inconsistency in recordkeeping. *RGSU* 3:511. In the seventeenth and eighteenth centuries, many parishes in the Church of Ireland contained baptism, marriage, and burial records for dissenting churches. Unfortunately, the destruction of the Public Records Office of Ireland in 1922, during the Irish Civil War, resulted in the loss of many of the church records stored there. Public Records Office of Northern Ireland, *Irish Genealogical Source*, 35.

They were likely part of the Presbyterian congregation at Brigh, which was located approximately one and a half miles from Annahone. Carson's parents may have eventually

mother and grandmother were especially dedicated to his religious upbringing, teaching him the doctrines and promises of the Scriptures.[3]

From an early age, Carson showed a strong inclination toward learning. This is evidenced, first, by his strong work ethic in school, even to the neglect of his physical health, and, second, by his academic achievements. Carson's parents provided a classical education for Carson's pre-ministerial training under a Mr. Peebles at the village of Tullyhogue, near Cookstown. Peebles trained many young men who would enter the ministry.[4] Carson continued his education at the University of Glasgow, where those planning to enter the pastoral ministry in the General Synod of Ulster normally enrolled. There may have been approximately one thousand students at the university during Carson's matriculation there.[5] Among those who attended the university during Carson's enrollment were those who would become theological allies and foes, such as Ralph Wardlaw (1779–1853),[6] a Scottish Congregationalist, and William Hamilton Drummond (1778–1865),[7] an Irish Unitarian. According

---

joined the congregation in Stewartstown, which was formed in 1788. *RCSU* 3:98, 112; Presbyterian Historical Society of Ireland, *History of Congregations*, 758.

3. Moore, *Life of Alexander Carson*, 1. Carson's mother is credited for being a "Eunice" to his "Timothy" in terms of spiritual upbringing, with his grandmother "Lois"; she had memorized the Psalms and sought to raise Carson in the faith.

4. Witherow, *Three Prophets*, 18.

5. A. Brown and Moss, *University of Glasgow*, 16.

6. Moore, *Life of Alexander Carson*, 152; Addison, *Matriculation Albums*, 162. Wardlaw was born near Edinburgh and raised in Glasgow. He matriculated at the University of Glasgow in 1791 and trained for ministry in the Associate, or Burgher, Synod from 1795 to 1800. During his university years, Wardlaw was apparently part of a philosophical society with Carson, where they had mock debates over philosophical topics. The tenets of Congregationalism had an impact on Wardlaw, and he joined their ranks in 1800. He was ordained as the minister of the Congregational church on North Albion Street in Glasgow in 1803. Wardlaw did not follow the Haldanes in becoming a Baptist in 1808 and remained a defender of infant baptism. His church ministry was supplemented by his professorship at the Glasgow Theological Academy, which was formed in 1811. Wardlaw's life was marked with activism in various arenas. He was involved in missions efforts through the British and Foreign Bible Society and London Missionary Society. His abolitionist views led him to help found the Glasgow Anti-Slavery Society. His views on the disestablishment of the state church are evident in his participation in the Voluntary Church Association. Finally, he remained committed to evangelical cooperation and was active in the Evangelical Alliance. The preceding information was taken primarily from the following sources: Stewart J. Brown, "Wardlaw, Ralph," *ODNB* 57:373–74; Alexander, *Ralph Wardlaw*.

7. Addison, *Matriculation Albums*, 174. Drummond, a native of County Antrim, Ulster, received ministerial training under the Armagh Presbytery, which did not require

to regulations passed in the General Synod of Ulster concerning the education of their ministers, Carson would have been required to study natural and moral philosophy, Hebrew, Greek, Latin, logic, metaphysics, church history, and theology.[8] He studied under John Young (ca. 1746–1820), a distinguished professor in Greek, and developed an appreciation for philology.[9] Of Young, Carson wrote, "With respect to Grammar, none who have had the advantage of hearing the profoundly philosophical Lectures on the Greek Language and General Grammar, delivered by Professor Young in the University of Glasgow, will be surprised at this doctrine. The unrivalled talents for critical analysis, possessed by that gentleman, enable him to unveil the whole mysteries of Language. The only merit I claim, on this occasion, is the extension of the principle over the empire of Figures of Speech."[10] The

---

subscription to the Westminster Confession of Faith. He was ordained at the Second Belfast Presbyterian church on August 26, 1800, under the Antrim Presbytery, which, while maintaining communion with the Synod of Ulster, was not under the authority of the synod. Drummond's pastorate in Belfast was coupled with his involvement with the Belfast Literary Society. Some of his literary works were *The Battle of Trafalgar: A Heroic Poem* (1806) and *The Giants' Causeway: A Poem* (1811). Drummond resigned from his pastorate over the Second Belfast congregation on November 1, 1815, after receiving a call to the Presbyterian congregation at Strand Street, Dublin. As in Belfast, his ministry was supplemented with more scholarly diversions, such as being a member of the Royal Irish Academy. Drummond also became active in promoting and defending Unitarianism through such works as *The Doctrine of the Trinity Founded Neither on Scripture, nor on Reason and Common Sense, but on Tradition and the Infallible Church: An Essay Occasioned by a Late Controversy Between the Rev. Richard T. P. Pope and the Rev. Thomas Maguire* (1827) and *The Life of Michael Servetus: The Spanish Physician, Who, for the Alleged Crime of Heresy, Was Entrapped, Imprisoned, and Burned by John Calvin the Reformer, in the City of Geneva, October 27, 1553* (1848). The preceding information was taken primarily from the following sources: R. K. Webb, "Drummond, William Hamilton," *ODNB* 16:995–96; *RGSU* 3:435.

8. *RGSU* 2:528–29.

9. Witherow, *Three Prophets*, 18.

10. A. Carson, *Treatise on Figures of Speech*, 15; *Works* 5:436. Carson was probably referring to John Young (ca. 1746–1820), a native of Glasgow. Young matriculated at Glasgow University from 1764 and received his MA in 1769. Young was installed as a professor of Greek at the university on June 9, 1774, and he taught there until his death in 1820. Young was known for his good sense of humor and enjoyment of the Greek language. "Professor Young, who filled the chair of Greek, was one of the few men of whom Scotland can boast, in modern times, as sustaining her ancient reputation for classical learning. Enthusiastic in his admiration for the literature of ancient Greece, . . . he was not less exact in his acquaintance with the grammatical structure and idioms of the noble language in which these treasures are contained. He had thought much on the philosophy of language in general, and was full of ingenious and learned speculations which he applied to the illustration of the Greek language in particular." Alexander,

General Synod also required a ministerial candidate to prove a minimum of four years of regular attendance at the university to proceed with his candidacy without delay.[11] Carson went on to receive both his BA and MA degrees at the university.[12]

On September 5, 1797, the Tyrone Presbytery reported that Carson, among several others, had entered on "first Tryals."[13] He was licensed by the Tryone Presbytery in May 1798.[14] Andrew R. Holmes describes what the entire process to become a minister in the General Synod of Ulster entailed: "Before being licensed to preach, the intending minister was placed on 'first trials' comprising a sermon, lecture, 'exercise and addition' (a critical examination of a text of Scripture and a discussion of its doctrinal implications), 'common head' (a paper on an important theological issue), and a popular sermon. He was also subjected to 'second trials' before ordination, which, again, included an exercise and addition, a common head, a popular sermon, and a lecture."[15] On December 11, 1798, Carson was ordained to the Presbyterian Church in Tobermore, at which time he subscribed to the Westminster Confession of Faith.[16] Moore wrote that the congregation at Tobermore made a unanimous decision to call Carson to be their minister after hearing him preach only once.[17] If true, this may indicate that his abilities as a preacher, as remembered and respected by others, were apparent from the beginning of his ministry.

Not many details of Carson's Presbyterian congregation are available, even in the earlier memoirs of his life. Yet, in his *Reasons for Separating from the General Synod of Ulster* (1805), Carson commented on several deficiencies in church congregations, which may indicate the problems he dealt with within his own congregation. He wrote that one of the issues that weighed most heavily on his conscience was "prostituting the ordinances

---

Ralph Wardlaw, 10. The preceding information was taken primarily from the following sources: T. W. Bayne and Campbell F. Lloyd, "Young, John," *ODNB* 60:918–19; Addison, *Matriculation Albums*, 74.

11. *RGSU* 2:529.
12. Joshua Thompson, "Carson, Alexander," *ODNB* 10:306–7, esp. 306.
13. *RGSU* 3:197.
14. *RGSU* 3:206.
15. A. Holmes, *Ulster Presbyterian Belief*, 137.
16. *RGSU* 3:217.
17. Moore, *Life of Alexander Carson*, 4.

of Christ, by promiscuous communion."[18] He devoted the whole chapter to the character of church members and the necessity of a pure communion. His primary concern was that a pure communion or church membership consist of only converted believers. This was a necessary characteristic of a church. He argued that while Presbyterian churches may "shut the gate against the openly profane, . . . the decent worldling may pass."[19] The true test of membership, for Carson, was credible evidence of the new birth, and he did not see this being used by any Presbyterian churches. While he applied this criticism against all the churches in the General Synod of Ulster, and possibly in other synods, it was arguably his experiences with unregenerate members in his own congregation that sparked this.

Carson also exhorted congregations to take responsibility for implementing discipline within their churches. He argued that this was not only the responsibility of the pastor, but of every church member.[20] This might reflect a lack of congregational participation in church discipline in his own church, or a strong resistance against being disciplined by those in his congregation, or both.

Fundamental weaknesses in congregations, such as those above, led Carson to question the ecclesiological practices in Presbyterian churches. For example, he argued that the use of communion tokens was motivated, in part, by the fear of man rather than obedience to Scripture: "Church leaders dare not professedly admit unregenerate men, from fear of offending God, and they dare not candidly deny them admission, from fear of men. They have, therefore, found out a way to compromise the matter between God and the world, by *fencing the tables*. Thus, they avoid giving individual offence, and driving unregenerate men away from their society, and imagine themselves clear as to the crimes of prostituting the ordinance of Christ."[21] Carson believed that pragmatic, yet unbiblical, expedients such as this were not effective. His observations of the inherent problems in Presbyterian practice and his studies of the New Testament eventually led him to reject the Presbyterian form of church government altogether.

As a minister within the General Synod of Ulster, Carson was active beyond the responsibilities of his local congregation, and he attended the

---

18. A. Carson, *Reasons for Separating* (1806), 87; *Works* 4:87.
19. A. Carson, *Reasons for Separating* (1806), 87; *Works* 4:87.
20. A. Carson, *Reasons for Separating* (1806), 92; *Works* 4:92.
21. A. Carson, *Reasons for Separating* (1806), 93; *Works* 4:93; emphasis in original.

synod meetings in 1799, during his first year in Tobermore, and in 1802.²² While there, he would have observed the continuing participation of those who did not subscribe to the Westminster Confession of Faith (the Presbytery of Antrim) and who were more theologically liberal, as well as the generally weak spirituality of the synod. Holmes points to the lack of fast days and spiritual reflection at synod meetings as a "reflection of the liberal theological opinion within the Synod."²³ In his *Reasons for Separating from the General Synod of Ulster*, Carson argued that he was unable to worship with Socinians and Arians, because they did not worship the same God.²⁴ Many believed that Arianism and other heterodox theologies reigned in the Presbytery in Antrim, and Antrim's continued presence at the General Synod of Ulster, though no longer under the authority of the synod, only served to strengthen and spread liberal views.

Ulster Presbyterianism was not devoid of evangelical efforts during Carson's time. Holmes sees the beginnings of a new surge of evangelical efforts at the end of the eighteenth century:

> The events of the final decade of the eighteenth century encouraged Presbyterian involvement in the formation of evangelical missionary societies, most notably the General Evangelical Society, founded in Dublin in 1787, and the Evangelical Society of Ulster, founded in Armagh in 1798. In the first decades of the nineteenth century, Presbyterian interest in home and foreign mission was channelled through the great voluntary evangelical societies of the day such as the London Missionary Society (LMS) and the Hibernian Bible Society (HBS). These societies were motivated to spread the gospel throughout the world by an eschatological belief that entailed "nothing less than the realization of the biblical vision of a world transformed by being filled with the knowledge of the Lord as the waters cover the sea."²⁵

The Evangelical Society of Ulster was the most prominent interdenominational organization during Carson's ministry within the General Synod of Ulster. James Seaton Reid (1798–1851), a historian of the Presbyterians in Ireland, wrote that the Evangelical Society of Ulster was formed on October 10, 1798, at Armagh "for the purpose of establishing a system of itinerant

---

22. *RGSU* 3:214, 251.
23. A. Holmes, *Ulster Presbyterian Belief*, 82.
24. A. Carson, *Reasons for Separating* (1806), 108; *Works* 4:109.
25. A. Holmes, *Ulster Presbyterian Belief*, 41; quoting Brian Stanley.

preaching throughout the towns and villages of the province."[26] From its inception the Evangelical Society was a cooperative effort, including thirteen ministers from four different Presbyterian denominations, including the General Synod of Ulster, plus a few from the Established Church (Anglican).[27] Reid notes the election of Carson's brother, Samuel Carson, to the position of treasurer for the society, which may be an indication that an evangelistic concern was shared within Carson's family.[28] The General Synod of Ulster would officially support the Hibernian Bible Society in 1811 and even receive someone on behalf of the London Missionary Society in 1812, both groups that Carson worked with. Yet, this was only several years after Carson had left the synod, one of his reasons being the synod's restrictions against cooperative efforts with such societies.[29]

The spread of the gospel as an important and necessary work of all Christians is evident in Carson's *Reasons*. Carson criticized the General Synod of Ulster for restrictions on itinerant preaching, which required itinerant preachers to submit their credentials to the presbytery of the area in which they wished to preach and await their approval. A minister within the synod who bypassed this rule by freely giving his pulpit to itinerant preachers would be rebuked for his first offense and suspended for his second.[30] In his *Reasons*, Carson wrote, "If I would dare to preach the Gospel out of my own bounds, or admit an evangelical minister of another denomination to occupy my pulpit, dreadful would be the thunder that would be hurled against me!"[31] Carson's frustration with the synod was due to what he saw as a restriction that limited the spread of the gospel.

The nominal faith of many in Carson's congregation and the synod's toleration of Arianism and other nonsubscribers eventually led Carson to leave the General Synod of Ulster and Presbyterianism altogether. Upon receiving a request to attend a presbytery meeting in May 1805, Carson responded with a letter declining "all connection with, and subjection to, the General Synod of Ulster," including some of his reasons and his intention to publish a more detailed explanation in due time.[32] While the synod

---

26. Reid, *Presbyterian Church in Ireland*, 3:415–16.
27. Hempton and Hill, *Evangelical Protestantism in Ulster Society*, 38–39.
28. Reid, *Presbyterian Church in Ireland*, 3:416.
29. A. Carson, *Reasons for Separating* (1806), 107; *Works* 4:108.
30. A. Carson, *Reasons for Separating* (1806), 107; *Works* 4:108.
31. A. Carson, *Reasons for Separating* (1806), 106; *Works* 4:107.
32. *RGSU* 3:296.

records show this as the earliest record of his separation from the synod, Carson was apparently convinced of his need to separate from the synod prior to 1805. In a written prayer, dated January 1, 1805, it is clear that Carson expected a significant amount of turmoil within the year as a result of his intended separation from the synod. He wrote, "What is to happen to me in the course of the present year Thou only knowest. I have to wade through deep waters. O Lord, let them not overflow me. Grant that if I live to look over this on the next new year, I may have cause of praise, and more ground for confidence, by seeing Thy hand to have led me when I gave up all. And when all men are against me be Thou my provider, protector, and comforter."[33] These words do not convey joyful excitement in Carson, but rather a sense of sober conviction.

Carson first published his *Reasons for Separating from the General Synod of Ulster* in 1805, where he systematically outlined his reasons for leaving Presbyterianism. Carson argued that the Scriptures provided a model of church government that is Congregationalism, as opposed to Presbyterianism. Related to this was that the Congregational model allowed for a regenerate membership, or a "pure communion." This was in reference to both the nominal Presbyterians in his congregation, and the ministers who did not believe in the biblical gospel. Carson's continuing concern for the biblical integrity of both the gospel and church government are respectively seen in his subsequent publications against Presbyterians, *Remarks on a Late Pastoral Address, from the Ministers of the Synod of Ulster, to the People Under Their Care* (1806) and *A Reply to Mr. Brown's Vindication of the Presbyterian Form of Church-Government, in Which the Order of the Apostolical Churches Is Defended* (1807).[34] In *An Answer to Mr. Ewing's Attempt Towards a Statement of the Doctrine of Scripture on Some*

---

33. Moore, *Life of Alexander Carson*, 12.

34. In his 1807 work (*Works* 4:127–553), Carson was replying to the work of John Brown (1778–1848), a minister in the Church of Scotland, called *Vindication of the Presbyterian Form of Church-Government* (1805), which was considered a standard work on this issue. Carson also wrote *Review of Dr. Brown "On the Law of Christ Respecting Civil Obedience"* (1838) against John Brown's *The Law of Christ Respecting Civil Obedience* (1837). Brown incorporated replies to some of Carson's charges in an expanded 1839 edition. Though Brown never left Presbyterianism, he was an early promoter of Evangelicalism in the Church of Scotland. The "Disruption" in 1843 in the Church of Scotland over state authority in the Church of Scotland resulted in a massive schism. As a result, Brown left the Church of Scotland for the Free Church of Scotland with over four hundred other ministers who had a more evangelical perspective. The preceding information was taken primarily from W. G. Blaikie and Rosemary Mitchell, "Brown, John," *ODNB* 8:76–77.

Disputed Points Respecting the Constitution, Government, Worship, and Discipline of the Church of Christ (1809), written in opposition to Greville Ewing (1767–1841), Carson argued that Scripture contained a definite model for the church.[35]

While Carson never expressed regret over his separation from the synod, he recognized what he had lost. In the preface of his *Reasons for Separating from the General Synod of Ulster* (1806), Carson wrote, "The day I gave up my connexion with the general synod, I gave up all that the world esteems. I sacrifice not only my prospects in life, and my respectability in the world, but every settled way of support."[36] As a minister in the General Synod of Ulster, a part of Carson's income came from the *regium donum* (royal bounty), which was a state grant to supplement the income of Irish Presbyterian ministers. From 1803, Carson was receiving £75 from the state each year, plus a stipend from his church. Prior to 1803, his share of the *regium donum* was variable. In 1799, for example, ministers in the synod were receiving £33.[37] Carson's stipend, the payment agreed upon between the

---

35. Greville Ewing (1767–1841) was ordained as a minister in the Church of Scotland in 1793. His preaching abilities made him popular in his ministry at Lady Glenorchy's Chapel, Edinburgh. Missions was a continual interest for Ewing, and he was involved in numerous missions efforts, including the Edinburgh Missionary Society and the *Missionary Magazine*. Though he was associated with the Haldanes at the turn of the century, ecclesiological disagreements led to public separation of ways. Ewing helped found the Glasgow Theological Academy in 1809 and the Congregational Union of Scotland in 1812. Ewing's controversial writings include *An Attempt Toward a Statement of the Doctrine of Scripture on Some Disputed Points Respecting the Constitution, Government, Worship, and Discipline of the Church of Christ* (1807) and *An Essay on Baptism: Being an Inquiry into the Meaning, Form, and Extent of the Administration of that Ordinance* (1824), which was against the Baptist position on the ordinance. The preceding information was taken primarily from the following sources: W. G. Blaikie and David Huddleston, "Ewing, Greville," *ODNB* 18:823–24; Matheson, *Memoir of Greville Ewing*.

36. A. Carson, *Reasons for Separating* (1806), iv; *Works* 4:xii.

37. Prior to 1803, the *regium donum* was a lump sum to be distributed equally among the ministers in the Synod of Ulster. In 1798, as a result of the Rebellion of 1798, Presbyterian leaders were eager to show their loyalty to the state, and the state desired to make the Presbyterian clergy more dependent upon and amenable to the government. The resulting effort to alter the *regium donum* was called the "Plan for Augmentation and Distribution of his Majestys Bounty." The two purposes outlined in the plan were to provide additional protection against the disgrace that comes with the disloyalty of an appointed minister, and a way for ministers to advance themselves through growing their congregations. The plan divided all the congregations in the synod into three classes according to their numerical size, with ministers in the first class receiving £100 per year, in the second class £75 per year, and in the third class £50 per year. The Tobermore congregation was categorized as a second-class congregation. The preceding information

congregation and pastor, in 1799 was £60.[38] Considering the loss of the *regium donum* as a source of income, Carson's separation from the synod was of economic significance, especially for one with a growing family. Those against his departure apparently saw Carson's responsibility to provide for his family according to 1 Tim 5:8 as a biblical rationale for him to reconcile with the synod. Carson's reply conveyed both a commitment to his family and to the Scripture: "I acknowledge the obligation of this Scripture in its fullest extent. But am I obliged to neglect one duty by attending to another? I am to provide for my family; but will any say, I should rob and murder to support them? I am to provide, but it is things that are lawful. I am not to support them at the expense of good conscience."[39] Carson's withdrawal from the synod also cost him the regard of many friends and relatives, who never forgave him.[40]

Of significance to Carson and those in the congregation who followed him in separating from Presbyterianism was the loss of the Tobermore meetinghouse. Though Carson's official departure from the synod was in 1805, there are conflicting accounts as to when he and his Independent congregation vacated the Tobermore meetinghouse. Moore wrote that Carson's Independent congregation was forced out of the meetinghouse in 1805, despite having a legal right to the building, and forced to be a nomadic congregation until 1814.[41] John Douglas agreed with the 1805 departure, but wrote that they were without a building for only two years.[42] By way of contrast, Joshua Thompson wrote, in the *Oxford Dictionary of National Biography*, that Carson continued to preach in the meetinghouse until his

---

was taken primarily from the following sources: A. Holmes, *Ulster Presbyterian Belief*, 64; Yates, *Religious Condition of Ireland*, 127, 145; Castlereagh, *Memoirs*, 2:384; *RGSU* 3:270–71, 289.

38. Yates, *Religious Condition of Ireland*, 145; Reid, *Presbyterian Church in Ireland*, 3:537.

39. A. Carson, *Reasons for Separating* (1806), 124; *Works* 4:124.

40. Hanna, "Alexander Carson," 192.

41. Moore, *Life of Alexander Carson*, 18–19.

42. Douglas, *Biographical Sketch*, 9. John Douglas was a Baptist minister in Newport, Monmouthshire, Wales. He membership in the Evangelical Alliance was announced at the meeting on July 14, 1881. Besides his biographical sketch on Carson, Douglas wrote several tracts, including one on the inspiration and canon of Scripture. The preceding information was taken primarily from the following sources: *Evangelical Christendom*, "New Members"; Starr, *Baptist Bibliography*, 6:165.

Independent congregation was expelled after a lengthy lawsuit.[43] Synod records support Thompson's account over those of Moore and Douglas.

According to records from the General Synod of Ulster in 1807, it is apparent that the Presbyterians at Tobermore did not have control of their meetinghouse, because they asked the synod to help them recover it.[44] Carson wrote in a letter, "We met as a church in May, 1807," which was two years after his formal separation from the synod and at least one year before he became a Baptist.[45] This may be an indication that Carson continued to preach in the Presbyterian meetinghouse without significant resistance until the first half of 1807. As a result of the Presbyterian congregation's request in 1807, a lawsuit began in the matter, and the synod's efforts in helping the Tobermore Presbyterians were ongoing throughout 1809 and part of 1810.[46] William Brown was ordained in Tobermore on November 20, 1810, which may indicate that the dispute over the meetinghouse had been resolved.[47] At the very latest, the Presbyterian congregation had recovered the building by mid-1811.[48]

After leaving the Presbyterian meetinghouse in Tobermore, Carson and his remaining congregation met in vacant barns and the outdoors until 1814, when a new meetinghouse was built at the expense of the congregation. It was a low, slated rectangular building of coarse stone, sixty-five feet

---

43. Thompson, *ODNB* 10:307.

44. "A supplication was presented to the Synod from the congregation of Tobermore, praying the Synod to devise & adopt such methods, as in their wisdom may seem most effectual, to recover for them possession of their meeting-house." *RGSU* 3:325.

45. Moore, *Life of Alexander Carson*, 77. Though his biographer seems to understand 1807 as when Carson came to reject infant baptism, it is more likely that it refers to a final separation from his Tobermore congregation. If Carson's change in sentiment over baptism came as an indirect result of Haldane's change, it could not have happened before 1808, after Haldane himself accepted believer's baptism.

46. "It was also resolved that our Agent be requested to continue his exertions to put the Congregation of Tobermore in possession of their Meeting-house, & that the expense be defrayed out of the same fund," at Cookstown, June 27, 1809. *RGSU* 3:334. "Dr Black stated the progress of the Suit respecting Tubermore. His conduct was approved of in this matter, & he was requested to persevere," at Cookstown, June 26, 1810. *RGSU* 3:360.

47. *RGSU* 3:364.

48. "Dr Black reported, that he had, under the advice of counsel, prosecuted the business of Tubermore, but the congregation having obtained the actual possession of the meeting-house further proceedings became unnecessary. Resolved, that Dr Black's conduct be approved of, & that he be requested, should any attempt be made to recover possession of the meeting-house by the opposite party to resist it by every legal means," at Cookstown, June 25, 1811. *RGSU* 3:374.

The Gospel-Centered Evangelicalism of Alexander Carson

by twenty-five feet, with a small sessions room attached to the western side. Seating for 270 adults was available, including the later addition of galleries, one on each end of the building.[49]

Soon after James (1768–1851) and Robert Haldane (1764–1842) came to reject infant baptism, Carson came into contact with their baptistic views in Tobermore.[50] It is unclear whether this contact was through a Baptist missionary or through James Haldane's *Reasons for a Change of Sentiments & Practice on the Subject of Baptism* (1808), but the conclusion was that Carson, ultimately through his own study of Scripture on the ordinance, came to reject infant baptism himself.[51] While Carson strongly

---

49. Day and McWilliams, *Parishes of County Londonderry*, 66. The galleries were built with funds donated by Robert Haldane. Moore, *Life of Alexander Carson*, 21.

50. Robert Haldane (1764–1842), James's older brother, served in the navy from 1780 to 1783. After settling in Scotland, he dabbled in numerous interests and married. Though the French Revolution sparked some interest in democratic politics, which led him to be labeled as a political radical by some, Robert's interests turned progressively toward religion. In 1797 he sold his wealthy estate with the intention of becoming a missionary to India. He was unable to obtain permission for his missionary venture, possibly due to his perceived political radicalism. Robert, instead, invested large sums of money into building preaching centers and tabernacles in Scotland to help spread the gospel. Besides creating venues for the itinerant preachers, he financed evangelical academies for their training. He followed his brother in rejecting infant baptism, which subsequently led to the divisions in their Congregational churches in Scotland. Robert's influence did not remain in Scotland. In Geneva, he taught through the Epistle to the Romans to students who had been primarily exposed to deism. His work in teaching orthodox doctrines of the gospel and the Bible helped to spark a revival in the French city. Robert was also a leading figure in the Apocrypha Controversy in the mid-1820s, during which he argued against the inclusion of the Apocrypha in the Bible. His *Review of the Conduct of the Directors of the British and Foreign Bible Society: Relative to the Aprocrapha, and to Their Administration on the Continent; With an Answer to the Rev. C. Simeon, and Observations on the Cambridge Remarks* was his first entry in the resulting pamphlet war. This controversy developed into discussion on the issue of the inspiration of Scripture, in which Haldane argued that Scripture was inspired in every word rather than in its ideas. The Haldane brothers were instrumental in spreading evangelical Calvinist doctrine and Congregational church polity. They were influential across numerous denominations despite their baptistic views. The preceding information was taken primarily from the following sources: Deryck Lovegrove, "Haldane, James Alexander," *ODNB* 24:505–6; Deryck Lovegrove, "Haldane, Robert," *ODNB* 24:523–24; A. Haldane, *Memoirs*.

51. Educated at the University of Edinburgh, James Haldane (1768–1851) became a midshipman in 1785. By 1793, he was the captain of his own ship, the *Melville Castle*. He was also married later that year. During his command, Haldane grew progressively concerned in religious matters, partly under the influence of David Bogue (1750–1825), a Congregational minister at Gosport, England. This growing focus on his religious state, desire to be with his wife, and encouragement from his older brother, Robert, led him to

believed in believer's baptism by immersion, his church apparently practiced open membership and open communion, simply requiring that one give credible evidence of regeneration to become a member.[52] While one biographer, John Young, attributed Carson's practice of not requiring baptism to his "extreme liberality and kindness of disposition," another biographer, George C. Moore, argued that Carson's practice was based on principle rather than "liberality of sentiment."[53] Even before becoming a Baptist, Carson argued that "baptism does not constitute church membership." Like John Bunyan (1628–88), Carson believed that baptism was for individuals as believers, not church members.[54] The Tobermore Baptist Church was noteworthy in a land with very few Baptists. In 1836, *The Baptist Magazine* included a "List of Baptist Churches in Ireland," which listed Carson's church in "Tulbermar," among thirty-one other churches, as having 300 members, which may have been almost a third of the total number of active members in Baptist churches in Ireland at the time.[55]

---

sell his command and settle in Scotland. By 1797, James was preaching as a lay evangelist in Scotland, provoking the status quo in parishes of the Church of Scotland. He helped establish the Society for the Propagation of the Gospel at Home, which sent out lay preachers. He became an Independent in 1799 and was ordained as a minister of a Congregational church in Edinburgh. His ongoing ecclesiological concerns were manifested in his written works, such as *A View of the Social Worship and Ordinances Observed by the First Christians, Drawn from the Sacred Scriptures Alone: Being an Attempt to Enforce Their Divine Obligation; And to Represent the Guilt and Evil Consequences of Neglecting Them*. His rejection of infant baptism in 1808 resulted in another separation, this time from many Congregationalist associates such as Greville Ewing. His theological concerns were not confined to ecclesiology. For example, he wrote *Refutation of the Heretical Doctrine Promulgated by the Rev. Edward Irving: Respecting the Person and Atonement of the Lord Jesus Christ* in reaction to Edward Irving's (1792–1834) views on the humanity of Christ. He also wrote on the biblical mandate for obedience to political authorities in *The Voluntary Question: Political, Not Religious; A Letter to the Rev. Dr. John Brown, Occasioned by the Allusion in His Recent Work to the Author's Sentiments Upon National Churches*. For reference, Carson had previously written against Brown's (1784–1858) views in 1838.

52. Young, "Memoir of Alexander Carson," xxxvi.

53. Young, "Memoir of Alexander Carson," xxxvi; Moore, *Life of Alexander Carson*, 84–85.

54. A. Carson, *Reply to Mr. Brown's Vindication*, 84. See also Moore, *Bigotry Demolished*.

55. Some data on Baptist churches in Ireland is included below the list from Reverend James Allen, of Ballina, Ireland. He "considers the aggregate number of members in actual fellowship with the Baptist Churches in Ireland to be about nine hundred and twenty." *Baptist Magazine*, "List of Baptist Churches in Ireland."

The Gospel-Centered Evangelicalism of Alexander Carson

Throughout the turmoil included with separating from the General Synod of Ulster and eventually shifting to baptistic convictions, Carson had the support of his wife. Soon after his ordination into the synod, he married Margaret Ledlie (1781–1844), who was a great support for Carson throughout his ministry.[56] Margaret came from a wealthy family where her father, George Ledlie, was successful in the linen industry in county Tyrone. In a memoir of Margaret's life, one of her daughters described her as being very active as a pastor's wife, visiting the sick and dying, both with her husband and alone.[57] Moore's high opinion of her is also evident in his memoir on Carson. Besides overseeing all the household responsibilities, Moore remembered Margaret for her faithful transcriptions of Carson's "hieroglyphics, which few mortals could decipher."[58] She apparently shared her husband's zeal for local and foreign missions, and she actively taught the gospel to those she encountered.[59] She was also careful to teach the gospel to her children.[60]

Carson and his wife had thirteen children together, five sons and eight daughters, four of whom died before Carson.[61] The available information about his children is primarily extant in memoirs and letters, though some have also published works. Two of Carson's sons, George and James, became medical doctors, and one daughter, Margaret, married a medical doctor. George Ledlie Carson (1803–38), the second-born son, was a surgeon

---

56. Thompson, ODNB 10:307.

57. G. Carson and Hanna, *Memorials*, 70.

58. Moore, *Life of Alexander Carson*, 5–6. Carson's poor handwriting is also noted in the "advertisement" prefixed to the posthumously published first volume of *Works*, in which the publishers "regret that [the volume] could not be issued sooner. The delay, however, was unavoidable, being in consequence of the great difficulty experienced in reading the manuscripts." *Works* 1:vii.

59. Matilda Carson Hanna shared an account in which her mother evangelized a fifty-year-old Roman Catholic widow by teaching her to read the Bible. G. Carson and Hanna, *Memorials*, 71–72.

60. G. Carson and Hanna, *Memorials*, 74–75.

61. Moore, *Life of Alexander Carson*, 100. Carson's children who died before him were Alexander Carson (ca. 1806–ca. 1822), Eliza Carson (ca. 1813–Mar. 17, 1837), Susan(na) Ledlie Carson (ca. 1811–May 1837), and George Ledlie Carson (1803–Jan. 5, 1838). Moore, *Life of Alexander Carson*, 47, 25, 32, 52. The other children's names were Margaret Carson Clarke (ca. 1810–Dec. 4, 1880), James Crawford Ledlie Carson (ca. 1815–June 2, 1886), Matilda Carson Hanna (dates unknown), Robert Haldane Carson (ca. 1821–Feb. 2, 1904), Sarah Carson, Charlotte Carson, Maria Carson, and a son and daughter whose names are unknown. Moore, *Life of Alexander Carson*, 38 32, 8, 36, 81, 36, 37.

and minister in the large town of Coleraine, approximately twenty-five miles north of Tobermore. He studied medicine upon his parents' advice, but he held an interest in ministry and "gratuitously officiated as pastor" of the Coleraine Baptist Church in tandem with his medical profession.[62] He also preached often at his father's church in Tobermore. George was buried in his family's plot at the Desertmartin Parish of the Church of Ireland. His younger brother, James Crawford Ledlie Carson (ca. 1815–86), completed his medical degrees at Glasgow University in 1837, and also practiced in Coleraine.[63] Though he did not also enter the ministry like his brother, James did write and lecture on theological issues, such as *The Heresies of the Plymouth Brethren* (1862).[64] Carson's daughter, Margaret Carson Clarke (ca. 1810–80), was married to a surgeon in Coleraine, Andrew Campbell Clarke. They and their children were buried at the same cemetery in Desertmartin, in a plot adjacent to that of her parents. Both James Carson and Andrew Clarke attended the dying Alexander Carson at Belfast in August 1844.[65]

Carson's youngest son, Robert Haldane Carson (ca. 1821–1904), followed his father into the ministry and eventually became the pastor of the Tobermore Baptist Church, though he became the pastor at the Baptist church in Perth, Scotland, beforehand, beginning in October 25, 1847.[66]

---

62. George's parents advised him to enter the medical field because there were no openings for Baptist ministers in Ireland at the time. Moore, *Life of Alexander Carson*, 52–53.

63. Boase, *Modern English Biography*, 4:610.

64. Like his father, James seemed to have been unafraid of wading into controversy. The 3rd edition of this work was published as a book in London, as opposed to a pamphlet, with his letters on the Revival of Ireland appended to the end.

65. Moore, *Life of Alexander Carson*, 146.

66. Douglas, *Biographical Sketch*, 7. "On Monday, October 25, Mr. Robert Haldane Carson, son of the late Dr. Carson of Tubbermore, who had ministered for some time to the church lately under the care of his venerated father, was publicly recognized as pastor of the baptist church in Perth. . . . Mr. Carson settles under encouraging prospects, and the church at Perth appears to be in a thriving, promising condition." *Baptist Magazine*, "Ordinations," 776. Interestingly, there seems to have been concern by those sympathetic to Campbell's restoration movement concerning Robert Carson's impending ministry in Perth. In a letter from Perth, dated November 14, 1847, a Robert Anderson wrote, "P.S. The Baptists here have hired the son of the late Dr. Carson of Tubbermore, to be their pastor; we can look for little favor from this gentleman, as we observe by the *Messenger* of last month, that he refused his chapel in Tubbermore, to brother Henshall, on the ground that Mr. Campbell is not a Christian? . . . On account of his views of divine truth, says Mr. Carson." *Christian Messenger*, "Items of News," 571–72.

He also served as the superintendent of the Sabbath school in Tobermore, where a number of his older siblings had been quite active in teaching the children in Tobermore.[67] His more widely published works were controversial in nature, such as *The Brethren: Their Worship and the Word of God at Open Variance* (1880) and *A Reply to the Late Work of the Rev. Thomas Witherow, on the Ecclesiastical Polity of the New Testament* (1856).[68]

Though Carson's writings during the initial years after his separation from the General Synod of Ulster dealt with church government and congregational polity, his shift to baptistic convictions were not immediately reflected in his writings. Rather, it seems that Carson was primarily focused on his pastoral ministry, though this is deduced more from a lack of published writings than positive evidence. Though it was not published until after his death, his evangelistic letter to Napoleon Bonaparte in 1814 is an example of his continuing evangelistic efforts beyond the boundaries of his Tobermore congregation.[69]

From 1820, Carson was periodically active in writing against Unitarianism and deism. In 1820, Carson wrote *The Truth of the Gospel Demonstrated from the Character of God Manifested in the Atonement: A Letter to Mr. Richard Carlile*, which was essentially a presentation of the gospel through a description of God's characteristics.[70] Carson also wrote *A Reply to Dr. Drummond's Essay on the Doctrine of the Trinity* (1831),[71] which was a defense of Trinitarian doctrine against William Hamilton Drummond's (1778–1865) *The Doctrine of the Trinity Founded Neither on Scripture, nor on Reason and Common Sense, but on Tradition and the Infallible Church* (1827).

In the early 1820s, Carson also published several works against Roman Catholicism. In 1823, Carson's *Strictures on the Letter of J. K. L. Entitled a Vindication of the Religious and Civil Principles of the Irish Catholics* was published anonymously in response to a letter by James Warren Doyle (1786–1834) or J. K. L. (James, Kildare and Leighlin), the Roman Catholic bishop of Kildare and Leighlin. In his *Strictures*, Carson addresses both

---

67. A. Carson, *Address to the Children*. Eliza and Matilda seem to have been especially committed to the Sabbath school. G. Carson and Hanna, *Memorials*, 13–14.

68. Witherow, who wrote a very positive biography of Robert's father responded to Carson's *Reply* in *Defence of the Apostolic Church* (1857). Alexander Carson's departure from the Synod of Ulster was Witherow's only criticism in his biographical sketch.

69. *Works* 1:279–94.

70. The second, enlarged edition was published in 1826 and reprinted in 1839.

71. *Works* 2:189–396.

Doyle's religious and political arguments.[72] Another anonymous work directed toward Doyle was "Remarks on the Late Miracle, in a Letter Addressed to the Rev. Doctor Doyle, Titular Bishop of Kildare and Leighlin" (1823), in which Carson discusses miracles performed by Satan through counterfeit churches.[73] Concerning Carson's view of the divine authority of Scripture and man's responsibility to read it was *The Right and Duty of All Men to Read the Scriptures: Being the Substance of a Speech Intended to Have Been Delivered at the Meeting of the Carlow Bible Society* (1824).[74] *The Doctrine of Transubstantiation Subversive of the Foundations of Human Belief: Therefore Incapable of Being Proved by Any Evidence, or of Being Believed by Men Under the Influence of Common Sense* (1825) reflected his belief in the Roman Catholic doctrine of transubstantiation as mere superstition.[75] Carson saw the Roman Catholic Church as a real threat to the spread of the gospel. His evangelistic overtures to Roman Catholics were not always appreciated and may even have endangered his life at times.[76]

Carson's *The Right and Duty of All Men to Read the Scriptures* foreshadowed, to a degree, the issues he would address in the later 1820s. Carson developed a close relationship with the Haldanes, and they published numerous works by Carson, often written at their behest. Possibly the most

---

72. *Works* 2:151–72. James Warren Doyle (1786–1834), an Irish native, was born and raised as a Roman Catholic in County Wexford, southeast Ireland. He matriculated at the University of Coimbra, Portugal, in 1807, but was subsequently arrested after the French invasion. He was recalled to Wexford in 1808, where he was ordained as a priest. In 1819 he was made bishop of Kildare and Leighlin in eastern Ireland. Doyle was an activist, working to improve the spiritual and moral condition of the priests and laity he was responsible for. He also became a political activist as far as it related to Catholics in Ireland. His *Vindication of the Religious and Civil Principles of the Irish Catholics: In a Letter Addressed to His Excellency the Marquis Wellesley* was published in 1823. He advocated both harmony and discord with Evangelicals, depending on the issue. For example, he promoted ecumenical education but was against Protestant schools because of their proselytizing goals. After his death, a controversy arose over Doyle's religious affiliation. Moore made reference to an 1834 article in *The Christian Freeman* that expressed belief that Doyle had been converted to a principally Protestant position prior to his death (Moore, *Life of Alexander Carson*, 41). William John Fitzpatrick argues strongly against Doyle's conversion to Protestantism, and he appeals to numerous letters that testify to Doyle's faithfulness to the Catholic faith up until his death. Thomas McGrath, "Doyle, James Warren," *ODNB* 16:833–35; Fitzpatrick, *Life, Times, and Correspondence*.

73. See Doyle, *Miracle*.

74. *Works* 2:1–46.

75. *Works* 2:47–128.

76. Moore, *Life of Alexander Carson*, 42–46.

well-known works were those dealing with the inspiration of Scripture. It began with the Haldanes' involvement in the Aprocrypha controversy, and their protest over the British and Foreign Bible Society's inclusion of the Aprocrypha in their Bibles.[77] Carson wrote numerous works dealing with the inspiration of Scripture from the latter 1820s through the latter 1830s, many of them written against John Pye Smith (1774–1851), a Congregational minister.[78] Carson's *Review of the Rev. Dr. J. Pye Smith's Defence of Dr. Haffner's Preface to the Bible and of His Denial of the Divine Authority of Part of the Canon, and of the Full Inspiration of the Holy Scriptures* (1827), written at Robert Haldane's request, espoused plenary verbal inspiration of Scripture as opposed to Smith's idea that Scripture was inspired in its principles.[79] *A Treatise on the Figures of Speech* (1827) was a hermeneutical work that classified figures of speech into nine categories; though Carson drew from numerous sources to illustrate the figures of speech, he likely meant his descriptions to be applied primarily to the proper interpretation of Scripture. In *The Theories of Inspiration of the Rev. Daniel Wilson, Rev. Dr. Pye Smith, and the Rev. Dr. Dick, Proved to Be Erroneous* (1830), Carson refuted various definitions of biblical inspiration that were contrary to the plenary verbal inspiration of Scripture.[80] In *Examination of the Principles of Biblical Interpretation of Ernesti, Ammon, Stuart, and Other Philologists*

---

77. The British and Foreign Bible Society, a nondenominational Bible society founded in 1804, had been including the Apocrypha in some of their Bibles from 1813, primarily to appease Roman Catholic and Greek Orthodox readers on the European continent. When Robert Haldane discovered the addition, he and others argued against its inclusion, saying that many lay people did not know how to discern between what was authoritative and what was man made. Protestants arguing for its inclusion believed that Roman Catholics who needed the Bible most would be allowed access only if it included the Apocrypha. When private discussions for the Apocrypha's removal failed, the controversy became a public affair. In 1825, the Edinburgh Bible Society published their *Statement by the Committee of the Edinburgh Bible Society, Relative to the Circulation of the Apocrypha by the British and Foreign Bible Society*, which began a pamphlet war. The Glasgow and Edinburgh chapters of the Bible society eventually separated as a result of the controversy, though the Bible society did stop including the Apocrypha in their Bibles. The preceding information was taken primarily from the following sources: A. Haldane, *Memoirs*; R. Haldane, *Review of the Conduct*; *Christian Guardian*, Unsigned review of *Statement*.

78. Smith viewed scientific studies very positively, and he would reject the literal biblical accounts of creation and the flood due to his geological studies.

79. *Works* 3:429–69.

80. *Works* 3:91–259. *The Orthodox Presbyterian* contains an overview of Carson's work, which is helpful in showing its positive reception among conservative evangelical groups. *Orthodox Presbyterian*, Unsigned review of *Theories*.

(1836), Carson critiqued how German philology was being applied to Scripture.[81] Though he previously bolstered Ebenezer Henderson's (1784–1858) earlier critique of an inadequate Turkish Bible translation, Carson attacked his view of degrees of biblical inspiration in *Refutation of Dr. Henderson's Doctrine in His Late Work on Divine Inspiration* (1837).[82] Like the Haldanes, Carson held to a plenary verbal inspiration of Scriptures, believing that the Bible was fully inspired by God in its very words, and not just in its ideas, as proposed by Smith and others. Carson's high view of Scripture was evident in all of his works, even those not dealing directly with inspiration, from the beginning of his ministry till its end.

Carson was also a source of aid for Robert Haldane's *Exposition of the Five First Chapters of the Epistle to the Romans* (1835–39). In the preface of the first volume, Haldane wrote, "I have also had the advantage of the assistance of Dr. Carson, whose profound knowledge of the original language, and well-known critical discernment, peculiarly qualify him for rendering effectual aid in such a work."[83] The description of Carson's linguistic skills points one back to Carson's training under John Young at the University of Glasgow. Interestingly, George Moore referred to a letter from Joseph D. Carson, a grandson of Carson, which led him to believe that Haldane's work was essentially from Carson.[84] In a copy of the letter included in the appendix, the younger Carson wrote, "I have heard it remarked by some that it was strange his works were not more voluminous, as they understood that a great part of his time was devoted to writing. But they are ignorant of the fact that for many years he assisted his friend, the late Robert Haldane, Esq., of Edinburgh, in writing his Evidences of Christianity, his Commentary on the Romans, and other works. I have myself, when but a boy, posted many a quire of manuscript sent from Tubbermore to Mr. Haldane."[85] Though Joseph Carson's experiences do not necessarily affirm Moore's suspicions, this does show that Carson had a close working relationship with Robert Haldane.

---

81. *Works* 5:223–423.

82. *Works* 3:261–402. In 1824, Henderson wrote *Appeal to the Members* (1824), to which Samuel Lee (1783–1852), professor of Arabic at Cambridge at the time, responded with *Remarks on Dr. Henderson's Appeal* (1824). Henderson responded, in turn, with *Turkish New Testament* (1825). Carson critiqued Lee's response in *Incompetency of Rev. Professor Lee* (1829), which was followed by his *Answer to Rev. Professor Lee* (1829).

83. R. Haldane, *Exposition of the Epistle to the Romans*, 16.

84. Moore, *Life of Alexander Carson*, 110.

85. Moore, *Life of Alexander Carson*, 151.

The Gospel-Centered Evangelicalism of Alexander Carson

Interestingly, Carson waited until 1831 to publish a work on baptism, *Baptism in Its Mode and Subjects Considered*, which sparked praise and debate throughout Great Britain and America. Carson was awarded honorary degrees from colleges in Kentucky and Louisiana.[86] Moore wrote that Carson waited over twenty years before publishing his views on baptism for two reasons. He wanted, first, to avoid using the common arguments used by those before him, and, second, to give further study on the subject and allowing his views to mature.[87] Carson wrote a second edition that excluded the use of Greek, thus making it more accessible to lay readers. Carson responded to various critics of his views on baptism for the remainder of his life. The most well-known debate was with Edward Beecher (1803-95), the president of Illinois College, whose father was Lyman Beecher (1775-1863).[88]

Carson was actively working to spread the gospel throughout his ministry, and his evangelistic efforts were not confined to his published works. For example, Carson and his Tobermore congregation were involved in mission work in Dublin with David Nasmith (1799-1839), who founded the Dublin City Mission.[89] W. D. Killen wrote that "a large proportion of

---

86. The colleges were Bacon College, Kentucky, and College of Louisiana. Bacon College no longer exists, but a number of Kentucky educational institutions have their roots, in part, in Bacon College, including the University of Kentucky and Transylvania University. The *Catalogue of Kentucky University* includes the following information about Carson: "Degrees Conferred by Bacon College, 1841–1850, Doctor of Laws: Alexander Carson, Tubbermore, Ireland." Kentucky University, *Catalogue*, 15. The College of Louisiana in Jackson, Louisiana, merged with Centenary College in Clinton, Mississippi, to form Centenary College of Louisiana in 1845.

87. Moore, *Life of Alexander Carson*, 23–24.

88. Beecher, *Baptism* (1840); A. Carson, *Baptism Not Purification* (1841). Edward Beecher was the third child of Lyman Beecher, and the brother of Henry Ward Beecher and Harriet Beecher Stowe. He graduated as valedictorian at Yale College in 1822. He became the president of Illinois College in 1831, only two years after it was founded by several Yale students committed to promoting education and religion in the West. During his time at Illinois College, Edward was involved in a theological controversy with Carson. He was also politically active as an abolitionist. In 1844, he left Illinois to minister at the Salem Street Church of Boston. He founded a Congregational church in Galesburg, Illinois, in 1855. He later preached at the Parkville Congregational Church in Brooklyn, New York, from 1884 to 1889. The preceding information was taken primarily from Stowe, *Saints, Sinners and Beechers*, 144–51.

89. A Glasgow native, David Nasmith was involved with religious and charitable societies from an early age. For example, he became the secretary of the Glasgow Youth's Bible Association at age fourteen. Nasmith founded the City Mission, a parachurch agency providing for spiritual and material needs, in the cities of Glasgow (1826), Dublin

the Scripture-readers belonging to the Dublin City Mission were at one period drawn from the congregation of Dr. Carson, of Tobermore."[90] Douglas wrote that the City Mission's "Scripture-readers" were examined in regards to their knowledge of Scripture and doctrine, as well as being asked to give a clear gospel presentation. The large proportion of readers from Carson's congregation that Reid referred to was presented by Douglas as being forty-four of fifty-four accepted candidates.[91] Carson was not an anonymous contributor to Nasmith's efforts in Dublin. In a letter to a Miss Oswald, dated January 22, 1835, concerning the raising of funds for founding a new mission in London, Nasmith mentioned "our friend, Carson, of Tubbermore," and his confidence that funds could be raised quickly for Nasmith's prospects in London.[92]

Carson, as a preacher, was primarily known for excelling in the preaching of the gospel, and never excluded presenting the gospel during a worship service. He regularly participated in evangelistic tours throughout Great Britain on behalf of the Baptist Missionary Society.[93] His reputation in gospel endeavors also led to an opportunity to preach at the fiftieth anniversary of William Carey's (1761–1834) missionary enterprise at Surrey Chapel, London, on October 12, 1842.[94] The sermon's title was "The

---

(1828), Edinburgh (1832), and London (1835). He also traveled and founded missions throughout America, Canada, and France. He was rebaptized by immersion in 1834, yet did not seek to join a Baptist church or be labeled as a Baptist. He founded the British and Foreign Mission in 1837, for the purpose of opening correspondence between existing missions and forming new ones where needed. The preceding information was taken primarily from the following sources: Gordon Goodwin and H. C. G. Matthew, "Nasmith, David," *ODNB* 40:243–44; Campbell, *Memoirs of David Nasmith*.

90. W. D. Killen, in Reid, *Presbyterian Church in Ireland*, 3:418n.

91. Douglas, *Biographical Sketch*, 14–15. Douglas's primary reason for mentioning the Tobermore congregation's participation in the City Mission was to show the effectiveness of Carson's expository preaching in instructing his congregation in the Bible.

92. Campbell, *Memoirs of David Nasmith*, 297–98.

93. Originally called the Particular Baptist Society for Propagating the Gospel Among Heathens, the Baptist Missionary Society was founded in 1792 by Baptist ministers such as William Carey, Andrew Fuller (1754–1815), and John Ryland (1753–1825). The society sent out Carey and John Thomas as their first Baptist missionaries to Bengal, India. The society acted as a catalyst for the formation of missionary societies in other denominations.

94. William Carey was born on August 17, 1761, at Northamptonshire, England. His father's occupation as a parish clerk and schoolmaster provided Carey with access to literature from an early age. While working as a shoemaker, he became a Congregationalist (1779) and, eventually, a Baptist (1783). He was baptized by John Ryland (1753–1825)

Propagation of the Gospel, with Encouragement to the Vigorous Prosecution of the Work."[95] It was during his return from one of these tours that Carson's life and ministry came to an unexpected end. On August 16, 1844, while waiting for a ship in Liverpool, he fell off the dock and was injured. Though he was able to return to Belfast the next day, he fell ill and died on August 24, 1844, in the presence of a number of friends and family members. Carson was buried in his family plot at the Church of Ireland parish of Desertmartin, which is approximately three miles from Tobermore. There, his body joined those of his wife, two daughters, two sons, and three grandchildren.[96]

---

in 1783. He preached and studied biblical languages while working as a shoemaker, though he would also become a pastor in 1785. His pamphlet *Enquiry into the Obligations of Christians* (1792) reflected his growing concern for evangelism beyond Europe. His arguments persuaded other Baptists, such as Andrew Fuller (1754–1815) and John Ryland, to join him in founding the Particular Baptist Society for Propagating the Gospel Among Heathens, which was later called the Baptist Missionary Society. In 1793, Carey and John Thomas, a surgeon, arrived in Bengal, India, as missionaries. Carey's work involved preaching, teaching, founding of mission centers, and Bible translation. Carey and his associates translated the entire Bible into six languages and partially into twenty-nine languages. Carey died in 1834, at Serampore, India. The preceding information was taken primarily from Brian Stanley, "Carey, William," *ODNB* 10:90–91.

95. Acworth and Carson, *Two Sermons*, 44–83.

96. His wife, Margaret; his sons, Alexander and George; his daughters, Eliza and Susan(na). It is unclear precisely which grandchildren were buried prior to Carson's burial, though two of the children belonged to Carson's oldest son, George. G. Carson and Hanna, *Memorials*. Other members of Carson's family, children, and grandchildren have joined his plot and an adjacent plot since his burial. They include his eldest daughter, Margaret Carson Clarke, d. Dec. 4, 1880; her husband, Dr. Andrew Campbell Clarke, d. Apr. 17, 1876; and Carson's youngest son, Rev. Haldane Carson, d. Feb. 2, 1904. Their graves can still be seen at the Church of Ireland parish of Desertmartin.

2

Alexander Carson on the Bible

DAVID BEBBINGTON ASSERTED THAT the common evangelical view of Scripture's inspired status in the early nineteenth century was the same as other theologians of the time, a view that rejected verbal inspiration, instead espousing the view that Scripture was inspired in degrees or modes.[1] He further claimed that a noticeable shift in evangelical attitudes towards the Scriptures and the way in which they were to be considered divinely inspired began with Robert Haldane. The Scottish Evangelical published *The Evidence and Authority of Divine Revelation* (1816) in two volumes, in which he rejected the "generally adopted" view that the Bible was inspired in different degrees and asserted that the Scriptures themselves claimed to be verbally inspired.[2] In contrast to Bebbington's opinion, Kenneth J. Stewart argued that Bebbington incorrectly portrayed "Haldane as the theological innovator."[3] Stewart argued that Haldane came from a lineage of those who also held to verbal inspiration, a group that included men such as John Gill (1697–1771), English Baptist theologian, and John Owen (1616–83), English Puritan theologian.[4] While Stewart was accurate to point out Haldane's position on biblical inspiration as part of a preexisting view, Bebbington's perceived view of Haldane as a innovator might be exaggerated. While Haldane was not alone in his views on Scripture, the view he opposed was well represented among Evangelicals. One supporter Haldane was able to enlist

1. Bebbington, *Evangelicalism in Modern Britain*, 86–37.
2. R. Haldane, *Evidence and Authority*, 1:135.
3. Stewart, "Evangelical Doctrine of Scripture," 410n58.
4. Stewart, "Evangelical Doctrine of Scripture," 410.

into his ranks was Alexander Carson, who had made ecclesiological shifts similar to Haldane's own. Carson's views on the Bible will be examined in the areas of inspiration, Bible translation, and the preservation of Scripture. The first two categories will be discussed in the context of Carson's polemical writings concerning those topics.

CONTEXT OF THE APOCRYPHA CONTROVERSY

In 1821, Robert Haldane discovered that the British and Foreign Bible Society had, to some degree unknowingly, funded the production of foreign Bibles that included the Apocrypha. The resulting controversy was initially kept from the public eye, and the Bible Society publicly resolved no longer to include the Apocrypha in 1822.[5] Yet, in 1824, the Edinburgh Bible Society, an auxiliary of the British and Foreign Bible Society, became aware of and addressed the main branch's practice of giving financial aid to foreign Bible societies that included the Apocrypha at their own expense. Though the British and Foreign Bible Society again made a resolution to abstain from directly funding the printing of the Apocrypha, the Edinburgh auxiliary was incensed that foreign societies were still allowed to append the Apocrypha to the society-funded Bibles as long as the printing of the Apocrypha was privately funded. The Edinburgh Bible Society's sentiment was grounded on the following beliefs: "The Apocrypha is not only an uninspired book, and therefore on a level with other human productions, but far below the level of many human compositions, as it is abundantly interspersed with falsehoods, false doctrines, superstitions, and contradictions of itself and of the Word of God ... and because these Apocryphal writings, laden as they are with such gross and palpable error, do advance a deceitful claim to reverence and attention, upon the pretext of their being inspired."[6] The Edinburgh auxiliary's sentiments were printed in a statement, which was sent to the Committee of the British and Foreign Bible Society on February 24, 1825. Though the committee was initially noncommittal to the Edinburgh Society's resolutions, the parent society finally capitulated by the end of that year. The three final resolutions were that the society would be "fully and distinctly recognized as excluding the circulation of the Apocrypha," that financial aid would not be given to foreign societies that circulated the Apocrypha, and that all issued Bibles would be bound

---

5. A. Haldane, *Memoirs*, 493–95.
6. Edinburgh Bible Society, *Statement*, 6–7.

with the "express condition, that they shall be distributed without alteration or addition."[7] The British and Foreign Bible Society's resolutions did not please everyone. The Frankfort Bible Society, for example, appealed to the fact that the German Bible had, since the Reformation, always included the Apocrypha as a separate section.[8] This sentiment was shared by numerous Bible societies on the continent, such as those in Basel and Berlin.[9] On the other hand, some Bible societies were pleased with the principle and the result. The Cologne Bible Society, for example, reported that only one in five hundred Bibles was returned "on the ground of its wanting the Apocryphal books. Some clergymen have complained of these books being wanting, but have not on that ground desisted from circulating them."[10]

Yet, these reforms made by the British and Foreign Bible Society did not conclude the controversy sparked by the distribution of the Apocrypha. In 1826, *The Evangelical Magazine and Missionary Chronicle* included a series of six intelligence reports on the state of religion in continental Europe by John Pye Smith.[11] Smith's fourth installment of the series appeared in the September issue of the magazine and included extracts from the *Report of the Eighth Annual Meeting of the Strasburgh Bible Society* and from a speech by Isaac Haffner (1751–1831), professor of divinity at the University of Strasbourg and vice-president of the city's Bible society, to describe the religious growth in Strasbourg.[12] The use of these two extracts led Alexander Haldane (1800–82), James Haldane's son, to send a critical response to *The Evangelical Magazine and Missionary Chronicle*, which was published in the following month's issue.[13] Haldane was especially critical of Smith's positive use of Haffner, a man he believed to be a rationalist, a

---

7. British and Foreign Bible Society, *Twenty-Second Report*, xvii.

8. Frankfort Bible Society, "From the Committee."

9. Basel Bible Society, "From the Committee"; Central Prussian Bible Society, "From the Committee."

10. Krafft, "From the Rev. Mr. Krafft."

11. J. Pye Smith: "State of Religion," nos. 1–3; "Extracts and Hints," pts. 4–6.

12. J. Pye Smith, "Extracts and Hints," pt. 4. Haffner was born December 2, 1751, in Strasbourg, France. Haffner was also the minister at St. Nichol's. Van Bemmelen, "Issues in Biblical Inspiration," 76.

13. Αληθεια [A. Haldane], "State of Religion at Strasburgh." Haldane used the pseudonym Αληθεια for this initial letter, which became a topic of contention in his subsequent discourse with Smith. Haldane was born in Edinburgh on October 15, 1800. He was the second son born to James Alexander Haldane's first wife Mary (1771–1819). He was educated at the University of Edinburgh. He later moved to London, where he was a barrister of the Inner Temple.

"*scoffer at vital Christianity*," and a denier of the inspiration of the Bible.[14] This, in turn, led to a published discourse between the two men, which was subsequently republished or noted in various periodicals.[15] While Haldane maintained his opinion of Haffner's heterodoxy, Smith's view of Haffner was more nuanced. Smith recognized theological differences with Haffner but argued that differences in conviction should not lead Evangelicals to demonize him.[16] While he admitted that Haffner was a German "*Rationalist*," he argued that not all rationalists were deists who denied the supernatural, though the term also included deists.[17] After an examination of some of Haffner's theological views, Smith concluded that "Dr. Haffner is, unhappily, far from the reception of the genuine evangelical doctrines; but that it is most *absurd, unjust,* and *untrue,* to call him an INFIDEL."[18] Concerning German higher criticism, Smith believed that the "fundamental *principles* of Bible-interpretation, which characterize these [rationalist] divines, are true and solid," and that the use of their principles were able to prove all the primary doctrines of the Christianity.[19]

Bebbington has accurately pointed out that Smith's work broached the "fundamental issue" of "the nature of inspiration."[20] It was because of the stakes involved in this crucial issue that Robert Haldane, in a letter to his nephew, described Smith's papers defending Haffner as "the most dangerous that have yet appeared in the Apocrypha business."[21] The elder Haldane also enlisted Carson to respond to Smith's views. This response, *Review of the Rev. Dr. J. Pye Smith's Defence of Dr. Haffner's Preface to the Bible, and of His Denial of the Divine Authority of Part of the Canon, and of the Full Inspiration of the Holy Scriptures* (1827),[22] was published as a sequel to Haldane's *The Authenticity and Inspiration of the Holy Scriptures* (1827), and it marked Carson's entry into the Apocrypha controversy as well as

14. Αληθεια, "State of Religion at Strasburgh," 438; emphasis in original.

15. J. Pye Smith, "Reply to Alethia"; A. Haldane and Smith, "Correspondence"; *Monthly Repository*, "Dr. J. P. Smith's Vindication"; *Monthly Repository*, "Dr. J. P. Smith and Mr. Haldane."

16. J. Pye Smith, "Reply to Alethia," 476.

17. A. Haldane and Smith, "Correspondence," 525; emphasis in original.

18. A. Haldane and Smith, "Correspondence," 526; emphasis in original.

19. J. Pye Smith, "Reply to Alethia," 477; emphasis in original.

20. Bebbington, *Evangelicalism in Modern Britain*, 88.

21. A. Haldane, *Memoirs*, 525.

22. *Works* 3:429–69. A section of Carson's critique of Smith was republished as a part of A. Carson, *Theories of Inspiration*; *Works* 3:91–259.

his first work specifically dealing with the inspiration of the Bible. Carson's role in the Apocrypha controversy had less to do with the Apocrypha and more with being an advocate for the plenary verbal inspiration of Scripture. Though he was initially brought into the controversy by his friend and patron, Robert Haldane, he did not see the role as a defender of plenary verbal inspiration as coming from Haldane or even himself. This role was committed to him from a much higher source: "The doctrine of verbal inspiration is one of the fortresses committed to Christians by Jesus Christ."[23]

CARSON'S DOCTRINE OF PLENARY VERBAL INSPIRATION

Carson's views on the inspiration of Scripture can be placed in two categories. First, he believed in plenary inspiration, that is, the entire Bible was divinely inspired. Second, he held to the verbal inspiration of Scripture, that is, it was inspired in its words as well as its thoughts and sentiments. It will be under these categories that Carson's doctrine of plenary verbal inspiration will be examined. As with most of his theological stances, Carson's views on inspiration were primarily conveyed to the public through his polemical works. It is within the context of these theological controversies that one is able to see the details and nuances of his views. His defense of the doctrine of plenary verbal inspiration included his criticism of what he believed to be the arbitrary theories of inspiration by Neologians as well as interaction with their use of Scripture.

Defense of Plenary Inspiration

Carson's defense of the inspiration of the whole Scripture is essentially found in two arguments. First, the nature and extent of the Bible's inspiration could only be learned from the Bible itself. This argument primarily consisted of Carson's dependence upon 2 Tim 3:16 as conclusive proof for the plenary inspiration of Scripture. His second point was that the Bible gave no criterion for determining which portions of Scripture were inspired or uninspired. Carson thus had to respond to numerous approaches for determining the inspiration of particular books or passages in Scripture.

---

23. A. Carson, *Theories of Inspiration*, 130; *Works* 3:192.

The Gospel-Centered Evangelicalism of Alexander Carson

The Nature and Extent of Inspiration Can Be Learned Only from Scripture

After charging Smith, a fellow Evangelical, with taking a more pragmatic approach to forming theories of inspiration, Carson asked, "What is the method that just criticism would adopt in ascertaining the nature and extent of inspiration? Undoubtedly it is by arguing, what saith the Scriptures?"[24] In answering his own question, he only referred to the first part of 2 Tim 3:16—"All Scripture is given by inspiration of God"—and he believed this to be sufficient evidence for the inspiration of the entire Bible. Both men were apparently asking the same question: What were the nature and extent of the inspiration of Scripture? In Carson's opinion, their answers were principally at odds. He believed that the only source that could provide an answer was the Scripture itself. Therefore, he rejected all external sources of evidence for and against inspiration as inconclusive. This conviction that the nature and extent of the Bible's inspiration could only be learned from internal evidence was a presupposition that influenced his arguments against those with whom he would disagree regarding the doctrine of plenary inspiration. While Carson believed that "there is as much evidence that the Bible is the Word of God, as there is that creation is God's work," he did not rely on quantitative evidence to establish his doctrine of plenary inspiration.[25] Instead, he found 2 Tim 3:16 to be clear in teaching the plenary inspiration of Scripture and, therefore, both sufficient in defending the doctrine and decisive in excluding any other view of biblical inspiration.

Carson also addressed this point in his critique of Ebenezer Henderson's views on inspiration.[26] In a series of published lectures on divine inspiration, Henderson was critical of those who based the doctrine of inspiration solely on what Stewart called "pillar" passages.[27] Henderson argued that it was wrong to receive the doctrine of inspiration "simply on the declarations of those by whom the Scriptures were written" for that would be taking "for granted the very point to be proved."[28] Another reason he disagreed with this type of reasoning for the inspiration of Scripture was that not all the writers of Scripture claimed any sort of inspiration.

---

24. A. Carson, *Theories of Inspiration*, 100–101; *Works* 3:171.
25. *Works* 1:284.
26. A. Carson, *Refutation of Dr. Henderson's Doctrine*; *Works* 3:261–402.
27. Stewart, "Evangelical Doctrine of Scripture," 410.
28. Henderson, *Divine Inspiration*, 281–82.

Alexander Carson on the Bible

Ultimately, Henderson believed that the demand for positive proof for the inspiration of Scripture must be more carefully and thoughtfully addressed. For Carson, on the other hand, it was sufficient that 2 Tim 3:16, which claimed the inspired status of Scripture, was just as inspired as any other part of Scripture: "Why do we believe that John i. 1, infallibly teaches the Deity of Christ? Is it not because all scripture is given by inspiration? And is not 2 Tim. iii. 16, equally inspired? If it is good proof for inspiration for all other parts of Scripture, surely it cannot be worse proof for the inspiration for itself?"[29]

Henderson presented three ways in which his contemporaries understood γραφή in the context of 2 Tim 3:16. The first interpretation was the most popular and understood γραφή to only refer to the Old Testament, though Henderson noted that advocates of this view were divided over whether it applied to the entire Old Testament or just parts of it. A second view was that γραφή referred to both the Old Testament and the New Testament writings that were already in existence when the epistle was written. The final viewpoint considered γραφή to only refer to the New Testament writings that were already written at the time of the epistle.[30] Henderson placed himself among adherents of the first view and did not believe that 2 Tim 3:16 provided sound proof of the New Testament's inspiration. Instead, he saw the ἱερὰ γράμματα in 2 Tim 3:15, which was a reference to the Old Testament, as a clear indication that γραφή also referred exclusively to the Old Testament.[31] This does not mean he denied the inspired status of the New Testament. Rather than using "presumptive arguments," he depended on "the authentic writings of the ambassadors of Christ" to prove the inspiration of the New Testament.[32]

Carson took issue with how Henderson limited the teaching of divine inspiration in 2 Tim 3:16 to the Old Testament. He argued that Henderson's position lacks force because γραφή lacks the article. Therefore, while he agreed that ἱερὰ γράμματα in the previous verse only referred to the Old Testament, the phrase "all Scripture" necessarily "embraces all that can be called Scripture."[33] More precisely, Carson believed that "all Scripture" included all of the Old Testament, the New Testament texts then in existence,

---

29. A. Carson, *Refutation of Dr. Henderson's Doctrine*, 4; *Works* 3:264.
30. Henderson, *Divine Inspiration*, 306.
31. Henderson, *Divine Inspiration*, 307.
32. Henderson, *Divine Inspiration*, 324.
33. A. Carson, *Refutation of Dr. Henderson's Doctrine*, 12; *Works* 3:269.

and all the New Testament texts that had yet to be written: "Should God this day give an additional communication of his will, calling it Scripture, 2 Tim. iii. 16, affirms its inspiration as directly as that of the Old Testament."[34] While the presence of an article would have implied that the text being referred to already existed, a lack of the article allowed for Carson's comprehensive application. His view was thoroughly explained in a series of letters to the editor of *The Christian Examiner, and Church of Ireland Magazine* in the early 1830s, in which Carson entered into a dialogue with another contributor, T. K., who was critical of the former's dependence upon 2 Tim 3:16 as one of the "pillars" for verbal inspiration.[35]

T. K.'s basic premise was that the appropriated sense of γραφή as a reference to the Christian Scriptures always required an article, and he concluded that the translators of the King James Version simply assumed the article was omitted at some point in the history of the Bible's transcription and that they translated the verse as though the article was present.[36] Carson's response was that while γραφή was typically used in its appropriated sense with the article, there were also instances in which γραφή was used anarthrously. He presented multiple examples of how γραφή was used in this sense without the article in both Scripture and the Church Fathers. He justified his use of the Church Fathers by reasoning that the question was one of Greek grammar: "And on such a question Justin Martyr is as competent an authority as the Apostle Paul. I appeal to the Fathers, not to sanction a theological sentiment, but to determine whether the appropriation of γραφη [sic] can subsist without the article. Inspiration did not give syntax to the Greek language."[37] While he gave multiple examples from various sources, Carson contended that a single positive example of γραφή used in the appropriated sense without the article would be sufficient to prove his point, because he was not trying to prove it as the general rule but as a possible exception.

Carson also argued that the article did not determine the sense of a word. Rather, the "situation, connexion, and circumstances" determined

---

34. A. Carson, *Refutation of Dr. Henderson's Doctrine*, 75; *Works* 3:317.

35. T. K., "Inspiration of Scripture." T. K., a frequent contributor to the magazine, was responding to Carson's use of 2 Tim 3:16 in *Theories of Inspiration*. Carson's letters were collated and included in his *Refutation of Dr. Henderson's Doctrine*, 133–87; *Works* 3:361–402.

36. A. Carson, *Refutation of Dr. Henderson's Doctrine*, 137; *Works* 3:366.

37. A. Carson, *Refutation of Dr. Henderson's Doctrine*, 143; *Works* 3:370.

whether the word was being used in an appropriated sense or not.[38] This point does not imply that Carson did not see an important role for the article. While he agreed that the presence of the article for γραφή would have been proper Greek, it would not have communicated the exact same meaning. The inclusion of an article would have been rendered as "all the Scripture" rather than "all Scripture." This would have resulted in the application of 2 Tim 3:16 being limited to at least the Old Testament or, at most, all the biblical texts in existence at the time of Paul's second letter to Timothy.[39] Carson saw the exclusion of the article as an example of the Holy Spirit's wisdom in choosing the individual words of Scripture so as to extend inspiration "to such parts of the Scriptures as were written after this Epistle to Timothy, as well as to the other scriptures."[40] Therefore, establishing the dates of individual books and letters in the Scripture had no bearing on whether they were inspired or not.

Carson believed that "disaffection to the truth contained in" 2 Tim 3:16 led opponents of the doctrine to reinterpret or retranslate the verse. For example, in his critique of Smith's defense of Haffner, Carson noted how Smith translated the first part of the verse as "every writing divinely inspired," which, he pointed out, was the translation also preferred by Unitarians.[41] From this translation of 2 Tim 3:16, Unitarians asserted that only all Scripture which was inspired was profitable. Carson argued that the false supposition leading from this interpretation actually proved its irrationality: "It supposes that there must be a standard or criterion by which, in reading the Scriptures, we may distinguish what is inspired from what is uninspired. If there is no such criterion, we cannot make the proper use of what is inspired. Now, as no such criterion is given in Scripture, there cannot be need for such criterion."[42] His conclusion on this point stemmed from his conviction that God would provide any necessary tools for people to be able to understand the divine revelation: "If such a criterion is necessary in reading the Scriptures, and if no such criterion is given, the Scriptures are an insufficient rule."[43] From the absence of any clear biblical standard for determining inspiration within itself, Carson argued that any standard put

---

38. A. Carson, *Refutation of Dr. Henderson's Doctrine*, 168–69; *Works* 3:389.
39. A. Carson, *Refutation of Dr. Henderson's Doctrine*, 170; *Works* 3:390.
40. A. Carson, *Refutation of Dr. Henderson's Doctrine*, 170–71; *Works* 3:391.
41. A. Carson, *Theories of Inspiration*, 137; *Works* 3:196.
42. A. Carson, *Theories of Inspiration*, 142–43; *Works* 3:200.
43. A. Carson, *Theories of Inspiration*, 146; *Works* 3:203.

forth was necessarily created by human ingenuity and, therefore, fallible. While such created criterion would not necessarily be unfounded, it could never be authoritative.[44] Yet, various standards for determining which passages of Scripture were inspired or uninspired did exist. The following discussion will present four different criteria that will act as case studies to examine how Carson viewed and addressed these different views.

Carson's Rejection of Novel Criteria for Distinguishing Between Inspired and Uninspired Biblical Texts

The first example will examine Carson's response to the views of William Parry (1754–1819), a Congregational minister of Little Baddow, Essex.[45] In *The Scripture Testimony to the Messiah: An Inquiry with a View to a Satisfactory Determination of the Doctrine Taught in the Holy Scriptures Concerning the Person of Christ*, John Pye Smith quoted Parry's views against plenary inspiration positively, an inclusion which became an object of Carson's censure.[46] What struck Carson was Parry's statement that particular details in Scripture "were not things of a religious nature, and no inspiration was necessary concerning them" and that, concerning the New Testament writers, "it is not necessary to suppose, that they were under any *supernatural* influence in mentioning such common or civil affairs, though they were, as to all the sentiments they inculcated respecting religion."[47] Parry's position on inspiration was that the apostles were under divine inspiration "as to every religious sentiment contained in their writings," though this did not

---

44. A. Carson, *Theories of Inspiration*, 143; *Works* 3:200.

45. Parry was born in Abergavenny, Monmouthshire, in Wales. Though he had Baptist roots, Parry later joined a Congregational congregation in London. His minister, Samuel Brewer, advised him to train for the ministry, and Parry entered the Homerton Academy. In 1780 he was ordained as the pastor of the congregation in Little Baddow, Essex, where he ministered until 1799. His pastoral ministry was followed by his teaching position at an academy established by the Coward Trust at Wymondley House. Though he enjoyed teaching and preaching, a combination of poor health, theological disunity at the academy, and accusations of Socinianism became a great hindrance to his work. Ironically, one of his major works (*Inquiry* [1797]) was an anti-Socinian work. The preceding information was taken primarily from the following sources: John Handby Thompson, "Parry, William," *ODNB* 42:901–2.

46. J. Pye Smith, *Scripture Testimony to the Messiah*, 1:110. Quoted in Parry, *Inquiry*, 26–27.

47. A. Carson, *Theories of Inspiration*, 144; *Works* 3:201; emphasis in original. Quoted in J. Pye Smith, *Scripture Testimony to the Messiah*, 1:110; and in Parry, *Inquiry*, 26–27.

extend to every word.[48] According to Parry, one of the advantages of his view on inspiration was that it removed the necessity of asking "whether *every thing* contained in [the apostles'] writings were suggested immediately by the Spirit or not."[49] The criterion Parry used to ascertain which texts were inspired was to limit inspiration to those passages that dealt with religious or moral matters.[50] While Parry emphasized the divine infallibility of Scripture, he only applied it to parts of the Scripture he considered to be inspired. That he did not teach the plenary inspiration of Scripture is further established by his statement that his criterion enabled the "plain Christian, in reading his New Testament, to distinguish what he is to consider as *inspired truth*."[51] What troubled Carson more than Parry's criterion for distinguishing "*inspired truth*" was Smith's use of Parry, for Smith also affirmed that 2 Tim 3:16 taught the inspiration of all the books of Scripture.[52] Carson argued as a principle that what was true of a portion might not be true of the whole, but what was true of the whole was necessarily true of every part.[53] Therefore, if a whole book was divinely inspired, as Smith professed, then every passage therein must be inspired.

One danger Carson saw in the creation of criteria for determining what passages were inspired was that it opened the door for progressively liberal theories. He wrote, "If Mr. Parry has a right to make one criterion, has not Dr. Priestly [sic] a right to make another? If the former is permitted, by his theory, to purge the Scriptures of certain useless, though harmless excrescences, shall not the latter be equally entitled to devise a theory that will expel all doctrines supposed to be derogatory to the human understanding? If the smallest license of this kind is permitted, nothing shall be left as God's in the Scriptures that atheistical impudence shall think fit to question."[54] It was not coincidental that Carson compared Parry to Priestley (1733–1804), because Parry was addressing Priestley and Socianism in his own work.[55] Yet, instead of contrasting them, Carson depicted them as having the same "spirit of infidelity" or being on the same path away from

48. Parry, *Inquiry*, 26.
49. Parry, *Inquiry*, 27; emphasis in original.
50. Parry, *Inquiry*, 26.
51. Parry, *Inquiry*, 27; emphasis in original.
52. A. Carson, *Theories of Inspiration*, 144; *Works* 3:201.
53. A. Carson, *Theories of Inspiration*, 145; *Works* 3:202.
54. A. Carson, *Theories of Inspiration*, 146; *Works* 3:203.
55. Parry, *Inquiry*, iv–v.

the plenary inspiration of the Bible.[56] Priestley was simply further along the path than Parry, and the latter had no right to criticize the former for simply acting more fully upon the same principles. Carson's fear of a snowball effect in doctrinal decline was evident, and, therefore, he was loath to make even relatively small compromises when it involved anything he considered to be biblical truth. He believed even "an inch of scriptural ground is worth eternal war."[57]

A second example of novel criteria for identifying inspired texts is found in Carson's response to an article in *The Eclectic Review* in 1827.[58] Originally attributing the article to Smith, Carson argued against the writer's suggestion that the books of Esther and the Chronicles were possibly not divinely inspired.[59] The author did not question their inclusion in Scripture, believing them to be "both authentic and true," but questioned their inspiration due to the lack of internal or external evidence for such a status. The external evidence that proved their inspiration and that Carson unsurprisingly pointed to was their inclusion in the Jewish canon, which Christ recognized as being inspired. Paul's words in 2 Tim 3:16 also pointed in this direction. In examining the internal evidences for their inspiration, though, Carson prefaced his argument by dismissing any arbitrary requirement that an inspired book prove its divine origin by "the nature and excellence of its contents."[60] He explained his criticism of this arbitrary standard in more detail: "I do not submit to the dogma on which some modern critics seem to act, that the authority of the canon is not sufficient to entitle a book to be admitted to the rank of inspiration, and that it is necessary for each book to be separately tried on the independent evidence from its own contents."[61] Carson compared the Bible to a human body, with each book playing a particular role.[62] Therefore, while such internal evidence was welcome, he reasoned that some books or parts of books were not in

---

56. A. Carson, *Theories of Inspiration*, 165; *Works* 3:216.

57. A. Carson, *Theories of Inspiration*, 139; *Works* 3:197.

58. See *Eclectic Review*, Unsigned review of *Vindication*. The excerpt he quoted is found on p. 390 (misprinted as p. 930).

59. Carson attributed that article to Smith based on hearsay. A. Carson, *Review of the Rev. Dr. J. Pye Smith's Defence*, 62. In *Theories of Inspiration*, which included a portion of the former work, Carson noted that Smith had denied authoring the particular article in *The Eclectic Review*. A. Carson, *Theories of Inspiration*, 155n*; *Works* 3:209n*.

60. A. Carson, *Theories of Inspiration*, 163; *Works* 3:215.

61. A. Carson, *History of Providence in Book of Esther* (1835), 110; *Works* 6:137.

62. A. Carson, *History of Providence in Book of Esther* (1835), 112–13; *Works* 6:138.

a style that would contain this evidence. For example, though genealogies may lack the content that could indicate a divine source, he argued they still had "their use in the inspired volume."[63] This meant that even genealogies were practical, thus fulfilling the characteristics of inspired Scripture found in 2 Tim 3:16. He agreed with words from Thomas Scott (1747–1821), an Anglican theologian and Carson's favorite commentator, "If we could not understand, or get any benefit from certain portions of the Scriptures, it would be more reasonable to blame our own dulness, than, so much as in thought, to censure them as useless."[64] In light of this, Carson urged his readers to approach any Scripture with a humble attitude, seeking to "discover its wisdom, and reap the instruction and comfort it is calculated to afford."[65]

One disputed book that Carson was able to find much instruction in was the book of Esther. While this conviction was, first and foremost, based upon his interpretation of 2 Tim 3:16, it was verified by the content within Esther. The theological instruction he found most evident in the disputed book was the doctrine of God's providence in all things, even in the "minutest concerns" of life.[66] This theme in Esther is discussed in detail in *History of Providence as Unfolded in the Book of Esther* (1833), which was one of three of Carson's works dealing specifically with the doctrine of God's providence. He wrote,

> The great design of this portion of the Holy Scriptures is to display the wisdom, providence, and power of God, in the preservation of his people, and in the destruction of their enemies. We learn from it, that the most casual events which take place in the affairs of the world are connected with his plans respecting his people; and that the most trifling things are appointed and directed by him to effect his purposes. . . . From this book the believer may learn to place unbounded confidence in the care of his God in the utmost danger; and to look to the Lord of omnipotence for deliverance, when there is no apparent means of escape.[67]

---

63. A. Carson, *Theories of Inspiration*, 163; *Works* 3:215.

64. A. Carson, *Theories of Inspiration*, 165; *Works* 3:216. See original quote in Scott, *Holy Bible*, 1:375. George Moore believed Scott to be Carson's favorite commentator. Moore, *Life of Alexander Carson*, 56.

65. A. Carson, *Theories of Inspiration*, 165; *Works* 3:216.

66. A. Carson, *Theories of Inspiration*, 166; *Works* 3:216.

67. A. Carson, *History of Providence in Book of Esther* (1835), 3; *Works* 6:73.

In this statement, Carson presented the purposes of the book and applications for Christians of his day. Specifically addressing the book's status, he noted two ways in which it contained internal evidence of being inspired. First, he argued that a product of human ingenuity attempting to present itself as a divine work would be saturated with supernatural events.[68] Throughout the work, Carson pointed how God worked without any miracles. Second, he argued that the narrative never satisfied "mere curiosity" and only contained the facts necessary to teach the divinely intended purpose.[69] In this sense, his commentary on Esther was also a critique of others' views on the book, and orthodox Protestants were among his targets. An ongoing theme in Carson's work was his criticism of the practice by commentators of "obliging with their conjectures" and "many a shrewd guess" whenever something was not fully explained.[70] His reply to this practice of filling in the blanks is not surprising given his conviction that God had given all that was necessary in his divine revelation. The strongest expression of this sentiment might be the following statement: "But it is the duty of a Christian to learn every thing that the Scriptures record; and it is equally his duty to remain in the most obstinate ignorance of every thing that they do not reveal." One sees this opinion manifested in his response to those who hypothesized the reason for Ahasuerus's banquet in Esth 1:3. Instead of giving his own theory, Carson simply stated, "I know not—I care not."[71] Another example of Carson's critique against commentators is found in his response to efforts by Thomas Scott and John Gill to justify Mordecai's "vile prostitution of Esther," in not only allowing her to marry Ahasuerus but even being "uncommonly solicitous to promote her exaltation."[72] Both Scott and Gill attempted to justify this marriage, forbidden by Jewish law, by hypothesizing that Mordecai and Esther had no choice in the matter. Carson, however, pointed out that Mordecai was willing to risk his own life and the lives of his people by opposing Haman, so putting his life on the line to withstand tyranny was not beyond Mordecai.[73] His critique of Scott, his favorite commentator, and of Gill show the degree of his disapproval of

---

68. A. Carson, *History of Providence in Book of Esther* (1835), 106; *Works* 6:134.
69. A. Carson, *History of Providence in Book of Esther* (1835), 106; *Works* 6:134.
70. A. Carson, *History of Providence in Book of Esther* (1835), 10; *Works* 6:77.
71. A. Carson, *History of Providence in Book of Esther* (1835), 10; *Works* 6:77.
72. A. Carson, *History of Providence in Book of Esther* (1835), 23–24; *Works* 6:85.
73. A. Carson, *History of Providence in Book of Esther* (1835), 23–24; *Works* 6:85.

giving into the temptation to find explanations for anything not taught in Scripture.

While he found the book of Esther to have an abundance of internal evidence for divine authorship, Carson still argued against this as a prerequisite for a canonical book to be considered inspired. Not only might some books or portions of books not contain internal evidence of inspiration, but they might have even been derived from human sources. Referring to the historical genealogies of 1 and 2 Chronicles, Carson wrote, "These tables may be taken verbally and literally from public documents; but as they are inserted in the inspired volume, they have the seal of inspiration."[74] For Carson, this seal also applied to the book of Esther, whose inspiration and inclusion in the Bible was challenged partly due to its unknown authorship and derivative character. Adherence to the theories of higher criticism concerning Esther, for example, can be found in the writings of Evangelicals. In his critique of plenary verbal inspiration, Henderson wrote that "the Book of Esther is for the most part a translated extract from the Book of the Chronicles of the kings of Media and Persia" and that these "are points which are now generally admitted among those who are conversant with Biblical criticism."[75] While Henderson referred to the derivative characteristics of Esther to specifically argue against the doctrine of plenary verbal inspiration, which will be discussed in further detail later, Carson's response is still applicable for his defense of plenary inspiration in general and of Esther's inspiration in particular. More than with Henderson's comments on Esther's derivative characteristic, Carson was critical of his dependence upon neological doctrines in opposition to what was taught in Scripture. Carson believed these theories were both unproven and unprovable. Concerning Esther's foreign origins, Carson argued that this, if true, did not have a negative impact on the book's inspired status or rightful inclusion in the Bible, solely based on 2 Tim 3:16.[76]

Daniel Wilson (1778–1858), an evangelical Anglican and the bishop of Calcutta from 1832 to 1858, also drew criticism from Carson.[77] Wilson

---

74. A. Carson, *Theories of Inspiration*, 163; *Works* 3:215.

75. A. Carson, *Refutation of Dr. Henderson's Doctrine*, 52–53; *Works* 3:300.

76. A. Carson, *Refutation of Dr. Henderson's Doctrine*, 53–54; *Works* 3:300–301.

77. Born in London, Wilson was raised with the expectation of inheriting his father's silk manufacturing business. After experiencing conversion in 1798 through the influence of his tutor John Eyre and John Newton, he enrolled in St Edmund Hall, Oxford, from which he received his MA in 1804. In 1808, Wilson began serving at St John's Chapel in London, which was a haven for Anglican Evangelicals. He was also deeply

extended inspiration to texts that did not have an apparent religious significance, but his reasoning was not based on pillar passages such as 2 Tim 3:16.[78] Rather, he used philosophic and pragmatic grounds to argue for the inspiration of these types of passages. Wilson's two reasons, in Carson's words, were "that philosophy has no objection to this view, and that practical uses may be derived from the slightest details, and most apparently indifferent circumstances." Carson's critique was a result of Wilson's pragmatic rationale for the inspiration of seemingly unimportant details in Scripture. While he agreed with Wilson that "Divine truth must be perfectly consistent with true knowledge of every kind, and must have some use," Carson also argued that "it is equally true that this is not a proper criterion for judging the contents of Scripture. A thing may be consistent with all other knowledge, and may have practical uses, yet not be a part of Divine revelation."[79] Carson recognized the importance of axioms for confirming doctrines, but he saw the initial and final determinant for inspired truth to be what was found in Scripture and not arbitrary principles created by people. Rather than accepting a passage of Scripture as inspired because it served a practical purpose, Carson believed that a passage was practical because it was inspired.[80]

Defense of Plenary Verbal Inspiration

As shown in his arguments for the plenary inspiration of Scripture, Carson believed 2 Tim 3:16 to be sufficient evidence to substantiate this doctrine. This verse also acted as a foundation for his conviction of the plenary verbal inspiration of Scripture and he was critical of those who rejected the verse as supporting the doctrine. In his critique of John Dick's (1764–1833) lack of dependence on the passage to bolster verbal

---

involved with the Eclectic Society, the Christian Missionary Society, and the British and Foreign Bible Society. In 1824, he took up the parish at St. Mary's, Islington, London, which was not known for its evangelical sentiments. It was during his time there that he published a series of lectures from 1827 to 1830 in *Evidences of Christianity*. In 1832, Wilson was ordained as the bishop of Calcutta. He devoted the remainder of his life towards strengthening and expanding the presence of the Anglican Church in India. The preceding information was taken primarily from the following sources: Andrew Porter, "Wilson, Daniel," *ODNB* 59:514–15; Bateman, *Life of the Right Rev. Daniel Wilson*.

78. Wilson, *Evidences of Christianity*, 1:325.
79. A. Carson, *Theories of Inspiration*, 34; *Works* 3:116.
80. A. Carson, *Theories of Inspiration*, 34; *Works* 3:116.

inspiration, Carson wrote, "And I complain that he does not rest verbal inspiration on its main evidence, 2 Tim. iii. 16. There are many other sound and substantial arguments, and these the author states in a very convincing manner. But the direct and main evidence, which applies to every case is 2 Tim. iii. 16, which I have not observed among the author's proofs of verbal inspiration."[81] The reason this passage was Carson's primary basis for verbal inspiration, as well as plenary inspiration, was due to his definition of inspiration. He believed that if God inspired the thoughts and sentiments of Scripture, the words, which conveyed the divine content, must also be inspired. In his "Remarks on the Review of the Rev. Daniel Wilson's Theory of Inspiration," which was published as a chapter in his *Theories of Inspiration*, Carson asked, "Does not [plenary inspiration] refer to every thing in the Scriptures, and to every word of the Scriptures?"[82] Carson's query clearly implies how he defined the phrase. The depth to which Carson believed Scripture to be inspired was accurately described by Ebenezer Henderson: "First, it is maintained, that as Scripture signifies writing, and all writing is made up of written words, or words, syllables, and letters, to say that a writing is inspired, while the words are uninspired, is a contradiction."[83]

As 2 Tim 3:16 taught the inspiration of all Scripture, as opposed to the inspiration of all the writers of Scripture, the subject of Carson's view of inspiration was the sacred writing itself and not the writers. This focus also gave validity to Carson's inclusion of words into his understanding of inspiration: "The writing is the thing whose inspiration is asserted. It cannot then be a question whether words belong to a writing."[84] Carson's response to Smith's objections to plenary verbal inspiration also reflected this conviction: "If any writing is inspired, the words must of necessity be inspired, because the words are the writing. . . . The Bible is said to be *a writing written by the Spirit of God*. A more express attestation of verbal inspiration could not be found."[85] This conviction, that "a more express attestation could not be found," was evident in his almost simplistic dependence upon 2 Tim 3:16 in rejecting all other views of inspiration, whether they held to a partial verbal inspiration or rejected verbal inspiration altogether.

---

81. A. Carson, *Theories of Inspiration*, 213–14; *Works* 3:254–55.

82. A. Carson, *Theories of Inspiration*, 73; *Works* 3:147.

83. Henderson, *Divine Inspiration*, 401. Quoted in A. Carson, *Refutation of Dr. Henderson's Doctrine*, 75; *Works* 3:317.

84. A. Carson, *Theories of Inspiration*, 214; *Works* 3:255.

85. A. Carson, *Theories of Inspiration*, 134; *Works* 3:194; emphasis in original.

Despite Carson's conviction that the doctrine of inspiration taught in 2 Tim 3:16 applied to Scripture itself and not to the writers, other perspectives on the inspiration of Scripture placed great emphasis on how the biblical writers were divinely inspired. This was an unceasing source of frustration for Carson, as he made clear to a reviewer of his *Theories of Inspiration*: "But will these men never learn, that inspiration in this celebrated passage [2 Tim. 3:16] is ascribed to the Scripture, and is not, as they perversely continue to suppose, predicated of the minds of the writers."[86] The focus that his opponents placed upon the way divine inspiration operated in the biblical writers were primarily concerned with two points. The first point dealt with the distinction between the matter, or content, of Scripture and its manner, or style. The second point, closely related to the first point, pertained to developing theories of inspiration that did not conflict with the writers' faculties. Carson believed this focus on the writers unnecessarily confounded the issue of biblical inspiration:

> In treating of the inspiration of the Scriptures, there is no necessity to enter into discussions about the Divine operation on the faculties of their mind.... On this there is nothing revealed, and all definitions with respect to this must, therefore, be the work of fancy. That the Holy Ghost spake and wrote through man is a fact attested by the Scriptures, but how he influenced their minds we are not informed. It is not, then, to be expected that we are to obtain much light on the subject from the definition of divines.[87]

Not only did his opponents' shift away from the written Scripture as the sole issue of topic confuse the discussion, according to Carson, but it also led to innovative, incorrect theories due to the lack of biblical testimony on how the writers were inspired.[88]

The Manner and Matter of Scripture

Carson's opponents frequently made a distinction between the content of Scripture, which typically pertained to the thoughts and message of Scripture, and the style of Scripture, which was concerned with the phraseology of the text. At least among Evangelicals, the message of Scripture was generally credited to God and, therefore, inspired. The style of Scripture

---

86. A. Carson, *Refutation of the Review*, 16; *Works* 3:415–16.
87. A. Carson, *Theories of Inspiration*, 213; *Works* 3:254.
88. A. Carson, *Theories of Inspiration*, 214; *Works* 3:255.

was another matter and became the grounds for much debate between Carson and his adversaries. While Carson was not especially concerned with how inspiration operated in the writers, he was concerned with the words written. Thus, theories that the style or phraseology of Scripture might be credited to human writers instead of to the divine writer forced Carson onto this battleground of theological controversy.

Carson described Daniel Wilson's view of inspiration as being a partnership between God and humans: "human in manner, divine in matter."[89] The following statement lists some of the evidence Wilson pointed to in crediting the style of Scripture to the writers instead of to God:

> We see, on the face of the whole, that the writers speak naturally, use the style, language, manner of address familiar to them. There are peculiar casts of talents, expression, modes of reasoning in each author. The language is that of the country and age where they lived. They employ all their faculties, they search, examine, weigh, reason, as holy and sincere men, in such a cause, might be supposed to do. They use all their natural and acquired knowledge; their memory furnishes them with facts, or the documents and authentic records of time are consulted by them for information.... The mind of man is working every where.[90]

These observations led Wilson to preserve the "free and natural exertion of the characteristic faculties of the writers."[91] In a sense, for Wilson, the freedom of the writer became sacred ground onto which any doctrine of inspiration could not encroach. This was a basic position for many theologians who rejected plenary verbal inspiration. Carson, on the other hand, completely rejected Wilson's idea of a "wonderful union of divine and human agency in the inspiration of the scriptures."[92] This did not mean he denied the evidence of human faculties in the style of the biblical text. In fact, he affirmed it, but he objected to the notion that the evidence of the writer's character within their writings excluded God's direct involvement. Carson asserted that God had the ability to imitate the style and manner of the various biblical writers so as to produce a text that would naturally appear as the writers' works. "When God speaks to man, he puts his thoughts and

---

89. A. Carson, *Theories of Inspiration*, 3; *Works* 3:94.
90. Wilson, *Evidences of Christianity*, 1:318.
91. Wilson, *Evidences of Christianity*, 1:319.
92. Wilson, *Evidences of Christianity*, 1:318.

words into the form which is natural to those through whom he speaks."[93] Next, Carson objected to the distinction Wilson made between the style and content of Scripture. While the former agreed that a distinction could be made between the style and content of the text, he believed that the "distinction between *matter* and *form*, as to their author," was a theological innovation to serve the purpose of supporting Wilson's bifurcated understanding of biblical inspiration.[94] Though style and content were distinct, they were both part of the written, inspired text. Therefore, it was natural for Carson to conclude that both the manner and matter of Scripture were authored by God. With the presupposition of plenary verbal inspiration according to 2 Tim 3:16, Carson was led to conclude, "He that is the author of a book, must be the author of the style of the book."[95] The cost of attributing even a small portion or aspect of Scripture to a human source would be to nullify plenary verbal inspiration, because it would not, "as a whole, be the word of God."[96]

Like Wilson, Ebenezer Henderson also attributed the variations in style to "a diversity of natural talent, to the various situations of the writers, to the character of the subjects on which they wrote, and to the impressions which such subjects were calculated to produce upon their minds."[97] However, unlike Wilson, Henderson used the various styles of writing found in Scripture to target specifically the doctrine of plenary verbal inspiration. Henderson never denied that the writers of Scripture were divinely inspired while they wrote their own particular styles. Rather, God was described as adapting "his inspirations to the physical and intellectual features of each, and rendered these, to the extent in which they were available, subservient to the revelation or the recording of his will."[98] Though recognizing that those holding to verbal inspiration also accepted the various styles of language in the Bible, Henderson believed that their position could not coexist with the variety of styles without contradiction. Henderson could find no middle ground between his position, in which the Holy Spirit used the various styles possessed by each writer, and the verbally inspired position,

---

93. A. Carson, *Theories of Inspiration*, 4; *Works* 3:95.
94. A. Carson, *Theories of Inspiration*, 13; *Works* 3:101; emphasis in original.
95. A. Carson, *Theories of Inspiration*, 41; *Works* 3:121.
96. A. Carson, *Theories of Inspiration*, 9; *Works* 3:98.
97. Henderson, *Divine Inspiration*, 393.
98. Henderson, *Divine Inspiration*, 394–95.

in which the Spirit "created" the styles used.[99] Carson, on the other hand, did not see any contradiction between plenary verbal inspiration and the various styles represented in Scripture. He believed the natural style of the writers to be so manifest that he would "not think of ascribing the style to the Holy Spirit, as well as to the writers," if "the divine testimony on the subject of inspiration" did not exist.[100] Of course, this "divine testimony," as found in 2 Tim 3:16, was the crux of Carson's argument. Any argument that stood in opposition to this foundational passage was, according to Carson, "a mere effusion of fancy" or a human theory not founded on Scripture.[101] Not only did Carson reject Henderson's view as unbiblical, but he also charged his opponent with confusing "style as it respects the genius, temperament, and habits of a writer, with style as it exists in a particular work."[102] As previously noted, Carson was concerned with the writings of Scripture and not with the writers themselves. While Henderson charged the doctrine of plenary verbal inspiration with "destroying and disturbing" the natural faculties of the writers, as though they experienced a suspension of their intellect and senses, Carson's view simply stated that the Holy Spirit "uttered his thoughts, reasonings, and words through the writers of Scripture, in the style of those writers."[103] While this seems similar to Henderson's position shown above, Carson clearly placed the authorship of the Scriptures with the Holy Spirit, and not with human writers.

Degrees of Inspiration

Henderson's concern over preserving the natural intellect of the writers from divine mind control led him, and other opponents of plenary verbal inspiration, to develop theories of inspiration that did not conflict with the writers' faculties. The theories developed by opposing Evangelicals contained degrees of inspiration, or ways in which the writers were inspired. Henderson, for example, categorized inspiration into five degrees: divine excitement, which was either a direct command to write from God or a providential setting of circumstance or state of mind that resulted in

---

99. Henderson, *Divine Inspiration*, 397.
100. A. Carson, *Refutation of Dr. Henderson's Doctrine*, 67; *Works* 3:311.
101. A. Carson, *Refutation of Dr. Henderson's Doctrine*, 69; *Works* 3:312.
102. A. Carson, *Refutation of Dr. Henderson's Doctrine*, 70; *Works* 3:313.
103. A. Carson, *Refutation of Dr. Henderson's Doctrine*, 70; *Works* 3:313.

inspired writing;[104] invigoration, which was an elevation of their natural intellect to comprehend, argue, and remember;[105] superintendence, in which the writers were left to their own abilities but divinely supervised to produce an infallible text;[106] guidance, which was basically a divine leading in what to write or, in the case of Moses, to compile;[107] and direct revelation, which was any worldly or divine knowledge that could not possibly be known to the human mind without being directly deposited by God.[108] Carson's refutation was essentially composed of two points. First, as has already been discussed, how the Spirit worked in the mind of the writer was distinct from the inspiration of Scripture. He then, somewhat caustically, applied Henderson's categories to the Scripture to show the incomprehensibility of the degrees: "Is the Scripture excited? Shall we say that *all Scripture is excited by God?*"[109] Carson's second critique was that Henderson's use of degrees was dependent on his own subjective perspective. The latter believed that the highest degree of inspiration was only necessary at times, but Carson countered that Henderson's standard for necessity could not be authoritative for anyone else: "Others will judge it unnecessary almost for anything."[110] This placed the status of the Bible in the hands of human subjectivity instead of upon what the Scripture claimed for itself.

Wilson also adopted a system composed of degrees. His degrees of inspiration were suggestion, direction, elevation, and superintendency.[111] Inspiration of suggestion was a type of verbal inspiration in which the Holy Spirit "suggested and dictated minutely every part of the truths revealed."[112] The inspiration of direction was when the Holy Spirit directed the human mind to use its native powers to express divine truth in the writer's own words.[113] The inspiration of elevation "added a greater strength and vigor to

---

104. Henderson, *Divine Inspiration*, 364.
105. Henderson, *Divine Inspiration*, 369.
106. Henderson, *Divine Inspiration*, 373.
107. Henderson, *Divine Inspiration*, 378.
108. Henderson, *Divine Inspiration*, 381.
109. A. Carson, *Refutation of Dr. Henderson's Doctrine*, 43; Works 3:292–93; emphasis in original.
110. A. Carson, *Refutation of Dr. Henderson's Doctrine*, 63–64; Works 3:308.
111. A. Carson, *Theories of Inspiration*, 3; Works 3:94.
112. Wilson, *Evidences of Christianity*, 1:323.
113. Wilson, *Evidences of Christianity*, 1:323.

the efforts of the mind than the writers could otherwise have attained."[114] The inspiration of superintendency was when the Holy Spirit simply made sure the writer did not write anything that would diminish the revealed truth. These categories were very similar to those later taught by Henderson. For example, Wilson's elevation, superintendency, and suggestion were essentially Henderson's invigoration, superintendence, and direct revelation, respectively. Though he did not present as detailed a system of the different modes of inspiration, John Pye Smith asserted that the writers each required "divine influences" that were tailored for themselves and what they were communicating through their writing. One example he gave dealt with a case in which verbal inspiration would be necessary. In the case of "a prophet penetrating into future ages, or declaring secret counsels of the Deity," he recognized that "there must be a direct communication of such intelligence as no created being could by any means or efforts ever acquire."[115] Though Carson's replies to both Wilson and Smith were in the same vein as his reply to Henderson, an additional number of his arguments warrant discussion. In regard to Wilson's four degrees of inspiration, Carson remarked that only "suggestion" could properly be considered as inspiration. Regarding the other three modes, Carson wrote, "Do not all the evangelical ministers of London claim these three? Do they not constantly pray for them?"[116] This critique would implicate most of Henderson's degrees as well.

Principle of Necessity

Smith's example of direct revelation mentions a principle that Carson would attack throughout his polemical works on inspiration. The principle is that of necessity. Carson's criticism of Henderson's requirement of necessity before allowing verbal inspiration has already been mentioned, and Carson's concern justifies a closer examination of Henderson's view on the issue. Henderson's criticism of plenary verbal inspiration and of those who held the doctrine did not signify he was against verbal inspiration per se. As Carson accurately observed, the extent of inspiration Henderson espoused was simply not comprehensive.[117] The latter's understanding of inspiration

---

114. Wilson, *Evidences of Christianity*, 1:323.
115. J. Pye Smith, *Scripture Testimony to the Messiah*, 1:96.
116. A. Carson, *Theories of Inspiration*, 24; *Works* 3:109.
117. A. Carson, *Refutation of Dr. Henderson's Doctrine*, 70; *Works* 3:313.

allowed for verbal inspiration in the following cases: when God spoke audibly himself or through an angel; when divine revelations and prophecies surpassed the writers' comprehension, thus requiring a divine source for the wording; and any other matter that would have been beyond the writers' ability to express in his own words.[118] Like Smith, he believed that verbal inspiration was not merely allowable in these cases but also necessary. Therefore, it would be more accurate to describe Henderson's critique as being aimed at plenary verbal inspiration rather than at verbal inspiration in and of itself.

Carson called Henderson's exceptions "an important admission; for if our doctrine is true in many instances, why may it not be true in all?"[119] The reason why Carson believed his question was valid was due to his conviction that variation in the mode of divine communication, whether speaking to the writer audibly or directly into his mind, did not affect the result of the inspiration. The differentiation Henderson pointed out was, in Carson's opinion, a false distinction. Concerning Henderson's pragmatic approach for allowing verbal inspiration, Carson agreed that some passages of Scriptures necessitated verbal inspiration, such as all "prophecies not understood by the Prophets," but he did not believe this negated verbal inspiration in other cases as a matter of course.[120] The latter's view "rests merely on views of necessity, and not on the divine testimony."[121] Again, one sees Carson's dependence on 2 Tim 3:16 as he evenly applied the inspiration taught therein to all Scripture. He believed that verbal inspiration could not be selectively applied; it was either necessary in all cases or necessarily excluded in all cases.

Variant Readings of Scripture Not Contradictory to Plenary Verbal Inspiration

Another objection to plenary verbal inspiration that Carson's opponents shared was the existence of variant manuscripts of Scripture. Smith wrote that the doctrine of plenary verbal inspiration gave "serious weight to the otherwise nugatory objection against the certainty of Scriptures, from the existence of various readings," because there was then no way for a person

118. Henderson, *Divine Inspiration*, 390.
119. A. Carson, *Refutation of Dr. Henderson's Doctrine*, 105; *Works* 3:339.
120. A. Carson, *Theories of Inspiration*, 102; *Works* 3:172.
121. A. Carson, *Refutation of Dr. Henderson's Doctrine*, 110; *Works* 3:343.

to be certain that he or she possessed the "one genuine reading."[122] Wilson believed that "the trifling inaccuracies which have insinuated themselves into the copies of the scriptures by the carelessness of transcribers, the various readings which have accumulated during eighteen centuries, and the further defects arising from translations" would no longer be "trifling" if all Scripture was considered to be completely inspired by the Holy Spirit.[123] Henderson argued that the existence of variant manuscripts overturned plenary verbal inspiration. He used John Owen, who "was clearly in the camp of those insisting not upon the creative individuality of the writers, but upon the overarching divine control of the process," as representative of those who held to plenary verbal inspiration.[124] By pointing out Owen's denial of even a single change in the transcribed manuscripts, Henderson indicated "the extreme folly of contending for a literal identity between any copies now extant, and the originals as published by the sacred penmen."[125] Variant readings from existing manuscripts were evidently seen as a force to be dealt with by many Evangelicals.

After dismissing Owen's "extravagant assertion" and agreeing on the existence of variant readings, Carson directed Henderson to his response to Smith's identical objection a decade earlier.[126] Based on Smith's admission that some portions of Scripture were necessarily verbally inspired, Carson responded, "As some parts of Scripture must of necessity have been verbally inspired, and as such parts are not better secured against the mistakes of transcription than the rest, if this objection cannot invalidate the verbal inspiration of the one, neither can it invalidate the inspiration of the other."[127] By "the other" Carson was referring to all the rest of Scripture. While he obviously meant this rejoinder to be sufficient for all his opponents' objections on this base, he added, in his reply to Henderson that God, in his providence and wisdom, had just as much reason to allow any words to "slip" in transcribed manuscripts as he had for dictating each of the words in the original manuscripts.[128] Carson believed one of the reasons for differences between manuscripts was to act as a "snare to worldly wisdom,"

---

122. J. Pye Smith, *Scripture Testimony to the Messiah*, 1:99.
123. Wilson, *Evidences of Christianity*, 1:327.
124. Stewart, "Evangelical Doctrine of Scripture," 398.
125. Henderson, *Divine Inspiration*, 426.
126. A. Carson, *Refutation of Dr. Henderson's Doctrine*, 114; *Works* 3:345–46.
127. A. Carson, *Theories of Inspiration*, 127; *Works* 3:189.
128. A. Carson, *Refutation of Dr. Henderson's Doctrine*, 114–15; *Works* 3:346.

and he seemed to be convinced that his opponents had been caught in that snare.[129] Finally, Carson denied any contradiction between variant readings and plenary verbal inspiration. The divine inspiration was "a matter of divine testimony," and that some of the original words had been lost was "a matter of fact." These were distinct matters, because 2 Tim 3:16 only applied to the original manuscripts.

Equipped with 2 Tim 3:16, Carson was bold in his refutation of anyone who undermined biblical inspiration, or plenary verbal inspiration. The "comfort and edification" this doctrine brought to the believer was a practical benefit he was loathe to lose. His commitment to the authority of every word of Scripture, coupled with his evangelistic zeal for all people to hear the gospel, naturally led to an interest in faithful Bible translation.

CARSON'S VIEWS ON BIBLE TRANSLATION

Controversy over Ali Bey's Turkish New Testament

In 1824, Ebenezer Henderson's *An Appeal to the Members of the British and Foreign Bible Society, on the Subject of the Turkish New Testament, Printed at Paris, in 1819* was published as an exposé on the deficiencies of that particular translation and the British and Foreign Bible Society's willingness to circulate it. His ultimate goal for its publication was "the total annihilation of this edition of the Turkish New Testament."[130] The translation he so strongly condemned was a seventeenth-century work by Ali Bey (ca. 1622–ca. 1676), a Polish native who served as a dragoman in Istanbul.[131]

129. A. Carson, *Refutation of Dr. Henderson's Doctrine*, 115; *Works* 3:346.

130. Henderson, *Appeal to the Members*, vi.

131. Wojciech Bobowski was Ali Bey's original name. He was known by numerous names throughout his life: Albertus Bobovius, which he used with Western scholars and diplomats; and Ali Bey and Ali Ufki, his common names with other Muslims and in the Ottoman court. He was captured by Tartars who invaded Poland ca. 1632. He was sold as a slave at the palace in Istanbul, where he served and was educated for approximately twenty-one years. After serving under a senior Ottoman officer in Egypt, he returned to Istanbul a free man. Afterward, he worked for the English ambassadors in Istanbul, Sir Thomas Bendish (ca. 1607–74) and Sir Heneage Finch (1628–89). It was while serving in this capacity that Bobowski completed the Turkish translation of the Bible, including the Apocrypha, over a three-year period, under the patronage of Levinus Warner, a Dutch resident in Istanbul. Prior to this, he translated the Catechism of the Church of England into Turkish for Isaac Basire (ca. 1607–76), a French-born English theologian. The preceding information was taken primarily from the following sources: Neudecker: "From Istanbul to London?"; "Wojciech Bobowski."

He encountered Ali Bey's Turkish New Testament after it was published under the auspices of the British and Foreign Bible Society, believing that it would be a helpful tool in studying Eastern languages. It was not long before Henderson found it to be inadequate: "But what was my surprise, after perusing a few verses, to detect liberties which I found it totally impossible to reconcile with the acknowledged principles of Biblical Interpretation!"[132] His concerns over the society's circulation of this Turkish New Testament led him to forego an appointment to their agency in Constantinople in 1820. Henderson focused his *Appeal* on the Turkish translation of Matthew, Romans, and Revelation due to the urgency of the matter.[133] He addressed five issues with the translation: "The mistranslation of proper names; the unnecessary use of synonymes; the want of consistency and uniformity; false renderings; omissions and additions."[134] Henderson also gave an account of how the British and Foreign Bible Society did not agree with his judgment of the Turkish New Testament, thus deciding to progress with its circulation.[135]

Henderson's critique of Ali Bey's mistranslation of proper names dealt primarily with the latter's tendency to affix epithets to what was originally a simple reference to "God." As an example, Henderson showed how Ali Bey either added to or substituted two thirds of the references to "God" in Revelation with epithets such as "Supreme God," "Glorious God," "Divine Majesty," "True Majesty," "Supreme Divinity," and "Illustrious God."[136] Ali Bey's "unnecessary use of synonymes" was a reference to his practice of adding synonyms to a present word. For example, he translated "sorrow" in John 16:6 as "anguish and sorrow."[137] Henderson's third criticism of Ali Bey's translation was the latter's tendency to vary his phraseology as much as possible. Henderson argued that when a reoccurring word also retained the same sense or meaning, it should be translated uniformly. He saw Ali Bey's tendency to render needlessly one Greek word into a variety of words as a "daring attempt to improve on the language of the Holy Spirit."[138] The fourth practice that Henderson took issue with was Ali Bey's "false

---

132. Henderson, *Appeal to the Members*, 14.
133. Henderson, *Appeal to the Members*, 14–15.
134. Henderson, *Appeal to the Members*, 19.
135. Henderson, *Appeal to the Members*, 53–54.
136. Henderson, *Appeal to the Members*, 20.
137. Henderson, *Appeal to the Members*, 29.
138. Henderson, *Appeal to the Members*, 29–30.

renderings." One significant example of this was in his translating "righteousness" as "righteousness and piety" in reference to Christ's righteousness with which believers are imputed by faith. Henderson believed Ali Bey's rendering changed the meaning of the original to the opposite: "But according to Ali Bey's version, we are accepted of God, and entitled to eternal life, on the footing of our own works!!!"[139] Henderson's fifth criticism was simply composed of examples of where Ali Bey added or omitted words from the original.[140]

Henderson's criticism of the Turkish New Testament did not go unanswered, and a reply to his *Appeal* was responded to that same year by Samuel Lee (1783–1852), professor of Arabic at Cambridge, in his *Remarks on Dr. Henderson's Appeal to the Bible Society, on the Subject of the Turkish Version of the New Testament Printed at Paris in 1819*.[141] Lee had been involved in examining Henderson's original remarks on the Turkish New Testament on behalf of the British and Foreign Bible Society.[142] Lee's lengthy treatise was a detailed response to Henderson's 1824 publication. While Lee did display a more thorough understanding of the Turkish language, the primary disagreements had to do with their contrasting principles of Bible translation. Lee discussed two schools of translation, which Henderson had also mentioned. He agreed with Henderson that one view was that translation should follow the letter of the original text as closely as possible, but they disagreed on the second method of translation. Whereas Henderson described the second method as focusing on elegance of style over accuracy, Lee argued that it emphasized translating the meaning of the text over the exact wording of the original.[143] This second method represented Lee's own position. He did not believe in the necessity of "verbal imitation of the original."[144] He argued that this was only possible when idioms from both languages were perfectly parallel, and to force a verbal translation otherwise would result in a translation that was "stiff, languid, and preposterous" in style and distorted in its sense.[145] This presupposition allowed Lee to

---

139. Henderson, *Appeal to the Members*, 33.

140. Henderson, *Appeal to the Members*, 44–48.

141. Lee was involved in examining Henderson's *Appeal to the Members* for the British and Foreign Bible Society.

142. Henderson, *Appeal to the Members*, 54–55n*.

143. Lee, *Remarks on Dr. Henderson's Appeal*, 9–10.

144. Lee, *Remarks on Dr. Henderson's Appeal*, 22.

145. Lee, *Remarks on Dr. Henderson's Appeal*, 61.

dismiss Henderson's arguments. For example, in response to Henderson's concerns over translating "righteousness" as "righteousness and piety," Lee simply replied that reduplication of words was used for emphasis.[146]

Henderson answered Lee with his own lengthy treatise, *The Turkish New Testament Incapable of Defence, and the True Principles of Biblical Translation Vindicated* (1825), later that year, though it was not published until the latter part of the following year.[147] He clarified his support for literal translations by contrasting it with "merely *verbal*" translations, which "consist merely of words inflexibly corresponding in number, and the order of their arrangement, to the words of the original."[148] Henderson pointed out three reasons for the necessity of a literal translation. First, it guards against the insertion of the translator's own biases and views; second, the reader is able to place his faith in the divine power that is conveyed through the Scripture; and third, the translated Bible is the textbook from which pastors and missionaries work and teach.[149] The bulk of the work contains a more detailed critique of Ali Bey's translation, a defense against Lee's critiques, and his own critique of Lee's principles of translation.[150]

In 1829, Carson's *The Incompetency of the Rev. Professor Lee, of Cambridge, for Translating, or Correcting Translations of the Holy Scriptures, Proved and Illustrated, in a Criticism on His "Remarks on Dr. Henderson's Appeal to the Bible Society"* (1829) drew Lee back into the debate over the proper principles of Bible translation.[151] Carson's critique was based solely on Lee's *Remarks on Dr. Henderson's Appeal to the Bible Society*. This is known because Carson later admitted to Lee, "I have not yet seen any one of Dr Henderson's productions on this subject. I know Dr Henderson's views only through you."[152] The implication from this is that Carson's work was motivated by a zeal for certain principles of Bible translation rather than a personal stake in the debate between Lee and Henderson. The significance

---

146. Lee, *Remarks on Dr. Henderson's Appeal*, 56.

147. Henderson explained the reason for the delay because he did not want readers to assume that he had difficulty in answering Lee's response. Henderson, *Turkish New Testament*, iii.

148. Henderson, *Turkish New Testament*, 4; emphasis in original.

149. Henderson, *Turkish New Testament*, 28–29.

150. Lee responded to Henderson's rebuttal the following year. Lee, *Some Additional Remarks*.

151. A. Carson, *Incompetency of Rev. Professor Lee* (1829). There is no explanation for the timing of Carson's critique of Lee.

152. A. Carson, *Answer to the Letter*, 1.

of Carson's treatise is that it displayed his views on Bible translation in more detail than shown in his critique of Smith's defense of Haffner's preface, as well as showing his firm view of the verbal plenary inspiration of Scripture. Carson critiqued Lee's, and Ali Bey's, principles of translation in five areas: first, the interchange of the exact term with another biblical term used for that elsewhere; second, omitting or adding words to the original text; third, allowing for the sense of a passage instead of the literal translation; fourth, a lack of uniformity in translating words; and fifth, the practice of modernizing the language as much as possible.

In arguing against the practice of interchanging original terms with terms found elsewhere in the text, Carson, like Henderson, centered on how Ali Bey translated "God." For example, Ali Bey translated Rom 10:13 as "the name of God" rather than "the name of the Lord," as shown in the Authorized Version. While Carson recognized that both terms were regularly applied to the same person, he argued that "the word *Lord* is not equivalent to the word *God*."[153] He made two points from this example: first, translators should translate faithfully rather than judge the text or inject their own views; and second, the original placement of the different names and titles for God were purposeful for instruction and edification.[154] He believed that this type of interchange was only suitable for commentaries and paraphrases, which led him to conclude that Ali Bey was not actually translating in these instances. Carson saw a clear distinction of roles to be played: "Let the translator give us God's words, as far as it is possible, and let the commentator assist us in discovering their meaning."[155]

The second false principle Carson attacked was the assumed liberty of omitting or adding words from and to what was found in the original text. He believed that omitting words stemmed from an arrogant assumption that the words God included were unnecessary. That he would even defend the words that some might deem unimportant shows Carson's commitment to the verbal plenary inspiration of Scripture. His distinction of roles between translators and commentators is seen again in his objection to adding words, even if the meaning is agreeable. Some examples he gave of additions were adding "like" to metaphors and explaining figures, such as when the term "Jacob" referred to the descendents of Jacob. Carson argued that metaphors and figures in the original text should remain as metaphors

153. A. Carson, *Incompetency of Rev. Professor Lee*, 4.
154. A. Carson, *Incompetency of Rev. Professor Lee*, 5.
155. A. Carson, *Incompetency of Rev. Professor Lee*, 6.

Alexander Carson on the Bible

and figures in the translation. He seemed especially offended that this practice would be defended by "an English professor of languages."[156]

Carson also addressed the view that the translator may "give what he deems the sense of a passage, instead of a strict translation."[157] This criticism is related to his critique of those who believe the Bible to be inspired in its thoughts rather than in its words. Carson pointed out that translators were not inspired, which could result in corruption of the translated text. Therefore, a literal translation was necessary and, as Henderson pointed out, guarded against the insertion of the translator's own theological bias.[158]

The fourth principle Carson argued for was "uniformity in translating words, as often as they occur in the same sense," or that a particular word used in a particular sense should always be translated the same.[159] Lee disagreed with this principle, which Henderson had also pointed out, rather requiring "only that the sense be accurately preserved."[160] Lee even noted that the New Testament writers did not observe this principle of uniformity when citing the Old Testament. Carson's response to Lee's appeal was that the New Testament writers were "inspired expounders, and not mere translators," who gave the sense of the Old Testament rather than the exact words.[161] Why then did Carson not allow Lee and Ali Bey the same privilege? "Professor Lee and Ali Bey may imitate this when they are inspired, but not sooner."[162] The confidence Carson placed in the New Testament writers could not be placed in a translation except in the degree to which its words corresponded with the original text.

Finally, Carson criticized the translator's apparent duty to modernize the language of the original. His concern for preserving the original age of the text was evident in later works, as well: "They must not in a translation be deprived of the venerable garb of antiquity. A picture of Adam or of Noah must not appear in the costume of a modern gentleman.... Any infusion of modern sentiment or phraseology would be considered as a flagrant violation of faithfulness."[163] With regard to the example he critiqued, Ali

---

156. A. Carson, *Incompetency of Rev. Professor Lee*, 8.
157. A. Carson, *Incompetency of Rev. Professor Lee*, 11.
158. Henderson, *Turkish New Testament*, 28.
159. A. Carson, *Incompetency of Rev. Professor Lee*, 12.
160. Lee, *Remarks on Dr. Henderson's Appeal*, 59.
161. A. Carson, *Incompetency of Rev. Professor Lee*, 13.
162. A. Carson, *Incompetency of Rev. Professor Lee*, 13.
163. A. Carson, "Characteristics of the Style of Scripture," 3:69. This work was

The Gospel-Centered Evangelicalism of Alexander Carson

Bey's translation of Rev 1:10, Carson took issue with how Ali Bey contextualized the text to make it understandable to Muslims, while missing the theological significance of the text completely. The passage was translated as "a market day" instead of as "the Lord's day," which Lee defended because by "Lord" "Mohammedans do not understand our Lord Jesus Christ, but God, to the exclusion of every other being."[164] Therefore, due to the theological ambiguity the term would introduce to Turkish readers, "Lord" was replaced. Carson responded with two points. First, a lack of familiarity with a biblical term should not lead one to change the text but to instruct the readers through teaching. "I ask Professor Lee, is the term *Lord's day* more unintelligible to a Turk, or to a modern heathen, into whose language the Scriptures are to be translated, than it was to the nations that spoke the Greek language, to whom the original was presented?"[165] Carson suggested that viewing unfamiliar biblical terms for the uninitiated in a translation as a deficiency would necessarily imply that the original text was also deficient, at least in this instance. Second, the alteration destroys biblical evidence for theological truths. In this case, "Lord's day" stood as evidence "for the sacredness of the day, and for the divinity of our Lord Jesus Christ."[166] Carson argued that the purpose of the original phraseology was not simply to act as a calendar marker but to point to the above theological points.

It is clear from Carson's arguments that he was a strong advocate for more literal translations of the Bible. Yet, like Henderson, he did not advocate a rigid literalism that resulted in the loss of the sense of Scripture. Throughout his critique of Lee, Carson qualified his demand for every "word of God" or "word of the Spirit" with an "as far as possible."[167] Against a literal translation that sacrificed the sense of Scripture, Carson wrote, "There is no greater mistake than to suppose that a translation is good, according as it is literal. It may be asserted, without exception, that a literal

---

published posthumously. In a biographical sketch of Carson included in an American edition of *Baptism in Its Mode*, Young wrote, "You will be glad to learn that he has left a good deal behind him yet unpublished. He had just completed a work on '*The characteristic style of Scripture*,'—showing its purity, simplicity, and sublimity, and contrasting the God of the Bible, as therein displayed, with the gods of the Heathen, as described by their poets." Young, "Memoir of Alexander Carson," xliv–xlv.

164. A. Carson, *Incompetency of Rev. Professor Lee*, 18–19; Lee, *Remarks on Dr. Henderson's Appeal*, 86–87.

165. A. Carson, *Incompetency of Rev. Professor Lee*, 19.

166. A. Carson, *Incompetency of Rev. Professor Lee*, 20.

167. A. Carson, *Incompetency of Rev. Professor Lee*, 5, 6, 7, 11, 17, 24.

translation of any book cannot be a faithful one."[168] In this respect, Carson's views on Bible translation reflect his views on the plenary verbal inspiration of the Scripture: "We maintain, . . . that the thoughts and sentiments are inspired, and the words also."[169] While these statements give a more balanced view of Carson's stance on Bible translation in nuce, the problem of his day was the surrender of the literal for the sense. These concerns for the proper translation of the Scripture were an ongoing theme until his unexpected death in 1844, as seen in his unfinished work on the *Characteristics of the Style of Scripture as Evidential of its Inspiration* (1854). Here to, he stressed the literal "as far as possible": "And not to translate literally, when the language of the translation can bear a literal rendering, is neither just nor faithful. Every translation of Scripture ought to be as literal as the idiom of the language of the translation will admit. The translator is never to depart from the idiom of the original till his language refuses the idiom."[170] The exception to a literal translation is more clearly stated here. Carson admitted that some idioms, specifically Hebraisms, could not be translated literally and still be intelligible to readers. Yet, even in regard to Hebraisms, he argued that a "strict exactness" be used "as far as our idiom will represent that of the original."[171]

Controversy in the British and Foreign Bible Society over the Translation of βαπτίζω

Carson's concern for maintaining the purity of Scripture in a translation is also seen in how he dealt with the conflict between this principle and sectarianism. One example of this type of conflict is seen in his participation in the controversy between the British and Foreign Bible Society and the Baptist Union over whether Baptist missionaries in India would be allowed to translate βαπτίζω using its literal meaning of "immersion" or if they would be required to perpetuate the practice of the English King James Version in leaving it untranslated. The British and Foreign Bible Society had aided in the funding of translation efforts by Baptist missionaries in Serampore since 1804, which they claimed amounted to "not less than

---

168. A. Carson, *Theories of Inspiration*, 139; *Works* 3:198.
169. A. Carson, *Theories of Inspiration*, 118; *Works* 3:183.
170. *Works* 3:4–5.
171. *Works* 3:69.

£27,000 in paper and money" by 1827.¹⁷² That year, they received a petition from twenty-one missionaries of various denominations, which objected to the Baptist missionaries who had translated βαπτίζω "to the one exclusive idea of Immersion."¹⁷³ Though one historian claimed that the funding of Baptist translators was not discontinued due to this controversy, the account given by the British and Foreign Bible Society implies that this was the case.¹⁷⁴ Though the Bible society agreed that translations of βαπτίζω should be more sensitive to pedobaptist convictions, its desire to reconcile with the Baptist Missionary Society led to decades of sporadic discussion on the matter.

In 1840, the Baptist Union gave their newest petition, *Memorial, Relating to the Bengali and Other Versions of the New Testament, Made by Baptist Missionaries in India*, to the British and Foreign Bible Society. The "Memorialists," as they referred to themselves as, responded to terms set for reconciliation by the Bible society in 1833, which stated, "That this Committee would cheerfully afford assistance to the missionaries connected with the Baptist Missionary Society in their translation of the Bengali New Testament, provided the Greek terms relating to baptism be rendered, either, according to the principle adopted by the translators of the authorized English version, by a word derived from the original, or by such terms as may be considered unobjectionable by other denominations of Christians composing the Bible Society."¹⁷⁵ The Baptists refused these terms, and the Memorialists detailed their argument in the 1840 petition. Their views were outlined into eight "particulars" by the subsequent statement by a committee of the Bible society. Though these proceedings were not initially made public, its publication was prompted by the Baptist Union's decision to publish their memorial.¹⁷⁶ The latest entries in the controversy between the two entities precipitated immediate reactions. Ebenezer Henderson, for example, wrote a critique of the Baptist Union's *Memorial* in *A Letter to the Rev. A. Brandram, M. A. on the Meaning of the Word ΒΑΠΤΙΖΩ, and the Manner in Which It Has Been Rendered in Versions Sanctioned by the Bible Society* (1840). Carson, who was no stranger to the debate on the meaning

---

172. British and Foreign Bible Society, *Proceedings*, 3.

173. British and Foreign Bible Society, *Proceedings*, 3.

174. Browne, *British and Foreign Bible Society*, 2:128.

175. Quoted in Committee of the Baptist Union, *Baptists and Bible Society*, 3, referring to appendix A, 55–56.

176. British and Foreign Bible Society, *Proceedings*, 4.

of baptism, expressed his own thoughts to the Bible society's response in *A Letter to the Rev. A. Maclay, M. A., of New York, on the Reply of the British and Foreign Bible Society to the Memorial of the Committee of the Baptist Union* (1840), in which he commented upon eight particulars to which the Bible society had reduced the Memorialists' views.[177]

The primary principle that Carson expressed in his *Letter* was that the goal of Bible translation, or of the translator, was to convey God's word faithfully. A clear supporter for the translation of βαπτίζω, as opposed to simply using a transliteration, he agreed with the Memorialists that to leave the word untranslated was "suppression of God's truth."[178] Carson's accusation against the Bible society was that "they have recommended the Serampore translators to conceal the meaning of a word, which with the most assured confidence they know; or to render it by a term which they believe to be a false rendering."[179] He saw it as one matter to leave an unknown word untranslated, but the meaning of βαπτίζω was known and therefore necessitated translation. Two implications became apparent from this principle. First, the translator must be explicitly nondenominational in how he translates, and, second, a part of Scripture that is not directly related to fundamental Christian doctrines is still God's divine revelation and must be treated as such.

Thus, the translator was not to translate with the purpose of promoting a denominational perspective, which was a rule the Bible society essentially accused the Baptists of trespassing. Carson's defense of his Baptist brethren was based on a principle of translation rather than on a supposed interest he had in the translation of this particular word in support of his own theological views, and he took great offense at the implication that the Baptists had partisan motives: "Our zeal is not confined to the word in question. We dare not falsify in translating the least important word in the book of God. The Committee do us the greatest injustice by supposing that our tenacity to faithful translation in this instance is sectarian."[180] Just as he argued in his critique of Ali Bey's Turkish translation, Carson insisted that a translation was to convey the original text and not serve as a commentary or paraphrase, because that was not a translation's purpose.[181] He was of the

---

177. A. Carson, *Letter to A. Maclay*; British and Foreign Bible Society, *Proceedings*, 6.
178. A. Carson, *Letter to A. Maclay*, 3.
179. A. Carson, *Letter to A. Maclay*, 5.
180. A. Carson, *Letter to A. Maclay*, 7.
181 A. Carson, *Incompetency of Rev. Professor Lee*, 6.

opinion that the meaning of Scripture must be decided by the reader based on internal evidence, and, by leaving a word untranslated, the Bible society was keeping important evidence away from the readers. Carson even argued that the Bible society made the controversy one of interdenominational harmony rather than about faithful Bible translation.

Moreover, though Bible translation may be facilitated by ecumenical efforts, the translator should not seek or be forced to reflect ecumenism in the translation. Carson believed the translator's allegiance was to God and shown through faithful translation: "If he is an honest man he must faithfully translate what he knows. He is in nothing to suppress or modify to suit parties. Is God's testimony to be concealed or falsified in order to produce co-operation among Christians?"[182] Based on the conviction that the Bible society disallowed the translation by Baptist missionaries because of the complaint received by pedobaptist missionaries, Carson accused the Bible society of being "guided by expediency and not by principle."[183] Rather than expediency, the principle for translation should be accurate conveyance of the original. Instead of supporting the production of accurate translations, the Bible society was actually keeping the translators in Serampore from doing their job. Though a faithful translation might cause "serious inconvenience" due to the theological differences between the various denominations, Carson argued that a translator could not please everyone without compromising Scripture itself and asked, "What sort of a book would the Bible be, if it is in translation, with respect to all matters of controversy, to be left untranslated, or translated by words which do not faithfully represent the original; but are chosen with the express purpose of giving equal countenance to truth and error?"[184] His conclusion was that it would be a product based on ecumenical syncretism rather than the word of God. Therefore, translators should not be required to accommodate the theology of other missionaries.

A second implication was that even words dealing with secondary theological truths should be translated faithfully. Carson asked: "But is it any relief from the charge of suppression of God's truth, that the thing is not considered a fundamental truth?"[185] His statement implied that baptism, as a biblical ordinance, was not necessary for salvation or should not be

---

182. A. Carson, *Letter to A. Maclay*, 5.
183. A. Carson, *Letter to A. Maclay*, 6.
184. A. Carson, *Letter to A. Maclay*, 6.
185. A. Carson, *Letter to A. Maclay*, 12.

regarded as a part of the gospel. His words on baptism in the following response to one of the critics over the meaning of John 3:5 shed some light on why baptism is not a fundamental truth:

> In whatever way its reference may be explained, it cannot possibly imply that baptism is essential to salvation. Were this the case, then it would not always be necessarily true that faith is salvation. Were this true, it would imply that an external work performed by man is necessary to salvation. I need not state the thousandth part of the absurdity that would flow from this doctrine. Whatever is the truth of the matter, this cannot be true; it is contrary to the whole current of Scripture. One fact will by example prove that baptism is not necessary to salvation: the thief who believed on the cross was saved without baptism. This single fact will for ever forbid such a meaning to be taken out of this passage.[186]

Carson could not be any clearer on where baptism stood in relation to the fundamental doctrine of Christianity, namely, the gospel. The secondary position that the ordinance of baptism had in Carson's theology was also evident in how it was practiced in his own church. Carson's church practiced open communion "to the utmost extent, by receiving members into their body simply upon evidence of their conversion, with but little inquiry whether they agreed with them on the subject of Baptism, expecting that whenever they became convinced of their duty to be immersed, they would attend to it."[187] Again, it is clear what Carson held to be integral to the Christian life, belief in the gospel, and what he did not, believer's baptism. Nevertheless, though it is clear that Carson did not see baptism as a fundamental doctrine on which one's salvation depended, it is just as clear that his conviction of the plenary verbal inspiration of the Scripture demanded he be under the authority of both fundamental and subordinate doctrines therein. This conviction motivated him to write his lengthy treatise, *Baptism in Its Mode and Subjects* (1831, 1844), and it motivated him to defend the translation of βαπτίζω by Baptist missionaries in Serampore.

---

186. A. Carson, *Baptism in Its Mode* (1844), 477. The original document (A. Carson, *Baptism Not Purification*), a response to Edward Beecher's *Baptism*, was included in the 2nd edition of Carson's work on baptism, which contained several of his responses to critiques of his views on the ordinance.

187. Young, "Memoir of Alexander Carson," xxxvi. While the author of the memoir in the American edition is unlisted, Moore attributes its authorship to John Young (Moore, *Life of Alexander Carson*, 83).

For Carson, to do otherwise "would show greater deference to man than to God."[188]

CARSON ON THE DIVINE PRESERVATION OF THE BIBLE

Carson's views on the inspiration of translations should not lead one to deduce that he minimized the value and importance of the transcribed and translated biblical texts that have come down through history. Almost a decade after his *Review of Pye Smith's Defence* (1827), Carson's *The God of Providence the God of the Bible* (1835) was first published.[189] Being a "companion" to his previous work on divine providence, *History of Providence as Unfolded in the Book of Esther* (1833), it had two stated goals: first, to direct readers to another testimony substantiating Christianity and, second, to teach Christians how to study history as Christians.[190] His approach this time was to trace the progress of the gospel after the New Testament, through "uninspired history," to show God's sovereignty towards the fulfillment of Matt 24:14.[191] While the treatise was primarily a case study of divine providence, it also reflected Carson's belief that the preservation of the Scriptures from their original form to his day was not simply based on a random series of events. Of the numerous proofs he presents, a number of them pertain directly to how the Scriptures were preserved and passed down throughout history. Therefore, one may reason from this work that, rather than having a dim view of contemporary biblical texts, Carson saw them as being personally handed to humanity by God. The relevant proofs are discussed below in the following categories: the unfavorable circumstances in which the Bible was preserved, availability of materials and inventions which enabled the preservation of Scripture, and revival or reforming movements that promoted the study and spread of Scripture.

One category of evidence for the divine preservation of Scripture focused on the immensely unfavorable circumstances in which the Bible was maintained and spread. In the second proof, Carson observed how the Scriptures were conserved during the reign of the Roman Catholic Church beginning with Constantine (ca. 272–337).[192] What was miraculous was

---

188. A. Carson, *Baptism in Its Mode* (1844), v.
189. A. Carson, *God of Providence* (1839); *Works* 6:17–69.
190. A. Carson, *God of Providence* (1839), 10; *Works* 6:20–21.
191. A. Carson, *God of Providence* (1839), 10; *Works* 6:20–21.
192. A. Carson, *God of Providence* (1839), 18; *Works* 6:26.

that the Bible was preserved in "purity and integrity" despite being in the hands of the "Man of Sin."[193] That an establishment who disagreed with what the Bible taught would preserve it was clear evidence of the Bible's integrity. Carson's antipathy toward the Roman Catholic Church and its doctrines is well documented in various works. In fact, he believed the Roman Catholic view of biblical authority to be so different from his own that he felt unable to refute their doctrines solely from Scripture, which makes this observation all the more striking for Carson and those who are familiar with his works.[194]

Another category dealt with particular inventions and availability of materials that encouraged the propagation of the Scriptures. Carson noted the significance of the invention of paper in the eleventh century as a replacement for prohibitively expensive parchment.[195] The high cost of books made them scarce and, therefore, the invention of paper was "absolutely necessary to the universal diffusion of the Scriptures," especially for "private persons."[196] One significant question Carson asked was why paper was not invented earlier, and his conclusion was, in part, that "God had determined to give up the world to the grossness of darkness during these ages."[197] This is somewhat similar to Carson's views on the style of Scripture and how God had purposely deviated from stylistic perfection in Scripture for providential purposes.[198] Another invention that Carson viewed as evidence of God's divine providence preserving and spreading the Scriptures was in the invention of the movable-type printing press in the fifteenth century, because it allowed the spread of "the resuscitated light of Divine truth."[199]

---

193. A. Carson, *God of Providence* (1839), 18; *Works* 6:27.

194. For an example, Carson's approach to the Roman Catholic view of the cross will be examined in detail in the following chapter.

195. Carson did not elaborate how he arrived at the eleventh century for the invention of paper. Neither did he give any information on the origin of paper, though he quoted James Beattie (1735–1803), who said that China had writing and printing techniques long before Europe. A. Carson, *God of Providence* (1839), 31; *Works* 6:36. This implied a medium useful for printing upon, but it is unclear if Carson knew of the origins of paper. Paper arrived in Europe from China via Muslims in the Middle East. Europe's exposure to Islamic culture, including paper, was a result of the first Crusades in the eleventh century, which might explain Carson's dating.

196. A. Carson, *God of Providence* (1839), 20; *Works* 6:28.

197. A. Carson, *God of Providence* (1839), 22; *Works* 6:31.

198. *Works* 3:7.

199. A. Carson, *God of Providence* (1839), 24; *Works* 6:31.

The seventh proof Carson noted was writing or, more specifically, a written alphabet. Though a very early invention, it allowed for the revealed will of God to be "conveniently, intelligibly, and securely conveyed to all ages."[200] Carson contrasted the alphabet with logographic systems such as hieroglyphics and Chinese characters, both of which he believed would not have been efficient for writing the Scriptures.[201] Yet, while the invention of a written language was neutral, it was not innocuous. Carson considered how writing was also used for evil purposes, but he argued that there were at least six benefits even when writing was misused. First, the "communication of error" was generally by unbelievers. Second, the evil use of writing could not injure the glory of the gospel. Third, these writings acted as a trial for a Christian's faith. Fourth, the practice of defending God's truth against error gave one a deeper knowledge of the Bible. Fifth, these errors humbled Christians. Sixth, this convinced the Christian of the need for the Spirit's teaching in conjunction with Scripture.[202] Carson gave an analogy to illustrate these benefits: "The best medicines may be used as poisons, yet they are still an immense blessing to the afflicted."[203] Also, the advantages of writing outweighed the disadvantages, for writing preserved not only Scripture itself but also reflections on Scripture.[204]

A broader category of revival movements is also referred to as evidence of God's providence in perpetuating the Scriptures. Carson points out three such movements. The first two movements were the revivals of literature and learning in the fifteenth and sixteenth centuries respectively. His reference to the Renaissance and humanism focused on two aspects. First, there was the renewed study of the biblical languages. Carson recognized the benefits of having access to Pliny and other Greek texts for improving our understanding of the Greek language. As a student of philology, Carson resonated with the humanist slogan *ad fontes*, but the merit was ultimately seen in how it aided in the study of Scripture: "Every discovery as to the syntax and laws of the Greek and Hebrew languages is a pearl of inestimable value to the Christian, and will ultimately serve to perfect the translation of the word of God."[205] Therefore, these revivals were not only

---

200. A. Carson, *God of Providence* (1839), 29; *Works* 6:34–35.
201. A. Carson, *God of Providence* (1839), 30; *Works* 6:35.
202. A. Carson, *God of Providence* (1839), 32–33; *Works* 6:37.
203. A. Carson, *God of Providence* (1839), 33; *Works* 6:38.
204. A. Carson, *God of Providence* (1839), 32; *Works* 6:37.
205. A. Carson, *God of Providence* (1839), 52; *Works* 6:51.

a return to the original languages of Scripture, but Christians everywhere would be able to reap the benefits of better translations. This statement also implies that Carson was not as opposed to better translations as Moore suggested.[206] The second aspect Carson emphasized was the importance of learning as a corrective for superstition and false science, or Roman Catholicism and Neologism respectively. He believed the Reformers' battle against Roman Catholic theology was ongoing, and Carson's Irish context made it especially relevant. He was a strong proponent for education, for literacy in particular, which he believed would provide "weapons for the children of light for the assault of the absurdities of superstition."[207] Bible translations also played a role in encouraging people to learn to read. Carson implied that Luther's translation of the Bible was his most significant legacy for the propagation of the gospel.[208] Concerning the "false science" of his day, Carson argued from his conviction of the plenary verbal inspiration of Scripture that any science that truly contradicted the biblical account could not be true science.[209] For example, he accused geology of often resembling a pseudoscience, because it threatened the Mosaic account of creation.[210] This particular denunciation may have included fellow Evangelical John Pye Smith, who clearly rejected a literal six-day creation of the earth because it did not harmonize with geological evidence.[211]

Possibly the most providential movement was the Protestant Reformation, which Carson described as "the re-appearance and progress of the Gospel in the very camp of the enemy."[212] While he clearly attested to God as the "First Cause" of the Protestant Reformation, he also noted the many secondary causes or means God used to bring it about. Many of the proofs that Carson pointed out were presented in relation to the Reformation. The revival of learning and literature previously discussed, for example, was seen as a harbinger of the Reformation, when the true benefits of that revival were able to be fully taken advantage of. Some of the providential secondary causes Carson reflected on were: the sales of indulgences that motivated Luther to speak out against the Roman Catholic Church; Luther

206. Moore, *Life of Alexander Carson*, 114–17.
207. A. Carson, *God of Providence* (1839), 50; *Works* 6:50.
208. A. Carson, *God of Providence* (1839), 52; *Works* 6:52.
209. A. Carson, *God of Providence* (1839), 49; *Works* 6:49.
210. A. Carson, *God of Providence* (1839), 49; *Works* 6:49.
211. J. Pye Smith, *Relation Between the Holy Scriptures*, 75.
212. A. Carson, *God of Providence* (1839), 34; *Works* 6:38.

being "such a prodigy of intrepidity, ardour, and unquenchable zeal" that he was enabled to challenge the establishment; the gradual progression of Luther's Reformed theology, which kept him from suspicion; the problems within the Roman Catholic Church, which made the people more receptive to Luther's teachings; and the economic burden the German princes were under while a part of the Catholic Church, which motivated them to aid Luther in his efforts.[213]

Not only did Carson believe that the promises made in the inspired Scriptures would be fulfilled, but he believed that the fulfillment of these promises made in the Bible confirmed the Bible's divine inspiration. From the proofs presented by Carson, it can be argued that his examination of the fulfillment of the promise in Matt 24:14 was designed to instill further confidence in Scripture's authority as well as in the providence of God at all times.

CONCLUSION

Carson did not take the Bible lightly, and the reason for this was that he believed it to be God's message to humanity. Therefore, when he believed that the Bible was being portrayed in a way that diminished the value of God's revealed word by incorrectly and overly emphasizing humanity's role in the writing of Scripture in opposition to the Holy Spirit's role, Carson fully immersed himself into the controversy that swirled around the issue of how the Scriptures were inspired. As shown, he clearly aligned himself within a more narrow understanding of the Bible's inspiration, called plenary verbal inspiration, which viewed the Bible to be completely inspired in its principles and in its words. How resolute he was in his convictions was apparent by the utter lack of compromise in his polemical works. This commitment to a completely verbally inspired Bible was also manifested in Carson's concern over the proper translation of the Scripture for the mission field. As each word of the Bible was originally inspired, Carson advocated the practice of translating with each word of the original in mind, as much as was possible. The gospel implications of this were apparent as well, because the translations were primarily for those in foreign nations who had not heard the gospel. They needed access to the Scripture in their own language to be able to learn about the gospel and the atoning work of Christ central to it.

---

213. A. Carson, *God of Providence* (1839), 37–48; *Works* 6:40–48.

3

Alexander Carson on the Cross

CARSON'S UNDERSTANDING OF THE GOSPEL could, in part, be understood by his belief that the word of God was "the only test of truth." While his commitment to the whole Bible as the word of God was evidenced in his polemical works, this conviction was also found in his proclamation of the gospel to unbelievers. Carson's evangelistic letter to the exiled Napoleon Bonaparte (1769–1821) is an example of this, and it shows the centrality of the cross in Carson's theology. In 1814, the defeated French Emperor was exiled by the British to the island of Elba. Anyone living through those tumultuous days would have been familiar with the events that led to his downfall. Napoleon's exile prompted Carson to write an evangelistic letter to him, though it is unknown whether this letter actually reached Napoleon or if Carson even sent it.[1] For the present chapter, it is significant that

---

1. The letter's existence and contents were made public upon its inclusion in the first volume of Carson's collected works, which was published three years after Carson's death in 1844. *Works* 1:279–94. If the publisher's introductory note of the first volume of Carson's works is accurate, his letter to Napoleon was copied from a manuscript (*Works* 1:vii). This manuscript can no longer be found. His letter was republished by an unnamed author in 1872 as part of an evangelistic letter to Napoleon III. A Carson, *Letter to the Emperor Napoleon* (1872). Despite its claim of being reprinted exactly as written in 1814, it most likely depended on the 1847 printing. The presence of the letter among Carson's belongings does not necessarily lead to the conclusion that he did not attempt to send his letter to Napoleon. Carson may have written a copy of his letter. Another possibility is that his wife wrote a more legible copy of the original letter to be sent. The publishers of his collected works noted the difficulty of reading Carson's manuscripts, and George Moore, who wrote a biography of Carson, noted that Carson's wife regularly acted as his copyist. Moore, *Life of Alexander Carson*, 6. As Napoleon gave no corroborating evidence of receiving the letter, it is arguably of little consequence whether Carson sent the letter or not.

he raises the issue of the cross. The following statement by Carson about Christ's crucifixion in his letter to Napoleon is significant: "The atonement by his death is the centre of revelation, in which all its numerous lines meet."[2] The "numerous lines" were the biblical texts on the atonement that were scattered throughout Scripture.[3] Therein lay the answer to redemption as Carson stated in numerous works that the way of acceptance with God, or redemption, was the most important subject man could consider. Carson understood the atonement through Christ's work on the cross to be the focal point of the gospel and Scripture. Since the question of redemption was the primary concern for man, Christ's work on the cross also became primary.

This chapter will explore Carson's view of humanity's need for the cross and the various aspects of Christ's atoning work discussed by Carson. This examination will show that Carson saw humanity's need for the cross to be the result of universal human sin. It will also show that Carson saw Christ's atoning work as the harmonization of God's justice and mercy, as a display of divine sovereignty, and as a completed work. Other themes that will be prevalent throughout this and subsequent chapters are Carson's refusal to go beyond the biblical account, either for pragmatic reasons or as a way to resolve hypothetical issues, and his disdain for human wisdom as a substitute for Scripture.

HUMANITY'S NEED FOR THE CROSS

Carson's argument in *The Doctrine of the Atonement* was presented through seven propositions: all of humanity is guilty of sin and thus exposed to God's wrath; Christ's death on the cross provides the only and complete atonement for even the chief of sinners; justification by faith alone; faith in Christ transforms the mind and lifestyle of the believer; the gospel is a product of God's wisdom and is rejected as foolishness by humanity's wisdom; rejection of the gospel will result in everlasting punishment; and the gospel promises everlasting glory and happiness.[4] In his first proposition, he argued that the entire human race was guilty and exposed to God's

---

2. *Works* 1:284.
3. A. Carson, *Reasons for Separating* (1806), 83; *Works* 4:83.
4. *Works* 1:8.

wrath.[5] This sinful condition, rooted in Adam's sin, had eternal ramifications, for the punishment of sin was not simply an untimely physical death, but "everlasting destruction from the presence of the Lord and the glory of his power."[6] Yet, everlasting destruction was not only the consequence of spectacular sins. Carson also believed that "eternal condemnation is the award of the smallest sin."[7] Now, it was common for him to tie what he considered to be indispensable doctrine to the gospel, the central message of the Bible. The doctrine of humanity's sin was no exception to this practice. Since "the way of acceptance with God" was the most important subject that people could consider, a correct understanding of the gospel was essential.[8] Yet, the doctrine of humanity's sin was necessary to understand humanity's need for God's acceptance, their need for salvation from God's wrath.[9] Christ, Carson noted, made it a point to expose the sinfulness of those who believed themselves to be without sin.[10] Carson also, comparing his own day's philosophers, men of science, and philanthropists to the New Testament Pharisees, sought to show them the reality of their sinful state.[11]

Carson believed that all people were dead in their sins, making humanity's sinful condition a universal one. In his evangelistic letter to Napoleon Bonaparte, Carson thus wrote that all men were guilty before God.[12] It was important for Carson that Christians also recognize themselves as sinners before their conversion. An article on evangelical preaching in *The Edinburgh Review* (1837) criticized the "evangelical" doctrine of universal depravity: "In the declarations made with such peculiar zest and complacency by the evangelical party on the depravity of human nature, we are apt to view them as merely indulging in feelings of deep humility, until it is recollected that, of this depravity, they themselves (at least by their own account) have ceased to be partakers. The depravity, then, which they so ingenuously confess, is the depravity of all mankind—except themselves."[13] The author accused Evangelicals of essentially judging only outsiders, or

---

5. *Works* 1:9.
6. *Works* 1:10.
7. *Works* 1:151.
8. *Works* 1:1.
9. *Works* 1:9.
10. *Works* 1:9.
11. *Works* 1:10.
12. *Works* 1:284.
13. *Edinburgh Review*, Unsigned review of *Mysteries*, 430n*.

maybe non-Evangelicals, as partaking in humanity's sin nature. Carson refuted this accusation in no uncertain terms in his response to the article. First, he claimed that Evangelicals did indeed include themselves in the "universal guilt of human nature." Second, he stated that there was an ongoing battle with a sinful nature, or "a law in their members," that struggled with the "law of their mind."[14] Therefore, Christians had past and present states of sin. Carson also responded by accusing the author of misrepresenting Evangelicals by applying beliefs to them that were "altogether *unevangelical.*"[15] In *The Doctrine of the Atonement*, he wrote, "Even Christians are said to have been, by nature, the children of wrath, even as others."[16] He reiterated the point later on, writing that people "are in no sense considered as godly until they are justified by faith."[17] Carson asserted that this doctrine of universal depravity was why all people were called to repent.[18] If humanity's universal sin was denied, the gospel no longer applied to all people. It became one option rather than the only option.

What then did Carson understand by the term "sin"? He defined sin as "the alienation of the heart from God, or [simply] alienation from God. . . . Whatever discovers most enmity to God is the most sinful."[19] This definition implied sin to be organized into degrees of sinfulness, though even the least sin still warranted separation from God. Carson believed that opposition to the gospel, to Christ and his atoning work on the cross, was the most contrary position to God. He wrote in his response to the critic of evangelical preaching, "that while faith is said to be the gift of God, unbelief is declared to be not only a sin, but the greatest of all sins."[20] Further evidence of Carson's view is seen in *The Knowledge of Jesus*: "Of all sins, enmity against God in the character in which he is manifested in the gospel, is the chief."[21] There were two reasons for this view. First, the gospel was at the center of God's special revelation, the Bible. Second, the gospel was the manifestation

---

14. A. Carson, *Letters on "Evangelical Preaching,"* 11; *Works* 1:322–23.

15. A. Carson, *Letters on "Evangelical Preaching,"* 11; *Works* 1:323; emphasis in original.

16. *Works* 1:19–20.

17. *Works* 1:82.

18. *Works* 1:9.

19. *Works* 1:23.

20. A. Carson, *Letters on "Evangelical Preaching,"* 17; *Works* 1:330.

21. A. Carson, *Knowledge of Jesus*, 149–50; *Works* 5:100.

of God's character to mankind. Therefore, rejecting the gospel was an absolute rejection of God.

This understanding of sin led Carson to see Saul of Tarsus, prior to his conversion, as the prime example of human sinfulness. "According to this standard, there is not in the human race to be found a greater sinner than the virtuous, the religious, the zealous, the sincere worshipper of God, Saul of Tarsus, when vice, adultery, drunkenness, stealing, and all the vile catalogue of gross sins do not discover so much hatred to God's character as opposition to the truth in which it is revealed."[22] Saul, as a persecutor of Christians, was in total opposition to the gospel, and, therefore, he was the chief of sinners.[23] Another biblical reference was to Jesus's words about the day of judgment being more tolerable for Sodom, Gomorrah, Tyre, and Sidon than for those who reject the gospel (Luke 10:12–14; Matt 10:15).[24] In this sense, there was a greater potential for opposition to God to be found in one's wrong beliefs than simply in one's immoral acts.[25] Just as the gospel of Jesus Christ was at the center of Carson's theology, the sin he was most concerned with was what he considered to be the greatest sin, the rejection of that gospel.

Carson used this idea as a foundational presupposition to his regularly-stated position that Christ's atoning work was able to save even the chief of sinners. If even Saul, the chief of sinners, could be saved, then any, regardless of how sinful they saw themselves to be, could be saved through faith in Christ's atoning work. For example, in *The Truth of the Gospel Demonstrated* (1820), Carson reasoned that Richard Carlile (1790–1843), an outspoken deist and convinced enemy of Christ, was not any more opposed to Christ than Saul of Tarsus was, and that Christ could also open his eyes to the truth.[26] Again, addressing any who may have rejected the gospel,

---

22. *Works* 1:23.

23. Carson believed that Paul was not calling himself the chief of sinners simply according to his personal feelings or false humility, but because he absolutely believed himself to be the chief of sinners, for "what he speaks of himself is spoken by the Spirit of inspiration." A. Carson, *Knowledge of Jesus*, 148; *Works* 5:99. It is unclear whether Carson interpreted the Scriptures to mean that Paul was chief sinner of all time only up to the time he wrote 1 Tim 1:15 or only at the time he wrote 1 Tim 1:15.

24. *Works* 1:23.

25. A. Carson, *View of Day of Judgment*, 23; *Works* 1:221.

26. A. Carson, *Truth of the Gospel Demonstrated* (1839), 14; *Works* 1:253.

Carson wrote, "Though you have spoken against [Christ], preached against him, you have not blasphemed him more than Paul did."[27]

Related to the universality of humanity's sinful condition was the extent of this condition. Carson affirmed the total depravity of all people and claimed that an unbeliever's every action, as the action of a sinner, was sinful. Yet, in response to criticism that Evangelicals believed that the natural person was "continually and wholly intent upon wickedness,"[28] Carson qualified his claim by explaining that it was the person who was sinful and not necessarily the nature of the act itself. This qualification was especially in regard to "duty" actions, such as providing food for one's family, which were not sinful per se. Carson's point was that any act, no matter how innocuous or good, was sinful when performed by someone who had not been saved by faith in the gospel.[29] In contrast, the Christian may do the same actions, but for the glory of God.[30]

Carson also insisted upon humanity's ignorance of the depth of their sin or the guilt of sin.[31] Though he believed that unsaved people were spiritually blind, he rejected an oversimplification of the evangelical position made by one critic, that sinners were completely blind to sin until their eyes were opened by the Holy Spirit.[32] Carson argued that while unbelievers did have some understanding of sin, "they do not have a sufficient view of the guilt of sin."[33] This lack of sufficient knowledge of one's own sin was significant to Carson, because a deficient understanding of one's guilt led to a deficient understanding of one's need for a savior. Another example of the unbeliever's spiritual blindness was evidenced by the practice of modifying God's righteousness to suit one's own subjective level of righteousness.

27. *Works* 1:66.

28. *Edinburgh Review*, Unsigned review of *Mysteries*, 430. While it is not clear if the author of the *Edinburgh Review* article claimed a particular religious party, at least one Unitarian, William H. Drummond, also had a critical view of the evangelical doctrine of humanity's total depravity, calling the doctrine an "infernal doctrine." Drummond, *Doctrine of Trinity* (1831), 67n*.

29. A. Carson, *Letters on "Evangelical Preaching,"* 10; *Works* 1:321.

30. Acworth and Carson, *Two Sermons*, 47; *Works* 1:426.

31. "[God] testifies that [the Gentiles'] understanding was darkened and alienated from the life of God, through their ignorance and blindness, notwithstanding all modern boasts of their piety and virtue." *Works* 1:19.

32. A. Carson, *Truth of the Gospel Demonstrated* (1839), 5–6; *Works* 1:247; *Edinburgh Review*, Unsigned review of *Mysteries*, 431.

33. A. Carson, *Letters on "Evangelical Preaching,"* 10; *Works* 1:322.

Carson argued that this was the only way any person could even attempt to be saved by one's own righteousness.[34] In the end, one's ignorance of the extent of sin or the standard by which it was judged did not mitigate one's responsibility to God and, therefore, made the conveyance of a proper understanding of the depth of sin that much more necessary.

Not only did Carson dwell on the sinfulness of unbelieving people, but he also delved into what the ultimate punishment for sin would be. "Yet such is the blindness of the human mind, that men often succeed in turning away their eyes from beholding that awful scene."[35] The blindness that kept people from seeing the extent of their guilt also kept people from seeing the final due for their guilt. Thoughts of the coming judgment were also often displaced by present concerns or pleasures. Though he did not dismiss present concerns as unimportant, Carson saw this lack of an eternal perspective as further evidence of humanity's fallen condition.[36] He described the way to be saved from divine wrath as "the most momentous of all questions," which is why he often brought the reader's attention back to the fact that there would be a divine reckoning for all people in the introduction of his evangelistic works.[37]

Unbelievers deserved hell because they have rejected the grace only conveyed through the gospel. "They shall live, only to endure merited wrath."[38] Not only was hell deserved by those who rejected the atoning work of Christ, but it was also an eternal punishment. Carson wrote that Satan's temptation of Adam and Eve was not the worst of his works. "[This]

---

34. "Man first moulds the law of God to his own supposed duty and taste, before ever he has hopes of living by the keeping of it." *Works* 1:14.

35. A. Carson, "Remarks on the General Resurrection," 1:198. This work was published posthumously from original manuscripts.

36. "To be supported comfortably in this world, and to be protected from the dangers to which we are exposed, are in themselves matters of great importance. But, compared with the salvation of the soul, they are as nothing." A. Carson, *Address to the Children*, 1; A. Carson, "Remarks on the General Resurrection," 1:198.

37. A. Carson, *Letters on "Evangelical Preaching,"* iii; *Works* 1:308. "Of all the subjects that solicit the attention of mankind, the way of acceptance with God is the most important." *Works* 1:1. "Whether is it possible to escape the wrath of God, and how we are to be saved from it, are questions, compared with which, all others are trifling." A. Carson, *Address to the Children*, 1. "You must grant, that to determine correctly on this subject, is a matter of the utmost importance. If the gospel is true, eternal damnation is the inevitable doom of all who believe it not." A. Carson, *Truth of the Gospel Demonstrated* (1839), *Works* 1:253.

38. A. Carson, "Remarks on the General Resurrection," 1:198.

is nothing compared with that everlasting misery which is denounced as the punishment of all evil doers. What a malignant mind must be in the Being that planned the everlasting ruin of the whole race of Adam."[39] In his address to the children at the Tobermore Sabbath school, he spoke of their eternal souls, the eventual resurrection of their bodies, and that they would either enjoy "everlasting and inconceivable happiness, or endure everlasting and inconceivable misery."[40]

Christ's Work on the Cross

Carson addressed humanity's sinful condition, but did not leave it at that. While universal sin was a necessary doctrine, it was only a stepping stone, albeit a necessary one, to the center of Carson's theology, which was the cross of Christ. Scripture taught the condemnation of all people, as argued in the first chapter of the *Doctrine of the Atonement*, but it also taught about salvation in Christ. There was no use in teaching the doctrine of total depravity if Christ's atoning work did not follow it. Carson made note of the atonement's exclusion during biblical times: "Instead of pointing to the death of the Messiah as a sacrifice for sin, [the Jewish teachers] taught their votaries to depend on the law of Moses, and traditions of human invention."[41] He encouraged Evangelicals of his own day to remain faithful in preaching the cross of Christ to sinners: "Why is a church called the pillar of the truth, if it is not a finger-board, constantly pointing to heaven? *Refuge, refuge*, ought to be so plainly inscribed on it, that he that runs may read."[42]

These exhortations were practiced in Carson's Tobermore church. According to Moore, Carson's preaching always addressed both unbelievers and believers: "[He] endeavored to scathe the impenitent with heaven's lightning; but he left them not long to quake in the vicinity of Sinai. No; Calvary and its Cross, and its omnipotent Saviour, constituted the refuge city to which he directed the perishing. Truly, the Cross was his Polar Star—Calvary was his much-loved home!"[43] Moore also records that those who sat under Carson's preaching over a span of decades testified that Carson

---

39. A. Carson, "Character and Empire of Satan," 1:297. This work was published posthumously from original manuscripts.
40. A. Carson, *Address to the Children*, 1.
41. *Works* 1:140.
42. Acworth and Carson, *Two Sermons*, 63–64; *Works* 1:439.
43. Moore, *Life of Alexander Carson*, 64–65.

never dismissed the congregation without having clearly shared "as much of Christ as would save, or condemn."[44] Thomas Witherow (1824–90), a Presbyterian minister, recognized Carson as a "deservedly esteemed" preacher of the gospel, especially for his ability to teach the Scriptures to even "some stupid block, into whose thick head it were a task indeed to hammer an idea"![45]

The reason that the cross of Christ was a refuge for sinners was because of the price Christ paid upon it. Carson described Christ's work on the cross as the ransom or price paid for the salvation of sinners. Two points were made about this. First, there had to be a price for the redemption of sinners, and, second, the price paid on the cross was the death or blood of Christ.[46] In *The Doctrine of the Atonement*, Carson wrote that the Father "provided a savior, who, by his death, has made atonement for sin, and through whom all his people have the gift of eternal life."[47] He believed the Bible was very clear that Christ offered himself as a sacrifice, bore the sins of his people, and cleansed them. As a propitiation for humanity's sin, Carson tied Christ's work on the cross to the sacrifices of the Old Testament. He made reference to 1 Pet 1:18–19, noting the contrast Peter made between the precious nature of Christ's blood shed for sinners with the normally precious, but here referred to as corruptible, silver and gold used to ransom prisoners. Carson also pointed out the sacrificial nature of Christ's blood in the passage, implied in "the expression, 'as of a lamb, without blemish and without spot.'"[48] He argued that Christ's sacrifice was the substance of Old Testament Jewish sacrifices; their value was that they pointed to Christ. Therefore, the Old Testament sacrifices were a type of Christ's sacrifice.[49] Using Heb 9:11–15, Carson argued that the atonement showed how Christ acted as humanity's high priest, not by giving the blood

---

44. Moore, *Life of Alexander Carson*, 71.

45. Witherow, *Three Prophets*, 22. Witherow was a Presbyterian minister in the General Synod and had a personal connection with the Carsons. Some of his published works were critiqued by Carson's son Robert Haldane Carson.

46. Carson discussed the necessity of a sacrifice in terms of God's justice and mercy, which will be discussed in a later section.

47. *Works* 1:42.

48. *Works* 1:44.

49. *Works* 1:51.

of animals, but his own blood, thereby acting as the mediator.[50] Christ was the church's Passover lamb who saved them from eternal destruction.[51]

Carson was clear in putting the cross, with its purpose and efficacy, over and above other aspects of Christ's ministry. For example, Christ was not simply, or even primarily, an example for righteousness. "Christ saves us, then, by giving a price for us, not by teaching us the way to happiness, giving us good example, and dying to confirm his testimony. His death not only teaches us to avoid sin, but through it we have the forgiveness of sins."[52] Carson drew attention to the necessity of the cross, that Christ died "not to teach us to save ourselves, but to save us from the wrath to come. By the death of Christ, they who were enemies to God are reconciled to him. The end of that death, then, is not the confirmation of doctrine, but the reconciliation of enemies."[53] Rather than being a lesson for people, Christ's death itself saves sinners. From 2 Cor 5:18–21, Carson argued, "They obtain acceptance with God, not as innocent or just in themselves, but as not being charged with their sins which are charged upon Christ."[54]

Carson believed that the Bible—the words of the Father, Christ, and the apostles—stated that Christ was the atonement for sins. The atonement was singularly associated with Christ, and, therein, lay the uniqueness of God's plan for the salvation of sinners.[55] "Many a scheme of righteousness has been invented by man, but the atonement of Christ is God's plan of righteousness."[56] Carson would regularly state that human wisdom could not and would not have come up with this plan for redemption. Rather, "all human schemes of religion save the sinner at the expense of some part of the divine character. The blood of the cross alone, adjusts the different and seemingly opposite claims of the divine attributes."[57] The harmony of God's attributes as manifested in the gospel was not only used as evidence for the uniqueness of the atonement, but also to show its necessity.

---

50. *Works* 1:50.
51. *Works* 1:51.
52. *Works* 1:44.
53. *Works* 1:48.
54. *Works* 1:48.
55. *Works* 1:43.
56. *Works* 1:45.
57. *Works* 1:123.

One of Carson's methods in defending the gospel was to present it as "a manifestation of the divine character," or divine attributes.[58] He believed that God revealed himself in two sources, which he called natural revelation and special revelation. God's natural revelation included his creative works and his providence. God's special revelation was the Bible. While both were inspired, Carson argued that the Scriptures went further than God's works by revealing "God in his character with reference to sin, and displays those attributes of his nature which secure the salvation of his people. On this subject the revelation of God in the heavens and the earth received no information: on this it communicates no instruction."[59] In fact, God's full character was only seen in the work of redemption.[60] Carson saw the gospel as the clearest display of God's character, compared to elsewhere in Scripture or in the created order. Of the various attributes Carson examined, he focused on God's justice and mercy more deeply and with greater frequency than the others. In addressing the corrupt gospels of both unbelievers and professing believers, Carson argued that God's justice and mercy were shown most perfectly in Christ's atoning work and also acted as evidence of the gospel's divine origin.

DIVINE JUSTICE AND DIVINE MERCY IN THE ATONEMENT

Only two of Carson's works were structured completely around the manifestation of God's attributes in the gospel, *The Truth of the Gospel Demonstrated from the Character of God Manifested in the Atonement: A Letter to Mr. Richard Carlile* (1820) and *The Knowledge of Jesus the Most Excellent of the Sciences* (1839). Each of these works discussed divine attributes such as divine wisdom, power, holiness, sovereignty, love, justice, and mercy. Of these attributes, justice and mercy were given the most discussion within and outside of his two works dedicated to divine attributes manifested in the gospel. For example, Carson devoted an entire letter out of five *Letters to the Author of an Article in the Edinburgh Review on "Evangelical Preaching"* (1837) to divine justice and mercy in the atonement.[61] They also have a strong presence in *The Doctrine of the Atonement* (1847) and *A Reply*

58. A. Carson, *Truth of the Gospel Demonstrated* (1839), 8; *Works* 1:249.
59. A. Carson, *Knowledge of Jesus*, iii; *Works* 5:xv.
60. A. Carson, *Knowledge of Jesus*, 224; *Works* 5:153.
61. A. Carson, *Letters on "Evangelical Preaching,"* 41–49; *Works* 1:359–68.

to Doctor Drummond's *Essay on the Doctrine of the Trinity* (1831). Carson described both justice and mercy separately, as well as how they worked together in harmony.

In his discussion of the divine attributes, Carson emphasized that they could never be compromised. God's divine justice was no exception, and thus required satisfaction from sinners. Carson wrote that removing what God's justice required resulted in a corrupt God: "You hope to escape punishment though you are not sinless; your God then is unjust."[62] Carson argued that nothing was allowed to take away from what divine justice had laid claim upon. In this case, justice required the sinner to be punished and, as a divine attribute, could not be compromised. Carson contrasted divine justice with that of human rulers who sometimes sacrificed justice to "expediency and popular clamor."[63] He wrote, "The God of the Scriptures is so just that no sin ever will be committed without being visited with adequate punishment; that neither angel nor man shall ever dwell in his presence tarnished with the slightest impurity."[64] Equating God's justice with his wrath, he also wrote, "Until you are delivered from your sins the curse of God rests on you, and Divine wrath must pursue you, both in this world and the next."[65] In both references, Carson argued that God would never go against his character, of which justice was a part. His justice also applied to all created beings, and not only mankind. Fallen angels, for example, were specifically identified along with mankind, partly to show the greatness of divine justice that extended even to these now demonic beings, but also against universalist theology that included fallen angels among those who would eventually be redeemed.[66]

A second point Carson made concerning divine justice was that God's justice required a sacrifice that only the divine could meet. Christ's death was able to atone for sin due to his divinity.[67] This is one reason Carson tied the knowledge of God to the atonement of Christ, especially in his

---

62. A. Carson, *Truth of the Gospel Demonstrated* (1839), 18; *Works* 1:256.

63. A. Carson, *History of Providence in Scripture*, 205; *Works* 6:299.

64. A. Carson, *Truth of the Gospel Demonstrated* (1839), 22; *Works* 1:258.

65. A. Carson, *History of Providence in Book of Esther* (1835), 86; *Works* 6:122.

66. Carson did not believe fallen angels would be redeemed. "The Divine mercy has utterly overlooked the whole host of fallen angels. It does not lay hold even on all the human race." A. Carson, *Knowledge of Jesus*, 157; *Works* 5:105.

67. "If Christ is God, his death is equal to the atonement of sin; and if sin is fully punished in him, his people must be freed from punishment." A. Carson, *Address to the Children*, 2.

writings against Unitarians, deists, and atheists. The deity of Christ was a necessary component of the gospel. In his letter to Richard Carlile, Carson wrote that "he who preaches the Gospel must exhibit the Saviour as a divine personage, making full atonement for sin. Without shewing the character of Jesus, to speak of salvation by him in the most correct and decided terms, fails of fully preaching the Gospel."[68] A deficient view of Christ's divinity also caused the atonement to fall short in a more practical manner, because it did not give people a sufficient reason to trust in the cross.[69] In *The Knowledge of Jesus*, he wrote, "It must be known who he is, as well as what he has done. . . . The name of Jesus is salvation, not by way of charm, or by its sound, but as it exhibits a character that is trustworthy. The mere letters of the name of Christ, or the sound of any of his names, will do no more than those of Mahomet. The character and work of him who bears the name must be known before that name becomes salvation."[70] The character to which Carson referred is the divine character made flesh in Jesus Christ. Carson contrasted Christ's perfection to man's sincerity, saying that sincerity could not satisfy God's justice. While sincerity was not a negative characteristic to have per se, it was unable to make up for a lack of righteousness. Human works, which were inherently imperfect despite any level of sincerity involved, were unable to serve as satisfaction for God's justice.[71]

A third point Carson made concerning divine justice in the atonement was that justice was most clearly seen on the cross. In fact, he argued that justice was fully served only in the death of Christ, and not in the punishment of man. He wrote, "In the atonement of Christ justice has a full compensation, which it never could have had in the punishment of the sinner himself."[72] While eternal punishment was the most a person would be able to pay for his or her sin, it was the very least that could be expected as a punishment for sinning against God. Christ's atonement was an actual payment in full. "The infinitely worthy Sacrifice gave justice a full

---

68. A. Carson, *Truth of the Gospel Demonstrated* (1839), 8–9; *Works* 1:249.

69. A. Carson, *Truth of the Gospel Demonstrated* (1835), 9; *Works* 1:249. "To men who do not know Jesus as a divine personage a call to believe in him, will not give a sufficient ground for hope. It is necessary to show them who Jesus is."

70. A. Carson, *Knowledge of Jesus*, 226; *Works* 5:154.

71. *Works* 1:13.

72. A. Carson, *Truth of the Gospel Demonstrated* (1839), 19; *Works* 1:256.

remuneration."[73] In response to William Drummond's horror at the idea of a father sacrificing his son, Carson replied, "This indeed gives the most awful and tremendous idea of Divine justice, and therefore, more than hell itself, proves the guilt and danger of sin."[74] Carson minimized the worth of man's punishment even more in *The Doctrine of the Atonement*. "The torment of hell does not exhibit the justice of God in as strong a point of view as the suffering of Christ. Those punished in hell never satisfy justice; but justice was fully satisfied in the death of Christ."[75]

According to Carson, God's mercy was often just as misunderstood as God's justice. People never portrayed divine mercy perfectly, not due to human inability, but due to human rebellion. As he wrote, "A salvation wholly of justice they fear, a salvation wholly of mercy they disdain. But the salvation of the gospel is of infinite mercy as well as of infinite justice. The mercy of God is unmixed mercy."[76] Carson argued that, though both divine justice and mercy were present in the gospel, mercy was not made less merciful by the presence of justice. Salvation by grace, without works, was not a human invention. "Since the foundation of the world, no man untaught by God ever looked for salvation in this way."[77] Salvation by grace was, for Carson, an example of God's mercy. Human wisdom diluted God's grace and mercy with works and merit: "Human wisdom . . . invariably expects that salvation will not be given without something on the part of the sinner himself to merit such a favor. The grace of God is not considered to consist in giving for nothing, but in giving at an undervalue. The great blessing of pardon is given for something done by the sinner, which in itself is not of adequate value."[78] Carson, therefore, saw divine mercy being devalued by human wisdom in two ways. First, it assumed that mercy must be earned in some way. Second, it presumed that God's mercy could be bartered for with something of lesser value, which, in this case, was human works. Carson saw yet another example of how human mercy was different from God's in the Jews' decision to deliver Barabbas from his just punishment. Their

---

73. A. Carson, *Truth of the Gospel Demonstrated* (1839), 19; *Works* 1:256.

74. Drummond, *Doctrine of Trinity* (1831), 7; A. Carson, *Reply to Dr. Drummond's Essay*, 23; *Works* 2:218.

75. *Works* 1:124.

76. A. Carson, *Truth of the Gospel Demonstrated* (1839), 23; *Works* 1:259.

77. A. Carson, *Truth of the Gospel Demonstrated* (1839), 23; *Works* 1:259.

78. A. Carson, *Truth of the Gospel Demonstrated* (1839), 23; *Works* 1:259.

mercy was not motivated by love for Barabbas, but from hatred toward Christ.[79] God's mercy, in contrast, was an example of divine love.

Carson also asserted God's mercy to be necessarily sovereign. Otherwise, divine mercy would not have legitimacy as long as any suffering existed in the world.[80] He demonstrated divine mercy to be sovereign in a number of ways. First, God's mercy overlooked a part of mankind. Carson wrote, "It not only extends to the chief of sinners, but, from among sinners, it takes one and leaves another, without any other reason than the will of God."[81] While the reason for divine mercy's application to some and not others was solely dependent on God's will, Carson reiterated that no person deserved God's mercy in the first place: "If all men are guilty and worthy of punishment, which most who are called Christians admit, a sovereign God may punish all. If his mercy cannot save one, and pass by another, he is no sovereign. Here then is an attribute of God necessary to the Divine perfection, which human wisdom, so far from discovering, cannot admit."[82] It is evident that Carson was just as concerned with preserving God's sovereignty as he was with preserving God's mercy.

In an experiential sense, Carson saw unbelief as that which excluded a person from mercy, for Mark 16:16 stated, "He that believeth . . . shall be saved." Yet, Carson saw that Scripture did not leave the application of God's mercy to people. He argued that biblical examples of those not reached by divine mercy, such as Judas Iscariot, were not due to the inability of divine mercy, but examples of divine sovereignty excluding one from faith.[83] Carson admitted that this aspect of God's mercy was difficult for many people to accept, even for those who admitted to believe in God's sovereignty.[84]

Second, God sovereignly granted mercy on whom he wished, regardless of human merit. In one sense, it was nonsectarian. Human wisdom expected God to favor a certain people. "There is a weak and wicked partiality which the gods of all nations are supposed to have for their favorite countries."[85] This view of a sectarian mercy might not only be driven by national affiliation but also religious affiliation. Carson continued, "This

---

79. A. Carson, *History of Providence in Scripture*, 201; *Works* 6:296.
80. A. Carson, *Knowledge of Jesus*, 159; *Works* 5:106.
81. A. Carson, *Truth of the Gospel Demonstrated* (1839), 26; *Works* 1:262.
82. A. Carson, *Truth of the Gospel Demonstrated* (1839), 27; *Works* 1:262.
83. A. Carson, *Knowledge of Jesus*, 151; *Works* 5:101.
84. A. Carson, *Truth of the Gospel Demonstrated* (1839), 28; *Works* 1:262.
85. A. Carson, *Truth of the Gospel Demonstrated* (1839), 28; *Works* 1:263.

sort of partiality many think that God will have towards the professors of Christianity, while he will more rigorously look to the conduct of infidels. While they drink, and swear, and lie, and cheat, without any dread of the Divine displeasure, they see the wrath of God coming on Mr. Carlile."[86] Carson insisted that this sort of sectarian "God" was a human creation, and not the God of Scripture. While God sovereignly chose on whom to have mercy, he also declared, according to Rom 2:11, that "there is not respect of persons with him."[87]

Concerning the presence of two opposing attributes, Carson presented two points. First, God's justice and mercy were distinct and, in a sense, mutually exclusive. Second, they were able to act in harmony without compromise. Concerning their mutual exclusivity, divine justice's inability to perform the work of mercy did not degrade the power of God, for there was a distinction between power and agency.[88] As Carson wrote,

> God, indeed, exercises mercy in consistency with justice, because, through the bloody sacrifice, "grace reigns with righteousness." But even God's mercy has nothing to do in judgment. His mercy does not judge the saved sinner to be less guilty than justice represents him, nor the punishment due to his sins to be less than the law awards.... Mercy forgives sin, but neither alleviates its guilt, nor lessens its punishment. Mercy never sat on the throne of justice to restrain its full exercise; nor justice on the throne of mercy to limit its extension. They both sit together on the same throne, demanding and obtaining their rights in infinite perfection and harmony.[89]

Their mutual exclusivity allowed them to act perfectly and without compromise, but they also worked in harmony. In contrast, Carson indicated that the Unitarian god was neither perfectly just nor perfectly merciful. "He saves the guilty by a compromise, and thus sacrifices both attributes. He cannot punish with all the severity and rigor that justice demands; nor can he save from punishment the exceedingly guilty."[90] Elsewhere, he stated that the man-made version of salvation was generally a mix of merit and mercy, with mercy making up for where merit fell short, at which point mercy

---

86. A. Carson, *Truth of the Gospel Demonstrated* (1839), 28; *Works* 1:263.
87. A. Carson, *Truth of the Gospel Demonstrated* (1839), 29; *Works* 1:263.
88. A. Carson, *History of Providence in Scripture*, 346; *Works* 6:402.
89. A. Carson, *Reply to Dr. Drummond's Essay*, 27–28; *Works* 2:225.
90. A. Carson, *Reply to Dr. Drummond's Essay*, 25; *Works* 2:221.

effectively stopped justice from being satisfied. Both mercy and justice were then compromised.[91] In response to an Unitarian's accusation of inconsistency, Carson wrote, "Instead of outraging either justice or mercy, our system is the only one which can give both attributes all their due. My God is so just, that no sin was ever committed, or ever will be committed, that hath not punishment according to its desert; yet he is so merciful that he can pardon the chief of sinners, through faith in the blood of his Son."[92] God's mercy was perfectly consistent with his justice because it reached the believer through the atonement. Through the atoning work of Christ, forgiving sins was not only merciful, but also just, for a just God would not punish the same sin twice. Once Christ paid for sin on the cross, it was paid for good, but only for those who took part in the atonement through faith.

DIVINE SOVEREIGNTY AND THE CROSS

That God's attributes could work in perfection and harmony is connected with divine sovereignty. The perfection of God's sovereignty meant that nothing external could restrain or influence him, because he was guided by his own perfections alone, which was to say by his own character. Though one may say God could not do certain things, it was only because those things were against his character. "He cannot do any thing inconsistent with the perfections of his own character."[93] Looking back to divine justice, for example, Carson argued that God could not punish unjustly, because that would be a denial of himself in his justice. It was because God's sovereignty was exercised within the bounds of his own character, such as his wisdom and goodness, that man could find great comfort in his sovereignty. This is completely different from being under the reign of an evil tyrant.

In *The Knowledge of Jesus the Most Excellent of Sciences*, one of the divine attributes Carson discussed was divine sovereignty. He did not consider God's sovereignty to be based simply in the actions themselves, but as rooted in his divine character. Manifestations of God's sovereignty, such as in the atonement, were a result of God's very character. Since Carson believed sovereignty to be a characteristic of God, he found the belief to be essential to a biblical understanding of who God was, writing that those "who

---

91. A. Carson, *Knowledge of Jesus*, 160–61; *Works* 5:108.
92. A. Carson, *Reply to Dr. Drummond's Essay*, 24–25; *Works* 2:220.
93. A. Carson, *Knowledge of Jesus*, 76; *Works* 5:48.

have not a sovereign God have not the true God in his true character."[94] He sought to defend the attribute itself rather than demonstrate how it was active within the atonement and redemption. Therefore, it is helpful to give an overview of Carson's understanding of God's sovereignty. The two sources of evidence Carson turned to for the doctrine of God's sovereignty were the Scriptures and the observable works of God both in his creation and his providence.

One evidence of God's sovereignty in creation Carson noted was how created beings were ranked, whether it was comparing humanity to the lowliest creature or contrasting an incredibly gifted man, such as Isaac Newton (1643–1727), with one whom Carson's society regarded as an ignorant savage.[95] Carson believed that the sovereignty of God was the only way to explain this discrepancy between created beings satisfactorily. God's sovereignty not only explained the created order, wrote Carson, but more importantly, it also enabled one to be satisfied with one's place in that order.[96] Carson applied this belief in his evangelistic letter to Napoleon. In reference to Napoleon's degraded position as the ruler of the small island of Elba, Carson wrote, "If then, sire, your loss of power would be the means of calling your attention to the gospel, if you would in this discover the pearl of great price, you would not only patiently acquiesce in the sovereign will of God in excluding you from power, but bless him for the exchange."[97] This implied that Carson saw God's sovereignty as having purpose rather than simply being arbitrary. This also led to his understanding of how God's sovereignty was worked out in one's daily life, which he referred to specifically as God's providence. He wrote, "In the providence of God, also, we see sovereignty every day before our eyes."[98]

Carson examined and defended divine providence in three works: *History of Providence as Unfolded in the Book of Esther* (1833); *The God of Providence the God of the Bible; or, the Truth of the Gospel Proved from the Peculiarities of Its Progress* (1835); and *History of Providence, as Manifested in Scripture; or Facts from Scripture Illustrative of the Government of God, with a Defence of the Doctrine of Providence and an Examination*

---

94. A. Carson, *Knowledge of Jesus*, 79; *Works* 5:50.

95. Carson's mention of "savages" was probably in reference to tribal peoples who were not seen as civilized according to British standards.

96. A. Carson, *Knowledge of Jesus*, 77–78; *Works* 5:49.

97. *Works* 1:291–92.

98. A. Carson, *Knowledge of Jesus*, 79; *Works* 5:50.

of the Philosophy of Dr. Thomas Brown on That Subject (1840). While his study of providence in the book of Esther tracked the depth and intricacy of God's providential actions within a single biblical narrative, his *History of Providence, as Manifested in Scripture* primarily focused on showing how God's providence was displayed throughout the whole of Scripture through a presentation of 141 examples from both the Old and New Testaments, as well as providing examples of Scripture teaching on the doctrine of Providence. Carson's subject in his second work, *The God of Providence the God of the Bible*, was an examination of God's providence in the spread of the gospel towards the fulfillment of his promise in Matt 24:14. From these works alone, it is clear that Carson did not ignore extra-biblical evidence, though he sought to base interpretation of this evidence on the principles of the Bible. Carson's hope was that his works would encourage Christians, in part, to see God's providence in everything. A detailed examination of Carson's views of the role of providence in the Christian's daily life is beyond the scope of this book, but it is sufficient to show that it was important to Carson's overall understanding of God's sovereignty.

Carson admitted that God's purposes behind the exercise of his sovereignty were often beyond the comprehension of mankind, and therefore confusing or dissatisfying. He wrote that dissatisfaction with how God's sovereignty was manifested often led to denials of particular providences.[99] The denial of God's sovereign mercy by many professing Christians has already been mentioned. He warned that people must not judge God according to their own understanding and standards, whether out of human arrogance or ignorance.[100] He described the danger of people's judgment of God in *The Doctrine of the Atonement*: "If the wisdom of men cannot reconcile [God's sovereignty] with their views of what is right, let them be prepared to dispute the matter with the Almighty in the day of judgment."[101] Yet, argued Carson, man could still trust in God's goodness. Though God's sovereign ways were often beyond human comprehension, the truth of the doctrine was unshakably rooted in Scripture. For example, "We see from other things mentioned in Scripture, the sovereignty of God in charging the offence of our first parents on their descendents. Eve's daughters had no more hand in her sin, than her sons, yet, females to the end of the world, have peculiar miseries on account of their mother, Eve, being first in the

---

99. A. Carson, *God of Providence* (1839), 8; *Works* 6:15.
100. A. Carson, *Knowledge of Jesus*, 76–77; *Works* 5:48–49.
101. *Works* 1:125.

transgression. It may be said, is this just? I reply, it is declared to be so in Scripture. . . . I cannot give any other reason for it, than that God has said it."[102] Carson also saw God's sovereignty in election as incomprehensible and held no qualms about leaving it as such. He made no efforts to explain God's reasons for choosing some for salvation and not others. On the matter of trying to explain God's reasons, he wrote, "It is not my business to justify God, for he scorns to give any account of his matters."[103] Carson chose to be dependent on the biblical account and argued that the Bible clearly taught that the sacrifice of Christ was made only for those who would eventually be saved by it. Carson pointed to 1 John 2:1–2 as evidence of this. When Scripture spoke of Christ as being a propitiation for the sins of the world, Carson did not understand this to be a universal propitiation. *World* referred to people all over the world in all ages who believed in Christ. Christ's atonement was not universal.

In terms of the application of the atonement, or for whom Christ died on the cross to save, Carson believed that Christ died only for those who believe. He wrote that atonement was limited, because "it can never be true of any that shall eventually perish, that Christ died for them."[104] Therefore the atonement was limited or applied specifically to those who believed, rather than to all individuals. In this sense, Carson was speaking from the perspective of the Christian's experience, which corroborated what was taught in Scripture. The doctrine of particular redemption was not an unimportant one for Carson. Rather, it was an essential part of the gospel. "What, then, is the gospel that the Apostle preached, that the Corinthian Christians received, and in which they stood; yea, more, by which they were saved? It is neither more nor less, than that Christ died for the sins of his people, that he was buried and rose again."[105] Carson wrote this in contrast to those who said that the gospel, what one must believe to be saved, was that Christ died for each person in particular. He argued that 1 Cor 15:1–4 was only directed to believers, and that Christ died for all who believe, rather than for every person.[106] Therefore, those who preached that Christ died for each person in particular were teaching a false gospel. Carson condemned this view strongly because it gave listeners a false hope

102. *Works* 1:29–30.
103. *Works* 1:125.
104. *Works* 1:92.
105. *Works* 1:91.
106. *Works* 1:91.

in their salvation. Interestingly, Carson said that those who preached this way were being inconsistent with their own beliefs.

> These persons do not believe that this is a truth. They hold with the Scriptures that Christ died for none, but for those who shall eventually be saved. What inconsistency, then, is there in calling upon all men to believe a thing that with respect to most of them is a lie? Can it be the duty of men to believe what is not true? Can their believing a lie, make it a truth? All men are called on in Scripture to believe the gospel, but there is no instance in Scripture in which all men are called upon to believe that Christ died for them.[107]

Returning to the subject of God's mercy, one can see Carson's point that while the atonement was not limited by the degree of one's wrongdoing, since mercy has been extended to the chief of sinners, "it takes one and leaves another, without any other reason than the will of God."[108] Carson made two points about this. First, this meant that God's mercy was truly sovereign in a way that did not compromise either his sovereignty or his mercy. Second, many, if not most, were offended by this idea of a sovereign mercy. He observed that most Christians who believed in the atonement could not "bear the thought that it was not made for every individual."[109] Carson saw it as being offensive to both the world and even to those who professed to hold this doctrine: "Nothing is more offensive to the world than this view of the Divine character. It is well known, that many who acknowledge this as a religious sentiment, are found to revolt at it in heart. . . . [Men] will not allow [God] to condemn or pardon the guilty as he pleases. He is not permitted to select a vile sinner, nor is he allowed to condemn those of a moderate character."[110] Carson saw this human revulsion towards God's sovereignty as further proof of the gospel's divine authorship.[111] Carson inextricably tied God's sovereignty in the atonement to his deity, and he argued that people who removed God's perfect sovereignty effectively removed his divinity.[112]

---

107. *Works* 1:92–93.
108. A. Carson, *Truth of the Gospel Demonstrated* (1839), 26; *Works* 1:262.
109. *Works* 1:125.
110. A. Carson, *Truth of the Gospel Demonstrated* (1839), 26–27; *Works* 1:262.
111. A. Carson, *Truth of the Gospel Demonstrated* (1839), 27; *Works* 1:262–63.
112. A. Carson, *Truth of the Gospel Demonstrated* (1839), 27; *Works* 1:262.

THE FINISHED WORK OF THE CROSS

Carson described Christ's work on the cross as a finished work in a variety of writings. In *The Doctrine of the Atonement*, he coupled belief in the finished work on the cross with salvation. "The work that pleases God has been finished by Christ;—believe in it and you shall find rest to your souls."[113] Furthermore, those who were not dependent on Christ's finished work on the cross could not be called believers.[114] Faith in the cross was not belief that Christ's work on the cross was only the beginning, but that it was also the end. Carson did not see the sufficiency of the atonement as a doctrine of lesser importance, but rather as a doctrine upon which salvation depended. This was made very apparent in his anti-Catholic writings, specifically in his references to the Roman Catholic understanding of the meaning of the Lord's Supper. As Carson's polemical work against Roman Catholicism was somewhat interrelated, it will be helpful to see the context of the individual works, before looking at Carson's critique of Roman Catholic views of the cross.

Carson's written efforts against Roman Catholicism seem to have been sparked in 1823 by the publication of Bishop James Warren Doyle's *Miracle, Said to Have Been Wrought by Prince Hohenlohe, in Ireland, on Monday, the 9th of June, 1823*, which gave an account of a miraculous healing of a young woman, through the remote intercessions of the German priest Prince Alexander of Hohenlohe-Waldenburg-Schillingsfürst (1794–1849).[115] Carson's immediate reply was called "Remarks on the Late Miracle, in a Letter to the Rev. Doctor Doyle, Titular Bishop of Kildure and Leighlin" (1823). His "Remarks" did not deny the supernatural healing, but, instead, attributed it to the power of Satan, who was simply cultivating the anti-Christian system of the Roman Catholic Church.

Soon after, Carson took issue with Doyle's *A Vindication of the Religious and Civil Principles of the Irish Catholics: In a Letter, Addressed to*

---

113. *Works* 1:106.

114. "You do not believe on the work that God had declared to you in his Word, that Jesus finished on the Cross." *Works* 1:54. "Never will [unbelievers] be able to say, as did the substitute of believers—'It is finished.'" A. Carson, *Knowledge of Jesus*, 175; *Works* 5:117–18.

115. Hohenlohe was known for working miracles from afar, and Doyle includes, in a letter to Hohenlohe, an account of a nun in England healed from a disease by an offering of the Mass on her behalf (Doyle, *Miracle*, 13). Doyle's *Miracle* was published before his *Principles of the Irish Catholics* and is found in a review of the latter work in *British Review and London Critical Journal*, Unsigned review of *Vindication*.

His Excellency the Marquis Wellesley (1823), in which he addressed a few religious and political accusations against the Roman Catholic Church during the early years of Catholic Emancipation in Ireland. Carson's response to Doyle's effort to exculpate Roman Catholicism, called *Strictures on the Letter of J. K. L. Entitled a Vindication of the Religious and Civil Principles of the Irish Catholics: Addressed to His Excellency the Marquis Wellesley, K. G. Lord Lieutenant General, and General Governor of Ireland, &c. &c. in a Letter to the Same Nobleman* (1823), was focused almost wholly on addressing what he called the "antichristian" doctrines and "superstitions" of the Roman Catholic Church and, at the same time, withheld lengthy commentary on the political aspects of Catholic emancipation.[116]

Carson's censures against Roman Catholicism in general and Doyle in particular continued in the following year, revolving primarily around restrictions the Roman Catholic Church placed on the laity's access to the Scriptures. Though Bible societies, such as the Hibernian Bible Society, advocated literacy and accessibility of English Bibles in Ireland,[117] the Roman Catholic Church resisted unrestricted Bible reading among their laity, which was evident through publications such as Doyle's *Letters on the State of Education in Ireland: And on Bible Societies; Addressed to a Friend in England* (1824). In *The Right and Duty of All Men to Read the Scriptures: Being the Substance of a Speech Intended to Have Been Delivered at the Meeting of the Carlow Bible Society; Containing a Refutation of Several Parts of a Late Pamphlet by J. K. L. Entitled "Letters on the State of Education, and Bible Societies,"* Carson responds to Roman Catholic criticisms of unrestricted Bible reading by the laity.[118]

In 1825, Carson wrote specifically against transubstantiation, attacking it primarily through a series of axioms and only secondarily through the use of Scripture, because the "Scriptures, though in some sense acknowledged, are not, with [the Roman Catholic Church], the only, nor

---

116. *Works* 2:151–72.

117. According to the general rules of the Hibernian Bible Society, which was originally established at the Dublin Bible Society in 1806, only the Authorized Version of the Bible, without any commentary, would be distributed. Dudley, *Analysis of the System*, 112–13. Schools established by private and public entities seemed to be generally popular and included both genders as well as a variety of age groups. "Evening and Sunday schools were attended by adults, whose employments did not admit of their presence at other times; and in various parts of Ireland, the whole face of the country was covered with schools, and the schools filled with eager learners." *British Review and London Critical Journal*, "Bible Society of Ireland," 132.

118. A. Carson, *Right and Duty*, 3; *Works* 2:3.

the ultimate standard."[119] He argued that, according to self-evident truths, transubstantiation defied human reason, and according to Scripture, there was no undeniable interpretation of any passage that required one to believe the doctrine of transubstantiation. In conclusion, Carson expressed his evangelistic motivation, stating, "I write to gain the souls of men, who are my flesh and blood," in reference to his Irish brethren.[120]

Carson's evangelistic motives were made the focus of his final anti-Catholic work, which came in the form of a letter to William Conyngham Plunket (1764–1854), the lord chancellor of Ireland, who had spoken out in the House of Commons against the Protestant Reformation movement in the county of Cavan.[121] In *A Letter to the Right Hon. William C. Plunket, His Majesty's Attorney General for Ireland: Containing Strictures on Some Parts of His Late Speech on the Roman Catholic Question in the House of Commons Touching the Cavan Reform* (1827), Carson criticized Plunket's reference of the Established Church's evangelistic efforts in Cavan as a "crusade," which was taken from Doyle's characterization of the so-called Cavan Reformation.[122] Plunket's speech was seen as essentially being an attack on religious liberty of conscience to evangelize, which, for Carson, meant "persuasion through the exposition of the word of God."[123]

In Carson's various works against Roman Catholic doctrine, he wrote on issues such as the authority of Scripture, the freedom and duty for all people to read Scripture, the freedom to evangelize Roman Catholics, and transubstantiation and miracles. According to a number of memoirs and his own writings, Carson was active in refuting Roman Catholic doctrines as well as in evangelizing Roman Catholics.[124] Though he did not specifically focus any of his anti-Catholic publications towards the atonement, he did include some of his thoughts on this issue where Catholic doctrine led people astray, primarily in his discussions about what he referred to as superstitions of the Roman Catholic Church. In *Strictures on the Letter of J. K. L., Entitled a Vindication of the Religious and Civil Principles of the Irish*

---

119. Carson continued, "Tradition has the better half of the empire of Revelation, and a Lord Paramount is acknowledged in the authority of the Church." A. Carson, *Doctrine of Transubstantiation* (1837), 4; *Works* 2:50.

120. A. Carson, *Doctrine of Transubstantiation* (1837), 111; *Works* 2:128.

121. The county of Cavan is located approximately eighty miles southwest of Tobermore.

122. A. Carson, *Letter to William C. Plunket*; *Works* 2:173–88; Doyle, *Doyle's Letter*, 4.

123. A. Carson, *Letter to William C. Plunket*, 8; *Works* 2:181.

124. Moore, *Life of Alexander Carson*, 39–50.

Catholics, written to the Marquis Wellesley, K. G. (1760–1842), Lord Lieutenant General and General Governor of Ireland, Carson argued that the Roman Catholic Church's gospel was a false gospel: "What then, my Lord, shall we say of the Church that has buried the Cross of Christ under mountains of superstition, and instead of directing perishing sinners only to the blood of Christ, that cleanses from all sin, has all heaven and earth, saints, angels, and men, at work to save sinners, and, after all, cannot accomplish it till they are purified after death in the fire of purgatory? Who, my Lord, shall dare to say that this is the Gospel of Christ?"[125] This superstition was the primary problem, and, in Carson's opinion, the most outstanding example of this was the doctrine of transubstantiation, his disdain for which he described in no uncertain terms: "Since God stretched the heavens over the earth, there has not been broached in human language, an absurdity so monstrous as that of Transubstantiation."[126]

For Carson, the real danger of the Roman Catholic Mass was the Mass's incompatibility with the finished work of the cross, with Christ's completed sacrifice. In *The Doctrine of Transubstantiation: Subversive of the Foundations of Human Belief*, Carson wrote, "The reason you so fondly cling to the doctrine of the Mass is, your blindness to the glory and efficacy of the atonement."[127] Carson specifically attacked the ongoing nature of the Mass's sacrifice. First, the Mass conveyed an incorrect understanding of the atonement's effectiveness. Carson argued that Christ's sacrifice was of infinite value and, as such, complete, unrepeatable, and eternally sanctifying. Second, the Mass's attempt to add to the efficacy of Christ's work on the cross actually kept people in their sins by keeping them under the law.[128] The Mass, as a continuation of Christ's sacrifice on the cross, necessarily contradicted the belief that Christ's work on the cross was finished.[129] Carson saw

---

125. A. Carson, *Strictures*, 11–12; *Works* 2:160. The Marquis Wellesley, Richard Colley Wesley, was an Anglo-Irish politician who filled a number of roles throughout the British Empire during his career. His significance in terms of the present topic was his advocacy for Catholic emancipation in Ireland while he served as the Lord Lieutenant of Ireland in the 1820s.

126. A. Carson, *Doctrine of Transubstantiation* (1837), 3; *Works* 2:49.

127. A. Carson, *Doctrine of Transubstantiation* (1837), 111; *Works* 2:128.

128. "This infinitely valuable sacrifice needs not to be continued or repeated. It perfects for ever those who are sanctified by it. To attempt to add to its efficacy, leaves men still in their sins, and makes them debtors to do the whole law." A. Carson, *Doctrine of Transubstantiation* (1837), 111; *Works* 2:128.

129. A. Carson, *Doctrine of Transubstantiation* (1837), 77; *Works* 2:103.

the Mass as "a doctrine that, by representing Christ as sacrificed from day to day, continually" overturned the gospel.[130]

CONCLUSION

Carson's theology of the cross was dependent upon a proper understanding of humanity's natural spiritual state, which was a sinful state. He defended the standard evangelical views of universal sin and total depravity inherited from the fall, as well as the eternal punishment that sin deserved. Reflecting the traditional evangelical views on the substitutionary atonement, the harmonization of divine justice and mercy was a major theme in a number of Carson's works, especially in his apologetical works aimed at atheists and deists. Another aspect that was important for Carson was how the atonement manifested God's sovereignty: it was particular with regard to whom it was applied, which made Carson's Calvinism apparent. Closely tied to the sufficiency of Christ's atoning work was Carson's understanding of Christ's work as a finished work, especially in regard to his anti-Catholic polemic.

Carson's understanding of the cross was not unique among Evangelicals. D. W. Bebbington stated, "To make any theme other than the cross the fulcrum of a theological system was to take a step away from Evangelicalism."[131] Claiming the Bible to be his "theological system," Carson's words to Napoleon, quoted at the beginning of this chapter, are a suitable reflection of Bebbington's assertion: "The atonement by his death is the centre of revelation, in which all its numerous lines meet."[132] Depending on one's opinion of Carson's status as an Evangelical, this can be seen as evidence for Bebbington's statement or evidence for Carson's Evangelicalism. Not only did Carson fit within this general characteristic of the primacy of the atonement, but his views on the finer details of the cross were also the standard views among Evangelicals. For example, Bebbington showed that the belief in a substitutionary atonement was a customary, though not uniform, evangelical view that distinguished them from other Christians.[133] Carson's arguments on divine justice and mercy in the cross clearly show him to fit within the mainstream of Evangelicalism in this area. Another example of how Carson reflected the primacy of the cross according to

130. A. Carson, *Strictures*, 9; *Works* 2:158.
131. Bebbington, *Evangelicalism in Modern Britain*, 15.
132. *Works* 1:284.
133. Bebbington, *Evangelicalism in Modern Britain*, 15.

Bebbington's definition of Evangelicalism was his moderate Calvinism. While Carson was not as moderate in his Calvinism as Bebbington saw the majority of Evangelicals to be in the early nineteenth century, how he applied his views on particular atonement demonstrated the inclusion of human responsibility.[134] Carson's views on Roman Catholicism also fit with Bebbington's description of the growing anti-Catholic sentiments within Evangelicalism in the early 1800s.[135] Yet, unlike Evangelicals in England, Carson's anti-Catholic views obviously were not coupled with a "traditional disdain for the Irish." These examples show that Carson's views on the cross, which were detailed throughout the chapter, were not views held at the periphery of Evangelicalism but within the mainstream of the movement.

---

134. Bebbington wrote, "Most Evangelicals were content to adopt a 'moderate Calvinism' that in terms of practical pulpit instruction differed only slightly from the Methodist version of Arminianism." Bebbington, *Evangelicalism in Modern Britain*, 17.

135. Bebbington, *Evangelicalism in Modern Britain*, 101.

4

Alexander Carson on Conversion

JUST AS CARSON DID not leave his audience with simply the doctrine of total depravity, he also did not leave them merely with the knowledge that Jesus died on the cross to save even the chief of sinners. His evangelical drive required him to examine the way "in which guilty sinners are interested in this atonement."[1] Carson recognized that there was much diversity in the way Christians answered the question of how a person might find redemption through the cross, yet he did not regard the various views as equally valid options. Rather, he framed the debate as a contrast between those who held to a biblical understanding of how sinners were saved and those who veered away from what the Scriptures taught. He grouped the latter together, not simply based on their shared divergence from Scripture, but on their agreement that "something is to be done on the part of the sinner, in order to entitle him to the benefits of Christ's sacrifice."[2] Carson believed the biblical gospel to be utterly opposed to salvation by works in any degree and called the requirement of works for salvation a deviation from the gospel. Therefore, the differences between these groups, "whether they be called Arminianism, or Pelagianism, or Baxterianism," were inconsequential for Carson's argument, which was simply to prove that salvation was only by faith in the atonement.[3]

---

1. *Works* 1:80.
2. *Works* 1:80.
3. *Works* 1:80.

CARSON'S DEFINITION OF SAVING FAITH

Within the bounds of his thoughts on the singular role faith played in justifying sinners, Carson also discussed the definition of saving faith. This question of the meaning of saving faith became an important one in light of what Carson saw as erroneous definitions of faith. His concern for this was especially evident in *The Doctrine of the Atonement*. Carson used James MacKnight's (1721–1800) understanding of faith as a foil for discussing his own views.[4] The Scottish scholar had defined faith as consisting "in a sincere disposition to believe what God hath made known," and not "in the belief of particular doctrines, but in such an earnest desire to know and to do the will of God, as leads them conscientiously to use such means as they have for gaining the knowledge of his will, and for doing it when found."[5] His definition of faith was set within a context of arguing against the idea that those who had not heard the gospel would definitely face judgment.[6] That Carson took offense to this portrayal of saving faith was evident in his describing MacKnight's definition as a "gross abuse of language."[7] Carson did not see MacKnight's understanding of faith as part of its proper definition but as a completely distinct category. What MacKnight called faith, the desire to know and do God's will, was actually an outgrowth of true faith and not faith itself. Therefore, while not denying the importance of the elements of this definition for the Christian life, Carson rejected their place in the meaning of saving faith.

In contrast to MacKnight, Carson presented a generic definition of faith that based faith only on belief: "The faith of any thing is neither more

---

4. James MacKnight was born in Irvine, Ayrshire, Scotland, in 1721 to William (1685–1750), a native Irishman, and Elizabeth Gemmil (d 1753). James graduated from Glasgow University (1742) almost half a century prior to Carson's matriculation. He was ordained in 1753 as a part of the general assembly of the Church of Scotland. He would become the moderator of the general assembly in 1769. In 1778, he was admitted to the collegiate charge of the Old Church in Edinburgh. He was primarily a biblical scholar, and his early work was focused on the Gospels, such as *A Harmony of the Four Gospels* (1756) and *The Truth of Gospel History* (1763). His magnum opus was *A New Literal Translation from the Original Greek of All the Apostolical Epistles* (1795), which appeared in four volumes and various editions through the first half of the nineteenth century. Lionel Alexander Ritchie, "MacKnight, James," *ODNB* 35:694–95; Addison, *Roll of the Graduates*, 391.

5. *Works* 1:89. Carson spelled his name as McKnight. Quoted from MacKnight, *New Literal Translation*, 1:187, 163.

6. MacKnight, *New Literal Translation*, 1:163.

7. *Works* 1:89.

nor less than the belief of it; and the belief of any thing is the conviction that the mind has of its truth, and implies no disposition about it, either good or bad."[8] Belief was the necessary ingredient of faith, and Carson regularly used the terms interchangeably or together. Applying his definition specifically to Christian faith, he wrote, "The belief of the gospel, then—or the belief that the sacrifice of Jesus is a sufficient atonement for the sins of all who receive it—is saving faith."[9]

In looking at how the Scripture presented belief, Carson examined distinctions between believing Christ, believing in Christ, and believing on Christ. Again, he began with a generic example, writing:

> To believe in a person, is to believe him to be what he is reported to be, what he professes to be, or that what he asserts is true. To believe in Christ is, in substance, the same as to believe him. The difference consists not in the thing believed, but in the testifiers. To believe Christ, imports that he himself is the testifier. To believe in Christ, includes the testimony of himself, of the Father, of the Spirit, and of the apostles. To believe Christ, imports the belief that the testimony which he gave of himself, as being the Messiah, is true. *To believe in Christ*, imports the belief of the same truth, without respect to the testifier. There is a further shade of distinction between these phrases. To believe a person respects his testimony only, whether that testimony regards himself or others; to believe in a person may include not only belief in his testimony, but belief in his pretensions to power.[10]

Despite the degrees of difference Carson detailed for his readers he concluded that all of these phrases had the same meaning in substance.[11] What is interesting in his discussion on belief is its simplicity. His definition of faith or belief, whether belief in general or in Christ, was stark. He did not discuss the need for loving Christ or feeling the guilt for sin. Rather, his definition of faith seems purely intellectual, at least on the surface. His general definition of faith even disregarded one's inclination to a particular truth. His view of justifying faith seems to have been just as devoid of affections.

Carson's thoughts on the relationship between faith and the affections are best seen in a mini-commentary on Rom 10:10 ("For with the heart man believeth unto righteousness; and with the mouth confession is

8. *Works* 1:89–90.
9. *Works* 1:103.
10. *Works* 1:100; emphasis in original.
11. *Works* 1:100–101.

made unto salvation"). Carson argued that those who disagreed with his definition of saving faith misinterpreted this verse, using it to create a false distinction between the heart and the mind: "The latter they call saving, the former they call speculative; the latter includes good affections, the former nothing but the understanding."[12] When referring to those who misused Rom 10:10, Carson may have had in mind MacKnight, for the latter wrote regarding the passage: "To believe with *the heart* is to believe in such a manner as to engage the affections, and influence the actions. This sincere faith carrying the believer to obey God and Christ, as far as he is able, it is called *the obedience of faith* and *the righteousness of faith*. Also, because God for the sake of Christ will count this kind of faith to the believer for righteousness, it is called *the righteousness of God*; the righteousness which God hath appointed for sinners, and which he will accept and reward."[13] Here, MacKnight clearly tied belief with the heart to the affections. He was not alone in such a theological conviction. For example, Carson's older Baptist contemporary, Andrew Fuller (1754–1815), also believed this Scripture passage taught the inclusion of affections in faith. He wrote that while believing the heart did not necessarily exclude understanding, it necessarily included the affections. For Fuller, belief of the heart had to do with more than just intellectual understanding.[14] Carson disagreed with any emphasis on the affections as a part of saving faith. In fact, he removed the affections altogether: "To believe with the heart is really to believe, and not to believe with good affections, for there are no affections in belief."[15] Rather, Carson argued, a "heart-belief" was typically a way to emphasize the reality of one's belief instead of a distinction between heart and mind.

Carson knew of one criticism of his definition of saving faith, noting that orthodox systematics referred to it as "historical faith." In *A Treatise on the Faith and Influence of the Gospel* (1831), Archibald Hall (1736–78) compared four types of faith: historical faith, the faith to do miracles, temporary faith, and saving faith.[16] Hall wrote that historical faith was typically

---

12. *Works* 1:98.
13. MacKnight, *New Literal Translation*, 1:405; emphasis in original.
14. Fuller, *Works of Rev. Andrew Fuller*, 1:133.
15. *Works* 1:98.
16. A. Hall, *Faith and Influence*, 240–41. This work was edited by James Peddie and first published posthumously from an unpublished manuscript in 1803. Born in Edinburghshire, Hall became a minister of the Burgher Secession church in Scotland. In 1765 he began ministering in London, where he was known to have an "energetic and evangelical ministry." T. B. Johnstone and Philip Carter, "Hall, Archibald," *ODNB* 24:588–89.

described as "a bare assent of the mind" to what the Scripture taught of the gospel, and added that those who held this type of faith saw the study of the Bible as a mere exercise of reason.[17] Carson's general definition of faith has already been shown to be more concerned with truth than with its source. It would be a mistake to reduce Carson's understanding of faith to what was called historical faith. Carson, himself, did not believe them to be synonymous. First, he saw the pejorative designation as purposely misapplied by critics.[18] Second, in *The Truth of the Gospel Demonstrated*, Carson argued that there was a difference between believing something to be true and understanding the object of belief. In terms of the gospel, one must understand the gospel to really believe in the gospel.[19] An incorrect understanding of the gospel meant that one's belief in it was actually a belief in something else. This was an important difference between those with a historical faith and those who possessed saving faith. In this sense, he agreed with Hall's definition of historical faith. When Carson wrote, "Many a learned and useful defence of the Gospel has come from the pen of those who do not understand it," it was with the view that simply knowing the facts of the Bible was not synonymous with understanding the message of the Bible.[20]

Therefore, Carson believed that the acceptance of any truth required one to understand the evidence on which that truth stood.[21] Yet, he also addressed the complex question pertaining to the divine and human roles within this equation. In speaking of the need for God's divine initiative for a person to come to faith, he wrote, "According to my doctrine, he cannot believe till God opens the eyes of his understanding."[22] Not only did these words show that understanding preceded belief but they also showed that understanding required a divine initiation. Yet, this divine initiation did not nullify the human role in believing the gospel: "Faith is the gift of God; yet it is the operation of the mind of man. Is he wise who attempts to comprehend the *manner* of the consistency of these two assertions? Shall we deny that faith is the gift of God, because it is the act of our own minds; or

---

17. A. Hall, *Faith and Influence*, 241.
18. *Works* 1:92.
19. A. Carson, *Truth of the Gospel Demonstrated* (1839), 8; *Works* 1:249.
20. A. Carson, *Truth of the Gospel Demonstrated* (1839), 8; *Works* 1:249.
21. A. Carson, *Knowledge of Jesus*, 30; *Works* 5:15.
22. *Works* 1:108.

that it is the act of the mind, because it is the gift of God?"[23] Carson retained the tension between the divine and human roles despite his inability to harmonize their coexistence. Two relevant ideas are present here. First, he accepted that some doctrines taught in Scripture, due to their divine source, would be incomprehensible to the human mind. Concerning the character of God, Carson wrote, "Certain attributes of God, as he is manifested in Scripture, are incomprehensible; but this is a very different thing from their being veiled in mystery. They are taught clearly, though in their own nature they are beyond our comprehension."[24] Another example that Carson gave of human incomprehensibility was the fact that while faith came from God, a person was held accountable for his or her lack of faith. Yet, the evidence for both in Scripture was clear and incontrovertible, rather than being "veiled in mystery." Therefore, while the coexistence of these two doctrines was incomprehensible, they were still true.[25] In contrast, many modern philosophers and even professing Christians mistakenly assumed that that which was incomprehensible was necessarily contradictory.[26]

Second, Carson did not belittle human intellect. He argued that faith was "the operation of the mind," and he was just as loathe to jettison human participation in saving faith as he was to compromise faith's divine source. He believed that all creation was a divine revelation, no less inspired by God than the Scripture, though it taught humanity less about God and his character than Scripture. The human mind, being created by God, was included as a source of divine revelation. Germane to the current discussion, Carson believed that one's God-given intellect could act, within its capability, as a test for the validity of doctrines. He wrote, "For the light of human intellect that God has poured into the mind of men is a previous revelation, which shows that a contradiction, or an impossibility, cannot be true. Were the doctrine opposed by such an enemy, it could not be entitled to a hearing."[27] For example, Carson effectively argued that transubstantiation, briefly discussed in the previous chapter, was a contradictory doctrine through the presentation of various extra-biblical axioms and biblical proofs.[28] If he did

---

23. A. Carson, *Refutation of Dr. Henderson's Doctrine*, 27; *Works* 3:281; emphasis in original.
24. A. Carson, *Knowledge of Jesus*, 315–16; *Works* 5:218.
25. *Works* 1:108.
26. A. Carson, *Knowledge of Jesus*, 124, 135; *Works* 5:82, 90.
27. A. Carson, *Knowledge of Jesus*, 121; *Works* 5:80.
28. A. Carson, *Doctrine of Transubstantiation* (1837); *Works* 2: 47–128.

not believe incomprehensible doctrines were necessarily false, he was just as convinced that genuine contradictions were necessarily false. Therefore, Carson's submission to the inspiration and authority of Scripture was balanced by the use of his God-given intellect to interpret and understand Scripture.

While Carson qualified and expanded on his understanding of saving faith in various works, his adherence to a simple expression of saving faith was prominent. He ultimately argued that his view was founded upon the authority of Scripture. He contrasted the authority of the Bible to the authority of systematic divines: "The man who believeth even the fact that Jesus is the Christ is born of God. They may degradingly call this historical faith; but the Holy Spirit designates it as the faith by which we are born of God. The divines tell us that many believe that Jesus is the Christ, who, notwithstanding, have no interest in him; but the Apostle John tells us that all who believe this are born of God. Which of the two, then, shall we believe?"[29] He admitted the difficulty encountered in human experience when many professing Christians did not show any evidence of being converted. Carson's view of saving faith was not aimed at contesting this reality. After all, one of his reasons for leaving the Presbyterian denomination and tradition was due to their toleration of the apparently unconverted within their churches. What Carson challenged was the practice of altering or adding to the biblical definition of faith to deal with problems within the church pragmatically. These alterations or additions resulted in contradicting a clear teaching of Scripture. Seeking to solve apparent contradictions between experience and biblical prescription by altering the Bible was not a solution.

Carson's Sandemanian View of Faith

David Kingdon described Carson's discussion of saving faith as "an echo of the controversy caused by the intellectualistic view of faith taught by Robert Sandeman," particularly in his exegesis of Rom 10:10. Kingdon regarded Carson's view of faith as a response to an unbalanced reaction against Sandeman's intellectual understanding of saving faith:

> Carson seems to have felt that the orthodox divines who opposed the "historical" faith of Sandeman to what might be called "vital

---

29. *Works* 1:94.

faith" or heart trust over-reacted and introduced a false distinction between faith of the head and faith of the heart. In my opinion he was right in his assessment of the situation, since he correctly saw that in Scripture the heart is the seat of man's personal, which includes his intellectual, life, not merely the centre of his emotions. Certainly many of our problems today, particularly in respect of both the necessity and the content of ministerial training, stem from a false dichotomy between head (which can be neglected) and heart (which must be cultivated).[30]

However, Carson's own words that set forth a very intellectual view of faith seem to indicate his perspective is more than an echo of the controversy caused by Sandeman's views. David Bebbington accurately described Sandemanianism as being at the "rationalist edge of Calvinism, maintaining that intellectual assent to the apostolic testimony concerning the work of Christ suffices for salvation, and that considerations respecting the believer's will, emotions and obedience are beside the point lest faith be mistaken for a work."[31] Carson's views on faith clearly reflect a Sandemanian view, especially in light of Bebbington's description above. The primary examples from Carson's works that appear Sandemanian are as follows. First, his definition of faith did not include the affections, only belief or assent. As previously quoted, Carson wrote, "The faith of any thing is neither more nor less than the belief of it; and the belief of any thing is the conviction that the mind has of its truth, and implies no disposition about it, either good or bad"; and "To believe with the heart is really to believe, and not to believe with good affections, for there are no affections in belief."[32] Second, Carson's arguments against other views of faith were very similar to Sandemanian arguments that came before him. This is especially evident in his argument that many definitions of faith have become bloated through the inclusion of what is legitimately categorized as a fruit or result of faith.[33] Third, his critique of a false distinction between the heart and mind through his exegesis of Rom 10:10 was regularly used by Sandemanians before him.[34] The strong emphases placed on belief, knowledge, and understanding of the gospel served to strengthen Carson's intellectualist view of faith. Coupled with his

---

30. Kingdon, "Theology of Alexander Carson," 58.
31. Sell et al., *Protestant Nonconformist Texts*, 98.
32. *Works* 1:89–90, 98.
33. *Works* 1:89.
34. *Works* 1:98.

denial of any place for affections in saving faith, these examples seem to indicate that Carson, rather than standing at the midpoint between the two parties referred to by Kingdon, could be more accurately described as a Baptist who held a Sandemanian understanding of saving faith. This can be shown most effectively by studying the progression of Sandemanianism from its founder, John Glas, to the Scotch Baptists who may have had a direct influence on Carson.

These examples reflect a Sandemanian understanding of saving faith, yet Carson never explicitly refers to Sandemanian sources. On the basis of the above quotations from *The Doctrine of the Atonement*, one can argue that Carson's definition of saving faith was essentially Sandemanian, but is there further evidence showing him to be influenced by Sandemanianism? One clue is found in an article on Carson in *Johnson's Universal Cyclopaedia*, where the Southern Baptist William H. Whitsitt (1841–1911) noted some of Carson's ties to Sandemanianism, "Throughout the remainder of his life he adopted the type of Sandemanian church order. The kiss of charity was observed every Sunday; there was weekly communion, and weekly exhortation by the brethren, in case any of them should desire it. At the time of his death he was claimed as an adherent by William Jones, the leader of the so-called Scotch Baptists in England. He was never in ecclesiastical fellowship with the regular Baptists of England."[35] Whitsitt's comments point out two connections Carson had to Sandemanianism, with a third comment noting his lack of fellowship with English Baptists. The first connection explicitly referred to church order. The church order Carson implemented in Tobermore reflected a literal application of New Testament practices, similar to what Sandemanians were practicing, and Whitsitt provided a few of the practices that reflected this. Sources closer to Carson show that Whitsitt's information was essentially correct. Moore described the order of worship in Carson's church in some detail:

1. Christians greeted each other with a holy kiss according to Rom 16:16.
2. Carson shared prayer requests and prayed.
3. Carson read a metrical Psalm, gave commentary on it, and then led the congregation in singing it.
4. He reviewed the previous week's sermon.

---

35. William H. Whitsitt, "Carson, Alexander, LL.D.," in Adams, *Johnson's Universal Cyclopaedia*, 2:99–100, esp. 99.

Alexander Carson on Conversion

5. The Scriptures were read.
6. This was followed by "his exposition, teaching, preaching, and exhortation."
7. A prayer was said, usually given by a qualified member of the congregation.
8. Another hymn was sung.
9. The admission and exclusion of members in the presence of the whole congregation.
10. The Lord's Supper was observed.
11. If time permitted, there was an opportunity for public exhortation by any who wished.
12. A final prayer was given.
13. A final hymn was sung.
14. Carson closed with a benediction.[36]

Ordnance Survey Memoirs written prior to Moore's account varied only slightly from the details of worship listed by Moore.[37] For the current discussion, the most significant difference is the Memoirs' mention of an

---

36. Moore, *Life of Alexander Carson*, 79–82.

37. In 1824, a committee in the House of Commons recommended a townland survey of Ireland with maps. The memoirs were descriptions meant to contain information that could not fit onto the maps. The memoirs covered topographical, economic, social, and religious topics. Beginning in 1830, officers were sent out to gather the pertinent information on various counties for the next decade. Though the memoir project collapsed by 1840 and the raw information was archived, collated volumes of the memoirs have been published in the 1990s. Several types of documents were created in the original project. "Memoir (sometimes Statistical Memoir): an account of a parish written according to the prescribed form outlined in the instructions known as 'Heads of Inquiry', and normally divided into three sections: Natural Features and History; Modern and Ancient Topography; Social and Productive Economy. Fair Sheets 'information gathered for the Memoirs', an original title describing paragraphs of information following no particular order, often with marginal headings, signed and dated by the civil assistant responsible. Statistical Remarks/Accounts: both titles are employed by the Engineer officers in their descriptions of the parish with marginal headings, often similar in layout to the Memoir. Office Copies: these copies of early drafts, generally officers' accounts and must have been made for office purposes." Day and McWilliams, *Parishes of County Londonderry*, ix–x.

unqualified "exhortation by the brethren."[38] According to Moore, Carson was not committed to a weekly practice of public exhortation.

Second, Whitsitt noted Carson's supposed connection to William Jones (1762–1846), which he most likely learned from at least one of three sources. First, Jones wrote a letter to the *Primitive Church Magazine* concerning Carson's views on church order, in which he claimed Carson for the Scotch Baptists.[39] Second, Alexander Macleod (1819–91), a Scottish Presbyterian minister, sent a letter to the *Primitive Church Magazine*, in which he dismissed Jones's claims and concluded that Carson's name could not be "fairly made a peg on which to hang the crotchets of either Scotch or English Baptists."[40] Third, Moore included an excerpt of Macleod's letter in his memoir on Carson, which saw at least three American editions in the 1850s.[41] While Whitsitt probably had knowledge of all three sources, it seems that he primarily relied on Jones's comments on Carson: "Assuredly he is not to be classed with the English Baptists either *particular* or *general*. . . . Dr. Carson is classed among the Scotch Baptists, and strenuously advocated the order of public worship, observed in those churches."[42] While Whitsitt might have been simply unconvinced by Macleod's dismissal of Jones's claim of Carson's adherence, the fact remains that the evidence Whitsitt used to show Carson's ties to Sandemanianism were all elements explicitly present in Jones's letter. This connection, if substantiated, would establish stronger evidence for a Sandemanian influence on Carson's thought. An overview of the key leaders of the Sandemanian movement leading up to Jones will help explain the nature of Jones's Sandemanianism as well as similarities between their views on saving faith.

What came to be known as Sandemanianism began with John Glas (1695–1773), who was from Auchtermuchty, a town in Fife, Scotland.

---

38. Day and McWilliams, *Parishes of County Londonderry*, 72; Stokes, "Memoir of J. Stokes," 24 (Public Records Office of Northern Ireland).

39. Jones, "Views."

40. Macleod, "Dr. Carson's Views," 12–13. After receiving an education at the University of Glasgow, Macleod was licensed as a minister of the Relief Church in 1843. He spent the bulk of his ministry at the Presbyterian Church in Claughton. He was known for a more ecumenical Evangelicalism, which might explain his apparent frustration more exclusive groups such as the Scotch Baptists, whom he said would not have ever received Carson in his lifetime though they claimed him after his death. Aird, *Glimpses of Old Glasgow*, 321–23.

41. Moore, *Life of Alexander Carson*, 4–5.

42. Jones, "Views," 563; emphasis in original.

His father, Alexander Glas (1653–1725), was a Presbyterian minister. The younger Glas received his MA from St. Leonard's College, St. Andrews, in 1713, and he prepared for the ministry at the University of Edinburgh. Ordained in 1719, his first charge was at Tealing, near Dundee. His concern for the destitute spirituality of his parishioners was coupled with his implementation of strict church discipline. The formation of a separate gathering of recognized believers within his parish would be part of the reason for his eventual deposition by the Church of Scotland in 1730. Another factor leading to his deposition was the publication of his views on the spiritual nature of the church as distinct from the state, which were published in *The Testimony of the King of Martyrs, Concerning His Kingdom, Explained and Illustrated in Scripture Light* (1729). Though Glas never received strong clerical support for his views, he did find a haven in Dundee where a group of supporters had gathered. Within thirty years, numerous Glasite churches could be found in small towns and larger port cities within a ninety-mile radius from Dundee. Glasite churches, founded in schism, became more isolated over time due to their intellectual view of faith, their literal implementation of New Testament practices, and the contentious writings of Glas's son-in-law, Robert Sandeman (1718–71).[43]

Regarding the meaning of saving faith, Glas put forth a couple of ideas. First, he wrote that faith was to believe something because God had said it. Second, how one came to believe in something determined the type of "faith" one had. He gave three examples: "If my persuasion be in the assent to the conclusion of a philosophical argument, then it is science, not faith; if my persuasion go upon evidence of human testimony, then it is human faith; and if my persuasion go upon evidence that the divine testimony carries in itself, then it is truly divine faith."[44] Therefore, not only did Glas believe that faith came from God, but the means God used were tied explicitly to Scripture. While the type of persuasion was a means for the resulting type of faith, he also believed biblical faith and secular faith were both essentially "a persuasion of a thing upon testimony."[45] Carson's own definition of faith, which he presented as simply a belief of something and a conviction of its truth in the mind, mirrored Glas's idea of an agreement to a given testimony.[46] Glas also described how the meaning of faith has

---

43. Derek B. Murray, "Glas, John," *ODNB* 22:429–31.
44. Glas, *Testimony of the King of Martyrs*, 1:103.
45. Glas, *Testimony of the King of Martyrs*, 1:116.
46. *Works* 1:89–90.

The Gospel-Centered Evangelicalism of Alexander Carson

been altered with elements added, while that "which is most properly faith, has been either shut up in a narrow and dark corner of the description, or almost excluded from it."[47] One example of this was shown in an example Glas gave:

> But it is evident it is not revealed unto every gospel hearer, that Christ is absolutely given unto him, and that he shall be saved; because this is not true; and therefore every hearer of the gospel is not bound to believe this concerning himself: nor will the hearers of the gospel that perish, be damned for not believing that they should never be damned. . . . [Seeing] it was never, nor can be at any time, a truth, that Christ is absolutely given certainly to save every gospel-hearer, or that every gospel-hearer shall be saved; we must have another notion of the assurance of faith. And the Scripture is very clear in this matter. When it speaks of the assurance of faith at its highest, it calls it the full assurance of understanding to the acknowledgment of the mystery of God, and of the Father, and of Christ, Col. ii. 2. And what is that, but a full persuasion of the truth of which Christ speaks, when he says, "Every one that is of the truth, heareth my voice?"[48]

There is a striking resemblance between Glas's words and those of Carson. The latter strongly criticized those who taught that what one must believe to be saved was that Christ died for each person in particular. In contrast, he argued that 1 Cor 15:1–4 taught that Christ died for all who believe, rather than for every person.[49]

Robert Sandeman was a native of Perth, and eventually became an elder at the Glasite church in his hometown after being influenced by Glas's teachings during his time at Edinburgh University. Sandeman's connection to Glas was only strengthened by his marriage to Glas's daughter Katharine (d. 1746). Sandeman's contentious style of writing tended to further isolate Glasite churches. His *Letters on Theron and Aspasio* (1757) were a prime example of his contentious style. For example, his negative views of John Wesley were very evident: "Mr. Wesley . . . may justly be reckoned one of the most virulent reproachers of that God, whose character is drawn by the apostles."[50] His criticism also extended to the followers of Wesley and other well-known Calvinistic Evangelicals: "I have nowhere observed the

---

47. Glas, *Testimony of the King of Martyrs*, 1:116.
48. Glas, *Testimony of the King of Martyrs*, 1:117–18.
49. *Works* 1:91.
50. Sandeman, *Letters*, 410–11n*.

Jewish disgust at the bare truth, or, which is the same thing, the bare work of Christ, more evident than among the admirers of the doctrine of Messrs. [Stephen] Marshall, [Thomas] Boston, [Ralph and Ebenezer] Erskine, [George] Whitefield, [John] Wesley, and such like."[51] Sandeman's views and controversial style quickly garnered opposition. John Wesley (1703–91), an object of Sandeman's reproach, immediately responded with *A Sufficient Answer, to Letters to the Author of Theron and Aspasio: In a Letter to the Author* (1757). Sandeman, who worked aggressively to expand the influence of Glas's teachings, subsequently founded a Glasite church in London, England (1762). Sandeman's writings and efforts to expand into England led to the movement becoming known as Sandemanianism, especially to those outside of Scotland. Sandemanianism spread to North America as well and Sandeman personally established small fellowships in Connecticut and Nova Scotia in the final years of his life.[52]

The third Sandemanian leader to be considered here is Archibald McLean (1733–1812), who was a Scottish bookseller and printer and who became a Sandemanian in 1762. McLean remained in fellowship with the Sandemanian church for only one year, for he came to hold the Baptist conviction of believer's baptism. These views were expressed in his *Letters Addressed to John Glas in Answer to His Dissertation on Infant-Baptism* (1767). Yet, the matter of baptism was not the only basis of disagreement between them. In his memoir on McLean, William Jones included a chapter entitled "The Scotch Baptists Not Sandemanians" in which he included a manuscript written by McLean illustrating several points of difference.[53] Jones's reason for including McLean's manuscript was to confute the perception that the Scotch Baptists only differed from the Sandemanians on the matter of baptism. McLean framed seven points of disagreement with the Sandemanians under the manner in which they opposed so-called Pharisaism: they labeled all who disagreed with them as Pharisees; the "spirit of ridicule and contempt" they held for those who had a "strict and serious religious appearance"; their laxness in abstaining from worldly activities and attitudes; their self-righteousness manifested by how they condemned the self-righteousness of others; though they criticized others for making new laws and dispensing with Christ's laws, the Sandemanians did the same; the

---

51. Sandeman, *Letters*, 86.
52. Derek B. Murray, "Sandeman, Robert," *ODNB* 48:857–58.
53. Jones believed that McLean wrote the manuscript at least twenty years before Fuller's *Strictures on Sandemanianism* (1810). Jones, "Memoir," xxxiv.

way they balanced their extreme pretension to genuine Christianity with "an affectation of singular humility"; and their "narrow party spirit," which kept them from co-operating with other denominations that differed from them.[54]

While the differences McLean cited were not trivial, they did not include other major characteristics such as their understanding of saving faith and ecclesiology. John Howard Smith has noted the ongoing similarities between the Sandemanians and Scotch Baptists: "The Scotch Baptists vigorously denied any connection to the Glasites and Sandemanians, even as they admitted to their admiration for John Glas's and Robert Sandeman's published works. . . . Nonetheless, a close examination of Scotch Baptist church discipline and doctrine reveals heavy Sandemanian influence, down to the particulars of Sunday worship."[55] Therefore, McLean's propagation of Sandemanian views in the Scotch Baptist churches was just as noteworthy as his departure from the Sandemanians, especially his eventual role as the primary theologian of the Scotch Baptists.

McLean was not as exclusive as the Sandemanians, and he was known for being an avid supporter of the Baptist Missionary Society. Despite his efforts to co-operate with English Baptists in evangelism, McLean's Sandemanian views resulted in division. Though McLean became friends with Andrew Fuller, their differing views on church order and the definition of saving faith led to the Sandemanian controversy within Baptist life. Fuller's response to McLean's criticism of his views on religious affections was included in an appendix to the second edition of *The Gospel Worthy of All Acceptation* (1801): "Mr. Mc. Lean, in a Second Edition of his treatise on *The Commission of Christ*, has published several pages of animadversions on what I have advanced on this subject, and has charged me with very serious consequences; consequences which if substantiated will go to prove that I have subverted the great doctrine of justification by grace alone, without the works of the law. . . . Our disagreement on this subject is confined to the question, *What the belief of the gospel includes?*"[56] McLean had apparently preserved a portion of Sandeman's controversial character as well as his views on saving faith. He had a very simple view of faith, which he saw the apostles present as "a single plain short proposition, such as that 'Jesus is the Christ, the Son of God,' or that 'God raised him from the

---

54. Jones, "Memoir," xxxiv–li.
55. J. Howard Smith, *Perfect Rule*, 89–90.
56. Fuller, *Gospel Worthy* (1805), 164–65; emphasis in original.

dead,' and declare that all who believe this truth upon the divine testimony will be saved."[57] Again, Carson's own view of faith can essentially be taken from McLean. McLean also separated the affections from faith itself and discussed them in relation to their effect on the Christian life.[58] McLean's voluminous writing, as well as his work as a printer, further helped spread Sandemanian views through literature.[59] The principles of the Scotch Baptists, including their Sandemanianism, continued to be spread through the work of McLean's protégé, William Jones.

Born in Gresford, Wales, Jones was baptized in Chester, England, in 1786 by Archibald McLean. Afterwards, Jones served as an elder in Scotch Baptist churches in Liverpool and London, while also working as a bookseller. From 1812, he took McLean's place as the primary writer for the Scotch Baptist movement. His publications included *An Essay on the Life and Writings of Mr. Abraham Booth* (1808) and a *History of the Waldenses, Connected with a Sketch of the Christian Church from the Time of Christ to the Eighteenth Century* (1812). He also served as the editor of the *New Evangelical Magazine* (1815–24) and *The Millennial Harbinger and Voluntary Church Advocate* (1835–36).

Jones's relationship with McLean naturally leads to the question of where Jones's theological inclinations lay. The answer in nuce is that his writings did indeed reflect a predilection for Sandemanian views. In *An Essay on the Life and Writings of Mr. Abraham Booth*, he generally described the writings of Glas and Sandeman as being filled with "the most rich and precious doctrine."[60] He also recommended Archibald McLean's writings to his readers a number of times.[61] On the topic of faith, Jones clearly understood Robert Sandeman's definition of saving faith to be "nothing more than *the bare belief of the bare truth*."[62] His partiality to this viewpoint was shown in his explication of Booth's own definition of faith: "'By believing in Jesus Christ,' says [Booth], . . . 'is intended *receiving him*, as exhibited in the doctrine of divine grace; or *depending upon him only*, as revealed in the gospel, for pardon, peace, and life eternal.' But these things are the effects of faith, and not faith itself; and it may be added, that not one of the texts

57. McLean, *Sermons on Doctrines and Duties*, 91.
58. McLean, *Sermons on Doctrines and Duties*, 298.
59. Murray, *ODNB* 22:431.
60. Jones, *Essay on Abraham Booth*, 69n*.
61. Jones, *Essay on Abraham Booth*, 69n*; 71n*.
62. Jones, *Essay on Abraham Booth*, 12; emphasis in original.

to which Mr. B. refers, prove that faith is any thing more than *belief*, or the *crediting of a report* founded on testimony."[63] In the *New Evangelical Magazine*, Jones responded to a letter in which the writer argued for a distinction between an intellectual faith, or "faith of assent," and a faith of the heart, or "faith of reception."[64] Jones strongly criticized this distinction as unbiblical and argued that to believe with the intellect or understanding included the heart. It would seem clear that Jones's definition of saving faith was in line with the views of Sandemanians before him. More importantly, Jones's words as well as Sandeman's have been mirrored in Carson's understanding of saving faith. The remaining question to answer is whether or not Jones's Sandemanian view of faith influenced Carson's understanding of faith.

Whitsitt's description of their connection is not conclusive evidence. In contrast, Jones, himself, did not specifically claim him as his adherent but wrote that Carson was "classed among the Scotch Baptists, and strenuously advocated the order of public worship, observed in those churches."[65] In his autobiography, Jones's reference to Carson expressed similarity with Carson rather than Carson as his adherent: "I may further add that the principles referred to as inculcated by Dr. Carson . . . differ but little from those of the Scottish Baptists."[66] Therefore, while Carson and Jones shared similar appropriations of Sandemanian practices of church order and understanding of saving faith, Macleod was probably correct in seeing enough differences between the two that he believed the Scotch Baptists "would not receive him, and never claimed him while alive."[67] Yet, a lack of established fellowship between Carson and the Scotch Baptists does not necessarily preclude a personal and influential relationship between Carson and Jones. Carson's personal tie to Jones is corroborated in two recommendations prefacing George Moore's memoir of Carson's life. One recommendation for Moore's work by Reverend John Dowling mentioned Jones: "The Rev. William Jones, the author of the Ecclesiastical History, had intended to prepare such a memoir, and would probably have done so had his life been

63. Jones, *Essay on Abraham Booth*, 68n*; emphasis in original.
64. Jones, "Rash and Unguarded Expressions," 107.
65. Jones, "Views," 563.
66. Jones, *Autobiography*, 124.

67. Macleod, "Dr. Carson's Views," 12. This is especially true if, according to Brian R. Talbot, the Scotch Baptists used McLean's "denial of the eternal sonship of Jesus" as a "test of orthodoxy for aspiring church members." Talbot, *Search for a Common Identity*, 33. Carson clearly accepted the eternal sonship of Christ, though he did not see it as a just cause for division. A. Carson, *Knowledge of Jesus*, 140–41; *Works* 5:93–94.

spared a few years longer."[68] That Jones's intention to write Carson's memoir was not simply owing to his own personal interest is proven by the fact that Carson's family requested Jones to write the memoir. In 1845 *The Primitive Church Magazine* included an announcement that "Mr. W. Jones, author of the 'History of the Waldenses,' &c. &c. has been requested by the family of the late Dr. Carson to write his life. We earnestly hope that his health may be spared to enable him to execute this important service for the church of Christ."[69] Jones's health was not spared, and he passed away before he could write Carson's memoir. Yet, Carson's daughter, Matilda Hanna, remembered Jones with high praise in a recommendation prefacing Carson's memoir by Moore: "Rev. G. C. Moore: My highly esteemed friend and brother—I can not express to you the pleasure it gives me to hear that you purpose to write a memoir of my late reverend father. Oh! how sorry I have often felt since the death of that devoted and excellent servant of God, the late Rev. William Jones, that there was no one else who would see it his duty to undertake such a task."[70] While the exact nature of her relationship to Jones is unknown, Hanna's admiration for Jones would have likely been a restatement of Carson's own sentiments. Carson and Jones also shared a common friend, James Buchanan (ca. 1851), the British consul to New York from approximately 1818 to 1844. William Hanna's biographical sketch of Carson stated that Carson and Buchanan were personal friends, and that Buchanan had encouraged Carson to begin a ministry in America in 1814, but Carson decided not to leave Tobermore due to the pleas of his congregation.[71] Moore called Buchanan a "respected friend" of Carson and included extracts from Carson's letters that Buchanan periodically delivered to American correspondents.[72] Jones, a friend of Buchanan as early as 1820, wrote that Buchanan "received his religious instruction under the ministry of the late eminently learned Dr. Carson, of Tubbermore."[73] The link with Buchanan could have easily developed into a direct relationship between Carson and Jones, and it serves only to strengthen the probability of a personal connection between them.

68. Moore, *Life of Alexander Carson*, iii.
69. *Primitive Church Magazine*, "Announcement."
70. Moore, *Life of Alexander Carson*, iv.
71. Hanna, "Alexander Carson," 198.
72. Moore, *Life of Alexander Carson*, 24, 74, 85, 89.
73. Jones, *Autobiography*, 123–24.

Does Carson's connections with the Scotch Baptists preclude a connection between Carson and the English Baptists? There is no evidence to support this. In fact, the evidence shows that there was a warm, though not regular, relationship with the English Baptists. On at least one occasion, he was invited to preach throughout Great Britain by the Baptist Missionary Society. This was during the notable fiftieth anniversary of William Carey's going to India in 1792. While this is clear evidence of cooperation between Carson and English Baptists, his jubilee sermon for the Baptist Missionary Society indicated that he spoke to them as one outside of the English Baptists. For example, he referred to the society as "your society" as though he was not a part of it.[74] And an article in *The Baptist Magazine* also seems to indicate that Carson's church was not connected to the Baptist Missionary Society.[75]

The evidence of a Sandemanian understanding of saving faith within Carson's written corpus, which is conspicuously similar to the views contained within the writings of key Sandemanians before him, along with the evidence of a personal relationship with various Scotch Baptists, leads to a number of conclusions. First, it is clear that Carson had a Sandemanian understanding of saving faith. The similarities between Carson in this regard and Glas, Sandeman, McLean, and Jones are too apparent to deny. Second, Carson's similarities and ties to Sandemanianism, primarily to the Scotch Baptists' embodiment of it, were recognized by both Sandemanian sympathizers and critics. Third, though one cannot irrefutably conclude that Carson came to a Sandemanian understanding of saving faith through the influence of Scotch Baptists or Sandemanians, their shared views allowed for an eventual relationship between Carson and Scotch Baptists such as William Jones.

CARSON'S VIEW OF WORKS IN JUSTIFICATION

In his *Letters to the Author of an Article in the Edinburgh Review, on "Evangelical Preaching,"* Carson presented a series of responses to a book review of *The Mysteries of Providence, and the Triumphs of Grace*, in which the unidentified reviewer criticized numerous doctrines commonly held by Evangelicals, including their belief that justification was by faith alone and not by works. Carson's third and fourth letters focused on the various

---

74. Acworth and Carson, *Two Sermons*, 78; *Works* 1:450.
75. *Baptist Magazine*, "Irish Chronicle," 47.

criticisms and misrepresentations given by his opponent concerning the subject justification by faith alone.[76] As previously shown, Carson believed that justification was by faith alone, and that the biblical gospel was diametrically opposed to salvation by works in any degree.[77] In the discussion on Carson's definition of faith, he was shown to have a very simple view of saving faith, which was a concept he included in his fifth letter to his opponent in the *Edinburgh Review*: "The faith that saves us . . . consists in believing in the Lord Jesus Christ."[78] While he had few words about what faith was, his words about what faith was not were numerous, especially as faith related to works. For example, some, out of strong desire to "assure men, that their works must have some share in their acceptance," described faith, itself, as a work.[79] Carson rejected this expedient without any ambiguity: "They who speak of salvation being by faith, on account of the excellence of faith itself, are virtually on the same foundation with those who preach salvation directly by works."[80] He believed that faith did not have an extraordinary or mysterious meaning, but that Scripture's use of the word was its common meaning, which was simply to believe.[81] Those who twisted the meaning of the word not only created a works salvation, but also altered God's revelation. This principle of faithfully interpreting the Scripture held true for works as well. According to the author of the *Edinburgh Review* article, evangelical preachers taught that "a text declaring that our salvation depends on our works, is made to declare that it does *not* depend on our works, but on our faith."[82] Denying this as an evangelical practice, Carson argued against changing the meaning of a word to appease one's theology, and that these words were present for a divine purpose and had a specific meaning.[83]

Carson also addressed the idea that the Bible's rejection of the efficacy of works, or the law, in one's salvation only referred to the ceremonial law, not the moral law. In a note, his opponent wrote that Paul's censure against the requirement of circumcision in Gal 5:2–6 disqualified only the

76. A. Carson, *Letters on "Evangelical Preaching,"* 12–21; *Works* 1:324–59.
77. *Works* 1:80.
78. A. Carson, *Letters on "Evangelical Preaching,"* 24; *Works* 1:338.
79. A. Carson, *Letters on "Evangelical Preaching,"* vi; *Works* 1:311.
80. A. Carson, *Letters on "Evangelical Preaching,"* 34; *Works* 1:350.
81. A. Carson, *Letters on "Evangelical Preaching,"* 37; *Works* 1:354.
82. *Edinburgh Review*, Unsigned review of *Mysteries*, 441n*.
83. A. Carson, *Letters on "Evangelical Preaching,"* 29–30; *Works* 1:345.

ceremonial law as efficacious for salvation, and this did not apply to the moral law.[84] Claiming that it was "as silly" as it was "wicked" to allege that Paul intended to deny the efficaciousness of only the ceremonial law for salvation, Carson quoted numerous verses from Galatians to show that Paul's references to the law included both moral and ceremonial.[85] Concerning Galatians, Carson concluded, "Circumcision, then, while it was the great, was not the only point in which they were attached to the law."[86] He also pointed out three passages in Paul's Epistle to the Romans as evidence that the apostle spoke "of the law without any reference to circumcision."[87] Carson argued that the biblical example of the rejection of the efficacy of a ceremonial rite to justify a person presented a principle by which all laws are rejected as efficacious for justification. For example, when the Scriptures prohibit the worship of Baal, the principle was that all idolatry was prohibited. Therefore, it was appropriate to apply the principle of Paul's rejection of circumcision in Galatians to other laws, moral and ceremonial.[88] Ultimately, Carson believed that Christians who instructed unbelievers to "obtain an interest in Christ by forsaking their sins, doing good works, and struggling with God in prayer" were just as mistaken as the Judaizers who required circumcision as well as faith for salvation.[89] The good works mentioned were supposed to be fruits resulting from faith rather than "an introduction to faith."[90]

Bebbington noted that critics of justification by faith alone believed the doctrine "to be subversive of all morality."[91] Carson's opponent in the *Edinburgh Review* was no different: "Here we are prepared to maintain, in spite of all the efforts of evangelical preachers to make the contrary to appear, that some of their most common representations [of justification by faith alone] must have the effect (if they have any effect at all), of relieving men from the duties of morality, of making morality utterly useless as

---

84. *Edinburgh Review*, Unsigned review of *Mysteries*, 440n*, 441n†.

85. A. Carson, *Letters on "Evangelical Preaching,"* 25–26, 31; *Works* 1:339–40, 346–47. Carson quoted Gal 2:16; 3:2, 10, 11, 12, 13, 21; 4:10, 21.

86. A. Carson, *Letters on "Evangelical Preaching,"* 31; *Works* 1:347.

87. A. Carson, *Letters on "Evangelical Preaching,"* 31; *Works* 1:347. Carson quoted Rom 3:20–21, 27–28.

88. A. Carson, *Letters on "Evangelical Preaching,"* 32; *Works* 1:348–49.

89. *Works* 1:105–6.

90. *Works* 1:107.

91. Bebbington, *Evangelicalism in Modern Britain*, 6.

regards salvation; and, of course, of removing all motives to the practice of moral virtue that may be drawn from that source."[92] Carson did not approve of the way his opponent characterized saving faith as the belief that works were worthless towards one's justification rather than as the belief in the Lord Jesus Christ: "Of course a faith that good works are useless will only produce bad works."[93] That aside, Carson disagreed with the critic's contention and gave a fourfold rationale for why Christians would not lose motivation for good works, even when those good works did not serve to gain them salvation. First, Christians obeyed God's commands out of gratitude for Christ dying on the cross to save them: "If even the rich grace and mercy of God could not reach us till our sins are removed by the death of Christ, shall we live in that which is so offensive to God?"[94] Next, Christians were motivated to do good works out of love for God, "because he loved us first." Another reason to remain motivated for good works was the promise that believers would receive an eternal reward based on their works. Finally, Christians were commanded to do good works, for "without holiness no man shall see the Lord."[95] Therefore, while good works did not justify a person, there were multiple motivations for good works.

Carson's fourth reason for the Christian to continue in good works received the most treatment. He emphasized that while both faith and works were important and taught in Scripture, they served different purposes. He contended that Scripture referred to salvation with different understandings: it could refer to either justification or admission to heaven. In terms of justification, salvation was only by faith and not by works. Christians were justified by the imputation of Christ's righteousness, "because they are one with Christ by faith."[96] On the other hand, "when it is asserted that a man cannot be saved without works, the meaning is, not that he cannot be justified without works, but that he cannot enter heaven without works."[97] These are works that the Christian, by faith in Christ, did on his own. In a sense, the Christian's works belonged both to the person and to Christ.[98]

---

92. *Edinburgh Review*, Unsigned review of *Mysteries*, 438.
93. A. Carson, *Letters on "Evangelical Preaching,"* 24; *Works* 1:338.
94. *Works* 1:117.
95. A. Carson, *Letters on "Evangelical Preaching,"* 23; *Works* 1:337.
96. A. Carson, *Letters on "Evangelical Preaching,"* 29; *Works* 1:345.
97. A. Carson, *Letters on "Evangelical Preaching,"* 27; *Works* 1:342.
98. A. Carson, *Letters on "Evangelical Preaching,"* 29; *Works* 1:345.

RECALLING ONE'S CONVERSION

The issue of whether one was always able to pinpoint the moment of conversion was also discussed. Though not of great significance in Carson's thought, his opponent in the *Edinburgh Review* thought the issue important enough to remark on it: "Now the impression which evangelical preachers constantly convey on this head, is that the effect that every man must, at a particular assignable period of his life, have made a *change* altogether different, in kind and degree, from any step in moral or spiritual improvement made either before or after."[99] The writer's remark was evidence of the topic's presence in the conversations of his day. Bebbington noted the debate over the issue, with mainstream denominations, such as the Established Church, generally accepting a gradual conversion or even nurture into the Christian faith, while the less methodologically conservative movements, such as the Methodists and revivalists, or dissenting denominations generally looked for a "particular assignable period" of conversion.[100] While the issue usually contrasted gradual with sudden, Carson seemed to see the issue in terms of assignable or unassignable. The reasons this issue can be said to be less significant for Carson are because he did not dedicate much writing to the issue and he chose to focus on the present state of the person in question rather than on the moment of their conversion. He did recognize that some sought after a recognizable moment of conversion, but Carson did not believe this view necessarily belonged to Evangelicalism.[101] Ultimately, he said, "The great matter with every individual is, not to be able to ascertain when he was made alive unto God, but that he is now actually alive."[102] This view of basing one's justified state on one's present beliefs was also how Carson approached assurance of salvation: "As [Christ] died for all that believe, as soon as a sinner is conscious that he believes the gospel, he have the same ground to believe that Christ died for him, as that he died at all."[103] Carson had a tendency to move his readers away from agonizing over the how or when and focusing the reader on the present situation instead.

---

99. *Edinburgh Review*, Unsigned review of *Mysteries*, 432; emphasis in original.
100. Bebbington, *Evangelicalism in Modern Britain*, 7–8.
101. A. Carson, *Letters on "Evangelical Preaching,"* 14; *Works* 1:326.
102. A. Carson, *Letters on "Evangelical Preaching,"* 14; *Works* 1:326.
103. *Works* 1:91.

DIVINE SOVEREIGNTY IN CONVERSION

Carson gave comfort to Christians who were anxious over whether they were among the elect or not, but this should not imply that he was unconcerned with matters regarding God's sovereignty in regeneration. As has already been shown, Carson held a strong conviction of God's sovereign rule over the Scripture, the atonement, and, as will be shown in the next chapter, in the evangelistic efforts of the church. In regards to human regeneration, Carson believed that it was God who gave life and faith to spiritually dead people, through Scripture by the Holy Spirit. All these elements showed divine initiative. Quoting the writer in the *Edinburgh Review*, Carson approved of the accurate description of his view on God's sovereignty in converting people: "'When one man has come into a state of salvation, another has not; this is not by the first person doing something which the other failed of doing, but by a supernatural intervention being made in behalf of the former which was not made in behalf of the latter;—in other words that a man's salvation has not been made to depend upon himself—has not been put in his own power.' This is the doctrine of your opponents. This is the doctrine of the Word of God."[104] This did not mean that Carson did not believe that people made a choice of whether to believe in Christ or not: "[Evangelicals] do not say that a man's choice and volitions are not his own, and that they are the choice and volitions of another being. But they say, that a man will not choose or will what is good, without the Spirit of God enabling him. They do not call our volitions God's volitions: they teach that God enables us to will."[105]

CONCLUSION

Carson's views on the effectiveness of the gospel, as seen through the conversion of people, reflected the issues Evangelicals in his day dealt with, but he primarily focused his attention on the way people could be connected to Christ's atoning work on the cross. Salvation could only be obtained through faith in the gospel, and not by works. It was seen that Carson objected to the efficacy of works in two senses. First, works could not justify anyone in and of itself. Second, works could not connect one to the atonement. Yet, Carson did not reject works per se, and his view of works was seen to have a

---

104. A. Carson, *Letters on "Evangelical Preaching,"* 15; *Works* 1:327.
105. A. Carson, *Letters on "Evangelical Preaching,"* 18; *Works* 1:331.

greater role in reflecting the true spiritual state of the believer than might be expected. Concerning the "question of timing" of conversion, as Bebbington called it, Carson showed himself to be against the requirement of having an assignable moment of conversion, which is not to say he was against memorable conversion experiences.[106] His Calvinism was also evidenced in his understanding of God's role versus the person's role in regeneration. The divine enabling of the person was necessary for someone to believe in the gospel. Carson's understanding of belief or faith was very simple and actually shared many qualities with Sandemanianism, a denomination many have considered to be a radical offshoot of English Protestantism. While Carson was never influenced directly by Sandemanianism, he had some connection to the Scotch Baptists whose formative theologian, Archibald Hall, came out of the Sandemanian movement. While Carson had much in common with the Scotch Baptists, especially in the areas of church order and view of saving faith, he was never officially associated with them or any other Baptist denomination.

---

106. Bebbington, *Evangelicalism in Modern Britain*, 7.

5

Alexander Carson's Activism

MANY EVANGELICALS WERE KNOWN for their commitment to social causes such as abolitionism, caring for widows, or founding orphanages. These endeavors of Evangelicals were arguably a product of their transformative experiences at conversion. One might say that they were living out the implications of the gospel. Therefore, while the activities of many Evangelicals "spilled over beyond simple gospel work," Carson's own efforts were almost exclusively evangelistic.[1] Carson's activism will be examined in four categories. The first will examine Carson's efforts focusing on the Scripture as an effective tool for evangelism, primarily through Sabbath schools and Bible societies. The second will examine Carson's evangelistic efforts within the political sphere, which will include his thoughts on freedom of religion. The third category will be an examination of God's providence in the evangelistic efforts of Christians in Carson's thought. The final category will be a study of Carson's views on the church's duty to evangelize.

TOOLS OF THE TRADE—
LITERACY, THE BIBLE, AND EVANGELISM

Carson's high view of Scripture, that all the words and thoughts contained therein were divinely inspired, meant that it served a practical purpose in exposing unbelievers to the gospel and in strengthening believers. This understanding of the role of Scripture in the spread of the gospel is evident

---

1. Bebbington, *Evangelicalism in Modern Britain*, 12.

in Carson's involvement with Sabbath schools and with the distribution of Bibles in Ireland by the Hibernian Bible Society.

Evangelism Through Sabbath Schools

Sabbath or Sunday schools began appearing in the Tobermore area in the early 1820s. Their goal was to spread the gospel through education and Bible reading; the overall effect of the Sabbath schools was deemed positive by Protestants. Observing the local impact of the Sabbath schools in 1836, John Stokes wrote, "The good effect of Sunday Schools has been made evident to disinterested individuals by the good effect in a religious point of view, produced in the minds of their parents by those children who were in the habit of attending at them."[2] There were at least six Sabbath schools in the Kilcronaghan parish, which included Tobermore. The six Sunday schools included Carson's school, the Kilcronaghan school connected with the Established Church, and four other schools that met in various homes. Carson's school was established in 1832 with two superintendents, Carson himself and John Wallace, a farmer. With 135 students, the Baptist, or Independent, Sabbath school had the highest attendance of the six area Sabbath schools. The second largest was the Kilcronaghan Sunday school, led by Carson's friend Reverend James Spencer Knox (d. 1862), with 98 students.[3] Over 80 percent of the students at the Baptist Sunday school were connected to Independent churches, many of whom possibly came from families in Carson's church. The remainder of students came from Anglican, Presbyterian, and Roman Catholic churches. Like most of the other Sunday schools, the Baptist Sunday school began and ended each session with singing and prayer. All the Sabbath schools had books provided by the Sunday School Society of Ireland for free or at reduced cost.[4] This

---

2. Day and McWilliams, *Parishes of County Londonderry*, 71; Stokes, "Memoir of J. Stokes," 21 (Public Records Office of Northern Ireland).

3. James Spencer Knox was the rector of the parishes of Maghera and Kilcronaghan. Carson considered Knox to be a friend and greatly appreciated the latter's irenicism: "While *you* are a very devoted, zealous, and active Minister of the Establishment, and *I* a Dissenter; from the first moment of your accession to the Parish in which I reside, you have not only shewn those ordinary attentions that discover a liberal mind, but you have solicitously sought opportunities to serve me." A. Carson, *Treatise on Figures of Speech*, 2; emphasis in original. He died on March 1, 1862, in Gloucester, England. District Registry of Londonderry, "Ireland Probate" (Public Records Office of Northern Ireland).

4. Day and McWilliams, *Parishes of County Londonderry*, 74–75; "School Statistics" (Public Records Office of Northern Ireland).

society, which was established in 1809 in Dublin, provided spelling books and Bibles specifically for religious instruction.[5] The Tobermore Sabbath school was something of a family affair. His youngest son, Robert Haldane Carson, eventually became the superintendent of the school.[6] At least two of Carson's daughters, Eliza (ca. 1813–37) and Matilda, were involved with the school, likely serving as two of the six female teachers.[7]

Carson's *Address to the Children of the Tubbermore Sabbath School, No. 2* (ca. 1837) gives insight into what he saw as the goals of the Sabbath school, the benefits of Bible reading, and the centrality of the gospel. He shared what motivated the teachers to "go through much drudgery" in teaching the students to read. First and foremost, the teachers were motivated by a love for the students' souls. The evangelistic motivation for the Sabbath school is clearly laid out at this point, because the teachers teach with the belief that what they are doing will be of eternal benefit to the students' souls. Carson said to the students, "Till you shall have known God, and been changed in heart by the power of his truth and Spirit, the object of your education remains unfulfilled."[8] Another motivation the teachers had for teaching the students to read was "to enable them to read the Word of God, that they may search the Scriptures, and in them find the pearl of great price."[9] This motivation to teach the children was thus evangelistic, to give them the skills to read the book that would teach them the way to salvation.

Carson contrasted this eternal benefit of the ability to read with the temporal benefits the students may have been expecting.[10] Rather than belittling the temporal benefits of reading, Carson attempted to put them in the proper perspective. He called the skill a "great temporal blessing."[11] This temporal blessing would make their lives better by enabling them to find better opportunities in the world, and he even encourages them to take advantage of the opportunities they are given. Yet, Carson reminded the students that all the learning in the world paled in comparison to the eternally

---

5. This society was originally called the Hibernian Sunday School Society of Ireland but changed it in 1816. Rice, *Sunday-School Movement*, 28.
6. See A. Carson, *Address to the Children*.
7. G. Carson and Hanna, *Memorials*, 18.
8. A. Carson, *Address to the Children*, 6.
9. A. Carson, *Address to the Children*, 6.
10. Hempton and Hill, *Evangelical Protestantism in Ulster Society*, 111–12.
11. A. Carson, *Address to the Children*, 6.

saving knowledge of the gospel: "The truth here asserted, eternity only shall fully reveal. Then shall earthly things be estimated at their real value. They shall then lose that tinsel which to the human mind is now captivating, and appear to be but 'vanity and vexation of spirit.'"[12] While Carson contrasted the temporal blessings of reading to the eternal blessings it gave access to, he did not ignore immediate blessings experienced by those who arrived at the eternal truths of the gospel.[13] An important aspect of this joyful Christian life was continued Bible reading: "If the Lord has opened your eyes to understand his Gospel, you will greatly value the Scriptures."[14] Therefore, while Carson's first concern in promoting and enabling Bible reading was for people to come to know the gospel, it is clear that the importance of Bible reading never diminished after one came to faith.

Carson's address made clear the motivations of the teachers and the purpose of Bible reading. Yet, the address also revealed that Carson was an opportunist when it came to evangelism. The Sabbath school did not box in his evangelistic methods to Bible reading with a hope that students would come to faith through the study of Scripture. The address itself was a clear gospel presentation, and it was not simply a "trite exhortation—'Sinner, come to Christ.'"[15] Carson spoke on such subjects as the eternity of the human soul, the universal sin of humanity, the impending judgment before Christ, the worldly temptations that draw one away from Christ, salvation through faith in the blood of Christ, and the present and future benefits of salvation.[16] This was followed by a personal inquiry into the students' spiritual state: "Let me ask you now, dear children, whether the Gospel has this effect on you. Has it delivered you from the fear of the divine wrath due to your sins? Has it given you joy on this account, as well as from the anticipation of future glory? If in some manner it has not had these effects on you, there is no evidence that you have understood it, though you may be able to give an account of it to those who examine you."[17] The context in which he was preaching allowed Carson to speak the gospel directly to his audience, and the use of personal language was meant to impact the listeners' emotions and thoughts. These methods were not always available

---

12. A. Carson, *Address to the Children*, 7.
13. A. Carson, *Address to the Children*, 7.
14. A. Carson, *Address to the Children*, 5.
15. Moore, *Life of Alexander Carson*, 71.
16. A. Carson, *Address to the Children*, 1–3.
17. A. Carson, *Address to the Children*, 3.

to Carson. While he had direct access to those who came to listen to him preach on Sundays or to students at his Sabbath school, his evangelistic goals extended beyond those in close proximity to him.

Promoting Bible Reading Among Roman Catholics

One of Carson's evangelistic targets was the Roman Catholic community. Though he and his church were able to make some connections with the Catholic laity through personal relationships and the Sabbath school, direct interactions also involved Catholic protests against Carson's evangelistic efforts and outspokenness against Roman Catholic beliefs.[18] Carson's conviction that Bible reading was useful as an evangelistic tool motivated him to extend his support for it beyond his own local domain. Bible societies, such as the Hibernian Bible Society, helped to promote the advancement of literacy in Ireland by spreading English Bibles throughout parts of Ireland.[19] Yet, there was substantial resistance by the Roman Catholic Church to unrestricted Bible reading among their people, which was evident through publications such as Doyle's *Letters on the State of Education in Ireland: And on Bible Societies; Addressed to a Friend in England* (1824) and this sometimes even manifested itself in mob violence. One such event occurred at the anniversary meeting of the Carlow Bible Society in 1824, where Carson had been invited as one of the speakers. After a formal dialogue began between Protestant and Catholic representatives concerning Bible distribution to the Catholic laity, a Roman Catholic mob formed at the venue where Carson was to speak, endangering the safety of the Protestant clergy. The Protestants had to escape by climbing over an eight-foot high wall.[20] Carson's *The Right and Duty of All Men to Read the Scriptures; Being the Substance of a Speech Intended to Have Been Delivered at the Meeting of the Carlow Bible Society; Containing a Refutation of Several Parts of a Late Pamphlet by J. K. L. Entitled "Letters on the State of Education, and Bible Societies"* was published later that year. In it, he addressed a number of the reasons Roman Catholic leaders objected to the "right and duty of all men, without restraint, to read what God has revealed for the instruction of

---

18. G. Carson and Hanna, *Memorials*, 71–73; Moore, *Life of Alexander Carson*, 43–46.

19. Other societies geared towards the evangelizing Ireland were the London Hibernian Society (1806), the Hibernian Sunday School Society (1809), the Irish Evangelical Society (1814), and the Irish Society (1818). Wolffe, *Expansion of Evangelicalism*, 170.

20. Carlow Bible Society and Skelton, *Speak-Out*, 2.

The Gospel-Centered Evangelicalism of Alexander Carson

the human race."[21] The Roman Catholic objections Carson addressed were taken from arguments presented by their representatives at the disastrous meeting of the Carlow Bible Society and from Doyle's *Letters on the State of Education in Ireland*.

One objection to which Carson responded was that portions of the Bible tended to be lascivious, thus having the potential to lead the laity into immorality. Carson's five-part response was primarily a defense of the Song of Solomon and, more importantly, a defense of the usefulness of divinely inspired Scripture, a view he grounded on 2 Tim 3:16. Carson's first point was that all Scripture was God's revelation and holy. If the Song of Solomon had a "necessary tendency to pollute the mind," it could not possibly be part of Scripture.[22] His second point was that marriage and all that it entailed was pure and holy, because it was a relationship created by God. Drawing from Eph 5:22–32, he asserted that nothing connected with the church could be unholy. Carson's next point was aimed directly against the Roman Catholic clergy. He argued that if anyone was in danger of being led into sexual immorality by the Song of Solomon, "priests are the men to whom above all others it is dangerous," presumably due to their mandatory celibacy.[23] His fourth argument was that legitimate fear of immoral influence upon the unmarried must logically extend to married people as well. His final response was to give five scriptural examples of possible offense in the laws of Moses that were publicly read in the presence of men, women, and children. His contention was that such laws were "as liable to be charged with grossness and indelicacy, as any contained in the Bible."[24] Yet this concern did not stand as a reason to restrict the hearing, or reading, of God's word. Rather, these examples stood as evidence that God's people had the duty to hear, or read, God's revelation.

Another objection to which Carson responded dealt with the "supposed impenetrable darkness of the Bible."[25] Against the accusation that the Bible was almost exclusively figurative, Carson argued that this exaggerated claim did not have a sound understanding of the figures of speech. Metaphors and such, which Carson would categorize as "figures founded

---

21. A. Carson, *Right and Duty*, 3; *Works* 2:3.
22. A. Carson, *Right and Duty*, 4; *Works* 2:5.
23. A. Carson, *Right and Duty*, 5; *Works* 2:5.
24. A. Carson, *Right and Duty*, 5; *Works* 2:5.
25. A. Carson, *Right and Duty*, 7; *Works* 2:8.

on resemblance,"[26] were generally not meant to confuse but to "bring an accession of light."[27] He considered most of the biblical metaphors to be quite intelligible, even for the uneducated, uncivilized, and young.[28] The only exception Carson allowed to the naturally enlightening characteristic of these types of figures of speech was allegory, which he described as placing a "thin veil over its subject."[29] Yet, he continued, these veils were always with a divine purpose and very memorable once explained. His belief in the general lack of obscurity in the Scriptures leads to one doctrine he believed to be clearly taught, that salvation was by faith in Christ's atoning work, a method of salvation that he believed was contradictory to orthodox Roman Catholicism.[30] "One thing, however, is abundantly plain, the way of salvation, through faith in the blood of Jesus Christ. If this is hid from any, it is hid from them that are lost, who are blinded by the god of this world."[31] His point was essentially that the gospel would be hidden from unbelievers, if the Bible was kept from them. This is one of the reasons for which Carson believed Bible reading was a practical method for evangelism. This is also why he believed that "the true cause of alarm [among Catholic clergy] is the general possession of the Scriptures by the people."[32]

Related to their concern over the obscurity of Scripture, Catholic leaders argued that "erroneous conclusions are the natural and necessary result of reading the Scriptures without an interpreter."[33] Carson found the Catholic leaders to equivocate on this topic. In another work, Carson pointed out that Doyle implied that the Catholic laity had the right to read the Scriptures, but that the clergy built up so many hedges around this liberty that it ceased to exist: "The people have a right to read the Scriptures, but the Clergy have a right, as often as they please, to keep them from reading."[34]

26. A. Carson, *Treatise on Figures of Speech*, 16; *Works* 5:437.

27. A. Carson, *Right and Duty*, 7; *Works* 2:8. Carson categorized metaphors with comparison and allegory as figures founded on resemblance. He defined these figures as those that have two objects, "the latter of which is the likeness of the former." A. Carson, *Treatise on Figures of Speech*, 16; *Works* 5:437.

28. A. Carson, *Right and Duty*, 7; *Works* 2:8.

29. A. Carson, *Right and Duty*, 8; *Works* 2:9.

30. Discussed in ch. 2.

31. A. Carson, *Right and Duty*, 16; *Works* 2:20.

32. A. Carson, *Right and Duty*, 12; *Works* 2:14.

33. A. Carson, *Right and Duty*, 15; *Works* 2:18; Carlow Bible Society and Skelton, *Speak-Out*, 50; Doyle, *Letters on Education in Ireland*, 58.

34. A. Carson, *Strictures*, 23; *Works* 2:170.

While Carson affirmed the indispensable role of teachers in the church, he disagreed that this necessarily nullified the mandate for people to read the Scriptures: "We do not disseminate Bibles in order to prevent preaching. These two divine ordinances do not oppose, but assist one another."[35] As previously shown, Carson actively used both mandates of preaching and Bible reading. Carson, in defense of the Bible society and for the salvation of unbelievers, pleaded that there was no reason for the Roman Catholic clergy to not take advantage of the Bibles being distributed. Using Rom 3:1; Col 4:16; and 1 Thess 5:27, Carson asserted that believers were commanded to read the Bible. Therefore, why would the Roman Catholic clergy keep from believers what they have been commanded to read? In one sense, Carson's argument is a ploy. He argued from the perspective of the Catholic clergy who assumed that their laity were true Christians, so that the laity would be given access to the Bible. Rather than believing that the Catholic laity were saved through knowledge of the gospel, Carson likely hoped that access to the Bible would show them that they had a defective gospel. His conviction as to what the clergy's "true cause of alarm" was serves only to strengthen this likelihood.

FREEDOM OF RELIGION—POLITICS AND EVANGELISM

Though Carson was not a politician, he was unafraid to be an activist when he believed the issues being dealt with in the political arena were germane to his evangelistic concerns. While he did not find any particular pleasure in the political marginalization of Irish Catholics, neither did he actively assert himself for the Catholic Emancipation. Though he expressed openness to political equality for people of any and all religious affiliations, his political concerns were driven by his evangelistic concerns.[36]

With the Act of Union in 1800, Britain was able to achieve, from its perspective, greater security from international threats, and Irish Catholics were able to hope for the fulfillment of Catholic Emancipation that would give them political representation in Parliament. Sadly for the Catholics in Ireland, emancipation did not come as soon as was hoped. Yet, efforts by both Catholics and many Protestants in Ireland for emancipation began to expand in the 1820s, with a growing number of members of Parliament and a grassroots movement that supported Catholic emancipation, which

---

35. A. Carson, *Right and Duty*, 19; *Works* 2:23.
36. A. Carson, *Strictures*, 24–25; *Works* 2:171.

coalesced into the Catholic Association, composed of both Catholics and Protestants.[37] James Warren Doyle, the Roman Catholic bishop of Kildare and Leighlin, was also very active in promoting the Catholic cause with his conciliatory writings to government officials and polemical writings to Protestant clergy. In 1823, Doyle wrote a letter, *A Vindication of the Religious and Civil Principles of the Irish Catholics*, to the Marquis Wellesley, in which the bishop addressed four accusations against the Roman Catholic Church. This letter was the occasion for Carson's letter to the marquis, *Strictures on the Letter of J. K. L. Entitled a Vindication of the Religious and Civil Principles of the Irish Catholics* (1823).

Carson's *Strictures* responded to each of Doyle's points. The first accusation against Roman Catholicism was that it was an anti-Christian religion and "so slavish a superstition as to unfit them for freedom."[38] While Carson left the issue of political freedom to politicians, he did agree that Roman Catholicism was, in fact, anti-Christian. He had equated the Catholic Church to the "man of sin" in 2 Thess 2:3 in his "Remarks on the Late Miracle, in a Letter to the Rev. Doctor Doyle" (1823), and he repeated that assertion here.[39] In reference to the nature of Roman Catholic miracles, Carson argued "that the strongly-marked features of the beast are all found in the Church of Rome, is as clear as that God made the heavens and earth."[40] The reason for Carson's judgment on Catholic miracles was due primarily to the incompatibility between the gospel of the Bible and the gospel taught by the Roman Catholic Church. His judgment of the Catholic Church was also due to his desire for them to believe the gospel of the Bible: "It may be thought that my opinions are uncharitable; but if they are the truth of God, I dare not, I ought not to dissemble them. I declare them freely, not for the condemnation of any of my fellow creatures, but solely for their salvation."[41]

The second charge Carson responded to was that the Roman Catholics "entertain the design of overthrowing the Established Church, and entering upon her possessions."[42] In contrast to Doyle's distinction between the Established Church and the constitution, Carson points out that the Established Church is a part of the British Constitution. Therefore, the Baptist

---

37. Yates, *Religious Condition of Ireland*, 45.
38. A. Carson, *Strictures*, 4; *Works* 2:154.
39. *Works* 2:139.
40. A. Carson, *Strictures*, 7; *Works* 2:157.
41. A. Carson, *Strictures*, 12; *Works* 2:161.
42. A. Carson, *Strictures*, 15; *Works* 2:163.

minister asserted, Doyle sought to modify the existing constitution to suit the Catholic Church. The third charge addressed was "that of intolerance towards the professors of other creeds; and an obstinate opposition to the diffusion of knowledge, and the progress of education."[43] While Carson admitted that Protestants are also exclusive in terms of their belief that salvation is only through faith in Christ, he asserted the Catholic Church was the only church that exclusively claimed "salvation to their own Church—a thing that finds no parallel in the opinion of Protestants."[44] This exclusivity of the gospel that Protestants claimed was the source of Carson's motivation for sharing the gospel, as well as his love for Roman Catholics. Carson's non-sectarianism is manifested to a degree by his statement that his only desire was for Roman Catholics to believe in the true gospel and not for them to join his denomination.[45] The fourth charge dealt with education, which, for Carson, concerned the Catholic laity's access to the Bible and has already been discussed above. In conclusion, Carson expressed his hope for the preservation of the English constitution which protected the religious liberty he was so thankful for. Interestingly, it would not be long before Carson would experience grave concern over the possibility of losing this religious freedom, particularly as it involved his freedom to share the gospel.

In the 1820s, wrote Nigel Yates, evangelistic efforts "entered a new phase . . . with the launching of what became known as the Second Reformation," primarily by Evangelicals.[46] This period of expanded proselytizing efforts focused primarily on Roman Catholics. Though the Second Reformation was active in all the areas where a strong evangelical presence existed, it was stronger in a few areas, one of which was in County Cavan.[47] One unique feature of the reformation at Cavan is that it was initiated by the local landowner, Lord Farnham, rather than by a clergyman. The Evangelical Lord Farnham, John Maxwell-Barry (1767–1838), served as a member of Parliament for Cavan until inheriting the barony in 1823. With the goal of combining "the moral improvement of the people with the increase of their comforts and wealth," Farnham instituted a number of regulations

---

43. A. Carson, *Strictures*, 16; *Works* 2:164.
44. A. Carson, *Strictures*, 22; *Works* 2:169.
45. A. Carson, *Strictures*, 19; *Works* 2:167.
46. Yates, *Religious Condition of Ireland*, 270.
47. Yates, *Religious Condition of Ireland*, 272. County Cavan is located in the southern part of Ulster, and its northwestern border is shared with present-day Northern Ireland.

for his tenants.[48] The portions dealing with moral and religious reform were a part of Farnham's apparent desire to evangelize his tenantry:

> To this end has a system of moral agency been established—to this end the course of education in the Schools will be directed—and to these subjects will the reports of the Inspectors principally relate. Parents of Families are therefore earnestly entreated . . . to train up their children in the paths of virtue, and in the habits of industry and strict sobriety; to withdraw them from Dances, Ball-alleys, Cock-fights, and all other scenes of dissipation; to lead them to keep the Sabbath-day holy; to avoid cursing and swearing, and every other evil habit contrary to the laws of God, and of their country. Upon these points, above all others, will the favour and regard of their Landlord depend, as upon the soundness of a man's religious and moral principles alone, can a confidence be placed in his faithful discharge of any of his social and relative duties.[49]

Farnham was not merely concerned with moral reformation, though, and this was made clear at a speech he delivered at a gathering of Evangelicals on January 26, 1827.

At this meeting, Farnham gave an account of Roman Catholic clergy and laity in his county who came to recant their Catholic beliefs, which raises some points for consideration. First, those seeking conversion were carefully examined to discover their motives.[50] Those wanting to join the Established Church were also warned that their conversion would not result in any temporal blessing.[51] Farnham's statements here were in response to accusations that he had offered bribes to "induce conformity."[52] Second, effort was made to "prevent any persons, but such as bear irreproachable characters, from coming forward," and many were discouraged from joining due to the lack of a favorable testimony of their character.[53] Doyle warned Farnham whether the latter was ready to add "some thousands of the vilest rabble" to his church.[54] It seemed that Farnham was concerned about whom he brought into the Established Church, but the criterion was

48. Maxwell-Barry, *Management of Farnham Estates*, 8.
49. Maxwell-Barry, *Management of Farnham Estates*, 16.
50. Maxwell-Barry, *Report of the Speeches*, 4.
51. Maxwell-Barry, *Report of the Speeches*, 5.
52. Yates, *Religious Condition of Ireland*, 273; Maxwell-Barry, *Report of the Speeches*, 5.
53. Maxwell-Barry, *Report of the Speeches*, 5.
54. Doyle, *Doyle's Letter*, 4.

based on the person's character and not the person's social status or level of education. Finally, Farnham made use of education and Bible reading as tools for evangelism. He wrote, "Notwithstanding all the efforts of the Romish Priesthood to keep the Bible a sealed book to the people, the light of the Gospel *has* broken forth, and shone over this benighted land in despite of their exertions. The thirst for Scriptural information is so great, and has already been indulged to such an extent, that those whose duty it is to examine the conformists, have expressed their astonishment at the progress in the knowledge of divine truth displayed by persons who laboured under such peculiar disadvantages."[55] The number of conversions in the county up to this meeting was 459 people, many of which he credited to people having read the Bible on their own or in a Sabbath school. Farnham's meeting established a society called the Cavan Association for Promoting the Reformation, which is evidence that he had no intention of putting a halt to his evangelistic efforts in the county. The stated goal of this association was to promote the Protestant Reformation through all suitable means, which included preaching the gospel and distributing Bibles.[56] At the same time, the association rejected the use of bribery and physical force.[57]

Roman Catholic clergy heavily criticized Farnham and others promoting the Second Reformation. On December 15, 1826, a party of four Roman Catholic bishops arrived at Cavan to assess the effects of Farnham's evangelistic efforts. Their report included the charges of bribery brought against Farnham. In *Doyle's Letter to Lord Farnham*, Doyle personally responded to Farnham's speech at the inaugural meeting of the Cavan Association for Promoting the Reformation, primarily focusing on political elements dealing with Catholic Emancipation. He argued that Catholic Emancipation was all but assured. He also criticized the Established Church, stating that it was motivated by "clamour, bigotry, enthusiasm, and spirit of selfishness."[58] Finally, he argued that this Second Reformation would serve only to strengthen the Roman Catholic Church's hold on Ireland.[59] Criticism of Farnham's efforts even appeared in the House of Commons, where the issue of Catholic Emancipation was debated. In March of 1827, William Conyngham Plunket (1764–1854), the attorney general of Ireland at the

---

55. Maxwell-Barry, *Report of the Speeches*, 5.
56. Maxwell-Barry, *Report of the Speeches*, 23.
57. Maxwell-Barry, *Report of the Speeches*, 21.
58. Doyle, *Doyle's Letter*, 3.
59. Doyle, *Doyle's Letter*, 5.

time, spoke in the House of Commons against Farnham's Reformation in Cavan.[60] Though Plunket deplored Doyle's language against the Established Church in the latter's letter to Farnham, the attorney general was more critical of the manner of Farnham's speech against Roman Catholicism: "Such is the manner in which it is attempted to disseminate the mild doctrines of Christianity, not by calm and sober reasoning, but by a sweeping attack on the alleged idolatry of the Roman Catholics. These are the means adopted for conciliating and converting the Catholics, so that the question of Catholic Emancipation should be lost, as the favourers of this New Reformation stated, in the great and glorious triumph of general Protestantism."[61] Plunket, who had been a political ally of Irish Catholics from the beginning of his political career, sought legal equality and religious harmony between Protestants and Catholics in Ireland. Men like Farnham, whose evangelical zeal Plunket did not share in equal parts, only drove the attorney general to work harder to fulfill Doyle's prediction of the conflict, further solidifying the Catholic position.

One of Plunket's criticisms was the zealous evangelism practiced by Farnham and other Evangelicals, because it disturbed the already fragile peace between Protestant and Catholics. It was primarily against this criticism that led Carson to write a response to Plunket. Carson took issue with Plunket's implication that "there is not unquestioned liberty of conscience for the clergy of the Established Church in extending the spheres of their religion."[62] Three points were particularly relevant to his views on evangelism to Irish Catholics. First, against Plunket's charge that Protestants

60. Plunket's speech was not wholly preserved (Plunket and Plunket, *Lord Plunket*, 2:243), but a portion of it was transcribed and included in Taylor, *Sir Robert Peel*, 1:280–82. Plunket was the youngest of four sons born to a Presbyterian minister of Enniskillen, the town where Plunket was born. He was raised in Dublin from a young age due to his father's new ministry position at the Strand Street Chapel there. Plunket matriculated at Trinity College in Dublin in 1779 and received his BA in 1784, after which he studied law at Lincoln's Inn. He entered the bar at Dublin in 1787 and practiced throughout northwestern Ireland until he was appointed as king's counsel in 1797. This marked his entry into politics. His Catholic sympathies led many accusations of radicalism to be made against him. As a result, his political career was not stable and he practiced law quite successfully during his interims away from political life. His time as the Attorney General of Ireland was actively spent fighting for Catholic Emancipation, which he helped achieve in 1829. He served as lord chancellor of Ireland from 1830 to 1839. The information above was primarily taken from J. A. Hamilton and Peter Gray, "Plunket, William Conyngham," *ODNB* 44:633–35.

61. Plunket's speech quoted in Taylor, *Sir Robert Peel*, 1:281.

62. A. Carson, *Letter to William C. Plunket*, 3; *Works* 2:175.

always focused on "a few invidious examples of individual intemperance" as evidence against the Roman Catholic Church, Carson argued that Plunket was doing the same to Protestants.[63] The difference Carson saw in this comparison was that, unlike the Roman Catholics, the Protestants were not unified. He argued no minister of the Church of Ireland could fairly represent the opinions of that denomination, while Doyle would be a fair representation of the Catholic Church's beliefs. On the other hand, argued Carson, even if an individual Catholic sincerely professed to have evangelical views, this would not change what the Roman Catholic Church believes.[64]

Carson also refuted Doyle's caricatured description of Farnham's evangelistic work as a "crusade."[65] The Tobermore pastor defined "crusade" as an "unjust frantic religious aggression, which aims to effect conversion by violence," and he claimed that only the Roman Catholic Church could properly claim the title of crusaders: "It is suitable to Popery only. From this it sprung, there let it live, with that let it die."[66] In contrast, he believed Farnham's efforts were more accurately described as a "peaceable triumph of truth."[67] Carson's argument made clear that he had read and believed the account given in Farnham's *Report of the Speeches Delivered at the Reformation Meeting Held at Cavan*.[68] It also showed that he viewed violence and coercion as unworthy and ineffective tools for Christian evangelism. The method of evangelism that Carson sanctioned was "persuasion through the exposition of the word of God."[69]

Finally, Carson defended the legitimacy of religious "controversy" or debate. Though written discussions served a purpose, he believed that live debate was able to reach further into the "cabins of the remotest parts of the country."[70] Carson argued that one who sought after truth would not fear these types of discussions. Plunket, who wanted to avoid controversy, believed that theological debates would "endanger the peace of the country," but Carson believed that they had the opposite effect as long as one avoided

---

63. A. Carson, *Letter to William C. Plunket*, 4; Works 2:177.
64. A. Carson, *Letter to William C. Plunket*, 12; Works 2:185.
65. A. Carson, *Letter to William C. Plunket*, 6; Works 2:180.
66. A. Carson, *Letter to William C. Plunket*, 8–9; Works 2:181.
67. A. Carson, *Letter to William C. Plunket*, 4; Works 2:178.
68. Maxwell-Barry, *Report of the Speeches*.
69. A. Carson, *Letter to William C. Plunket*, 8; Works 2:181.
70. A. Carson, *Letter to William C. Plunket*, 13; Works 2:186.

"inflammatory language."⁷¹ This topic brought Carson to his main point, which was that Christians must have the liberty to evangelize, whether it be through religious debates or other methods. At the very least, Carson asked that Protestants be allowed the same freedom of conscience that Roman Catholics were allowed in Ireland.⁷² While Carson wished to avoid persecution, he did make clear that he was willing to be persecuted for exercising liberty of conscience if outlawed. In other words, he would not allow human restrictions to keep him from sharing the gospel with others. It would probably be mistaken to think Carson was advocating civil disobedience, for, as he would later write, "Even when [Christians] are persecuted in his own cause, they are forbidden to fight. They may fly; but they must not resist."⁷³ The importance of sharing the gospel, in this case, and obedience to Christ, in general, are made evident in his willingness to endure persecution if needed.

AN EVANGELISTIC GOD— DIVINE PROVIDENCE IN THE SPREAD OF THE GOSPEL

Carson's understanding of God as a sovereign deity who actively participates in and directs the world is clear from his writings on providence as well as in other works. His view of divine providence in preserving the Scripture and divine sovereignty in the cross-work of Christ have already been examined in previous chapters. Another aspect of divine providence that Carson examined had to do specifically with the spread of the gospel, which is found primarily in his *The God of Providence the God of the Bible* (1835). The present discussion will focus on Carson's thoughts about the providential spread of the gospel in two eras, namely, the spread of the gospel in the early Christian church and, second, the spread of the gospel through the progression of international missions in Carson's own day. As will be seen, Carson believed God to be both desirous for the spread of the gospel and actively involved in achieving that goal, both of which reveal his deep convictions about divine providence.

The first proof that Carson presented as evidence of God's providence in the spread of the gospel focused on how quickly and extensively the gospel advanced during the New Testament period and the early centuries of

71. A. Carson, *Letter to William C. Plunket*, 13; *Works* 2:187.
72. A. Carson, *Letter to William C. Plunket*, 14; *Works* 2:188.
73. A. Carson, *Review of Dr. Brown*, 12.

the Christian church. The evidence he put forward was multifaceted. Carson first looked at how contrary the gospel was to the existing Graeco-Roman and Jewish culture during the apostolic age. In reference to 1 Cor 1:23, he described the gospel as a stumbling block to the Jews and foolishness to the Greeks. In fact, the gospel opposed multiple levels of the Graeco-Roman society: "It had to encounter all the prejudices of ancient systems of religion, strengthened by the interests of the teachers that lived by them, and the trades and manufacturers to which they gave employment."[74] Therefore, the natural resistance to the gospel was not simply in the religious arena, but aspects of the Graeco-Roman economy were also predisposed against the Christian Faith. Despite these hostile conditions, many people from various levels of society were converted by the gospel. This progression of the gospel among people naturally disinclined toward the gospel was, for Carson, well-founded evidence that it came from a divine source.

The tools God used to disseminate the gospel throughout the Roman Empire were also seen as evidence of God's providential work in the spread of saving knowledge. The earliest of these tools was "a number of illiterate fishermen" who were chosen to "sustain the claims of an unpopular truth, against all the power and learning in the world," which included Greek philosophy.[75] The divine purpose in using tools so inadequate by worldly standards was, according to Carson, to show that the propagation of the gospel was dependent upon God's power, and this divine support for the gospel's spread continued through three hundred years of persecution from the Roman Empire.

Carson stressed that God generally avoided using miraculous means after the initial spread of the gospel. For example, God "delivered the apostles, forwarded them on their journey, and gained them friends and protectors" by ordinary means.[76] Carson also detailed how God established three large-scale conditions to assist the gospel's spread beforehand. First, there was the general peace of the period, which was not the norm throughout Roman history. A second characteristic of the age was that there was, for a time, one ruler over the largest unified empire the world had ever seen, which gave the apostles easy access to numerous peoples and ethnicities. Finally, the empire was relatively developed with its vast system of roads, thus easing the gospel's dissemination. The divine purpose, according to Carson,

---

74. A. Carson, *God of Providence* (1839), 13; *Works* 6:23.
75. A. Carson, *God of Providence* (1839), 14; *Works* 6:24.
76. A. Carson, *God of Providence* (1839), 15; *Works* 6:24–25.

was "that it might hear God's message respecting the salvation of sinners through his Son Jesus Christ."[77] In the midst of detailing God's providence in orchestrating events in the spread of the gospel, Carson referred to God's initiative in opening "the hearts of men to receive" the gospel.[78]

The propagation of the gospel through the burgeoning international missions movement of Carson's own day was included as another area in which God's providence was evident. Four of the proofs related to modern missions are germane. First, some people have been given a talent for learning foreign languages. In his sermon given at the jubilee of William Carey's India mission for the Baptist Missionary Society, Carson said, "Jesus confers certain talents on his servants; and that he requires the diligent use of these talents."[79] In this case, Carson wanted to make clear that effort or zeal alone was not sufficient to succeed on the mission field. God providentially gave the requisite skills to the missionary. Therefore, Carson's contention was that those without the God-given talent of learning languages should not seek to be a missionary in a foreign land. The prime example of a talented missionary, according to Carson, was William Carey: "All the qualifications that fit for missionary work were found almost miraculously combined in the late Dr. Carey, the missionary of India."[80]

Another act of providence that affected the missions movement was Britain's naval strength. Carson argued that God chose "the land of Bibles" to be the naval power, so that Bibles could be carried to every port.[81] Britain's influence was not just in the seas, but also within the foreign governments, which presents another of Carson's proofs. He specifically referred to opportunities for missionaries in India that had improved with men such as Daniel Wilson, the bishop of Calcutta, who was "not likely to be less useful than his predecessors in advancing the cause of Christ in the regions of the East."[82] That Carson would be grateful for an Anglican bishop, let alone one with whom he had had grave disagreements with on the issue of biblical inspiration, is evidence of the importance of evangelism for Carson.[83] Carson

---

77. A. Carson, *God of Providence* (1839), 16; *Works* 6:25.
78. A. Carson, *God of Providence* (1839), 18; *Works* 6:26.
79. Acworth and Carson, *Two Sermons*, 47; *Works* 1:426.
80. A. Carson, *God of Providence* (1839), 53; *Works* 6:52.
81. A. Carson, *God of Providence* (1839), 64; *Works* 6:60.
82. A. Carson, *God of Providence* (1839), 67; *Works* 6:62–63.
83. A. Carson, *Theories of Inspiration*; Wilson, *Evidences of Christianity*.

The Gospel-Centered Evangelicalism of Alexander Carson

was most irenic when it came to evangelism, because he saw the gospel as something that transcended denominational barriers.

Carson was convinced that India had been given to Britain for the purpose of giving "the Bible to the hundred millions of idolaters" in that land.[84] Britain's political, economic, and naval strength were given for an evangelistic purpose by an evangelistic God. Carson also believed that this purpose was a responsibility given to Britain, which, if unfulfilled, would be taken away: "If ever she loses India, it will be the forfeiture of her treachery to the God of Providence in withholding the Bible from her Indian subjects."[85] He compared this potentiality to the current events of his own homeland of Ireland: "To what is it owing that Great Britain is now in danger of losing Ireland? To her unfaithfulness in not evangelizing it."[86] Carson expressed frustration over the establishment of the Irish education system in 1831. This system was based on the two principles put forth by Robert Peel (1788–1850) in 1824, then home secretary of Great Britain, which were, "first, to unite as far as possible, without violence to individual feelings, the children of protestants and catholics under one common system of education; and secondly, in so doing, studiously and honestly to discard all idea of making proselytes."[87] The final implementation of these principles was to have combined literary education and separate religious instruction, an outcome that only dissatisfied those who were truly religious.[88] Carson, in particular, believed it damaged the efforts of the London Hibernian Society, which had worked to integrate the Bible with education.[89] As the chief purpose for education, for Carson, was to teach the Bible, it is not completely unexpected to find such a bitter comparison here. Yet, his bitterness was over those whom he believed were without the gospel: "The injury is to the Roman Catholics, who, by this contrivance, are kept from the Bible."[90]

A final proof worth examining is Carson's observation of the growing number of missionary societies. He believed that the increased desire by Christians to evangelize the world was a result of God "putting his engines

---

84. A. Carson, *God of Providence* (1839), 69–70; *Works* 6:64.
85. A. Carson, *God of Providence* (1839), 70; *Works* 6:64.
86. A. Carson, *God of Providence* (1839), 71; *Works* 6:65.
87. Peel, *Speeches*, 1:293.
88. Hempton and Hill, *Evangelical Protestantism in Ulster Society*, 94.
89. A. Carson, *God of Providence* (1839), 71; *Works* 6:65; A. Holmes, *Ulster Presbyterian Belief*, 267.
90. A. Carson, *God of Providence* (1839), 71; *Works* 6:65.

in motion" for the fulfillment of his promise in Matt 24:14.[91] He also cited a renewal of evangelistic efforts towards Roman Catholics in Ireland, which he found particularly inspiring: "Does not Providence declare by this, that the period of the tenure of the man of sin is nearly at its close, and that he must shortly surrender his usurped dominion?"[92] The "man of sin" in Carson's writings is almost always a reference to the Roman Catholic Church. Finally, Carson found great encouragement in the interdenominational efforts of the missionary societies, and he saw them as proof of the "gradual extinction of party spirit."[93] What Carson disliked most about sectarianism in evangelism was that the denominations would put their own sectarian interests before the conversion of sinners. Carson may have been reminded of how evangelistic efforts in the past had been stifled by denominational differences and loyalties during the controversy between the Baptist Missionary Society in Serampore and the British and Foreign Bible Society over the translation of βαπτίζω.[94] Now, "zeal for the Gospel is evidently paramount.... Without respect to the interest of particular denominations, Christians unite their efforts for the salvation of sinner."[95] Carson found great comfort in his belief that God was providentially active in the evangelistic work being carried out by the societies.[95] Clearly, Carson did not believe that evangelism, both at home and abroad, was being worked out by people alone; rather, they worked as they were empowered by a sovereign God interested in fulfilling his evangelistic goals.

THE CHURCH'S MISSION—SERMON AT THE BAPTIST MISSIONARY SOCIETY MEETING

Though Carson's evangelistic work never took him outside of Great Britain, he was still active in promoting international missions, as well as domestic missions. The sermon he preached at the fiftieth anniversary of the Baptist Missionary Society, published as "The Propagation of the Gospel, with Encouragements to the Vigorous Prosecution of the Work: A Sermon in

---

91. A. Carson, *God of Providence* (1839), 72; *Works* 6:66.
92. A. Carson, *God of Providence* (1839), 73; *Works* 6:67.
93. A. Carson, *God of Providence* (1839), 73; *Works* 6:67.
94. A. Carson, *Letter to A. Maclay*; British and Foreign Bible Society, *Proceedings*; Committee of the Baptist Union, *Baptists and Bible Society*.
95. A. Carson, *God of Providence* (1839), 73; *Works* 6:67.
96. Acworth and Carson, *Two Sermons*, 75; *Works* 1:448.

The Gospel-Centered Evangelicalism of Alexander Carson

London" (1842), provides insight into Carson's views on evangelistic endeavors at home and abroad. Particularly noteworthy is Carson's view that all Christians were called to engage in evangelism, at home and abroad, and that God had equipped all his people for the work.

In terms of God's call to missions, he stated, "The gospel being destined to pervade the earth, Christians are the appointed means to convey it to its destination."[97] In one sense, this divine appointment was a continuation of God's providence in using, at least according to human wisdom, a less effective method for the spread of the gospel.[98] More efficient options, Carson theorized, would have been to reveal his truth to people directly, or to deliver the gospel via angels or through the powers of the civil government.[99] Instead, God chose Christians, who were usually "poor and despised" and at odds with the world's rulers, to disseminate the good news. This, Carson argued, was clearly an example of God's power.[100] Yet, despite being a display of God's power in propagating his gospel, Carson emphasized that God was using "the zeal and devotedness of his disciples."[101] The Tobermore pastor was convinced that this was no call to wait passively for a fulfillment of God's promises.

Carson also asserted, "The duty of exertion to propagate the gospel extends to all Christians without exception."[102] He did not limit the church's mission to teaching the gospel in foreign lands or to large assemblies at home. While most Christians could not speak effectively in large gatherings, Carson was confident that "there is not one of them who may not tell his neighbour the way to heaven."[103] Every Christian was to be directly involved with the spread of the gospel. Carson did not allow anyone to be confined simply to the task of funding missionaries, though giving financially was necessary, or simply to the task of praying for missionaries and the unsaved, though prayer was also vital. In one sense, special training was not required to spread the gospel, for, Carson asserted, if a person knew the gospel well enough to be saved by it, he or she knew it well enough to share it with others so they might be saved. Included in this exhortation

---

97. Acworth and Carson, *Two Sermons*, 47; *Works* 1:427.
98. A. Carson, *God of Providence* (1839), 14; *Works* 6:23–24.
99. Acworth and Carson, *Two Sermons*, 48–50; *Works* 1:428–29.
100. Acworth and Carson, *Two Sermons*, 48; *Works* 1:427.
101. Acworth and Carson, *Two Sermons*, 51; *Works* 1:430.
102. Acworth and Carson, *Two Sermons*, 53; *Works* 1:431.
103. Acworth and Carson, *Two Sermons*, 53; *Works* 1:431.

was his critique of those who restricted preaching the gospel to an office or license. Carson's sentiments on this were evident from the early years of his ministry while a part of the General Synod of Ulster, which, with other Presbyterian synods, was "hostile to itinerant evangelical preachers.... The Synod of Ulster passed resolutions in 1789 and again in 1804 forbidding ministers to allow unapproved preachers into their pulpits."[104] 1804 was also the year Carson decided to leave Presbyterianism, partly for the reason above.[105] This critique also extended to High Church attitudes towards apostolic succession in the Anglican Church: "And whatever may be the mode of conveying office, the preaching of the gospel, either publicly or privately, is not confined to office. Every Christian has a right to preach the gospel."[106] Carson even criticized dissenting churches for possibly being influenced by "Puseyism" and tying "preaching inseparably with office."[107] It needs bearing in mind again, as previously discussed in Carson's critique of Roman Catholic restrictions, that Carson did not at all despise the pastoral office.[108]

Carson's exhortation for all Christians to participate in spreading the gospel applied to when Christians were together or alone. Carson encouraged believers to motivate one another to evangelism, and he noted that some were especially gifted in this ability.[109] Carson's own abilities in this regard were manifest: "[Carson] called every member to 'build the wall before his own house.' He had them every Sabbath evening scattered over the country, preaching, exhorting, and praying."[110] This example also gives credibility to his conviction that "a church, in its meetings for its own edification, ought to have constantly in view the conversion of sinners."[111] Carson was described as having "never dismissed a congregation without having presented as much of Christ as would save, or condemn."[112] An article in *The Primitive Church Magazine* (1844) thus stated: "His preaching was characterized by great originality. He possessed the secret of making

---

104. A. Holmes, *Ulster Presbyterian Belief*, 153.

105. Moore, *Life of Alexander Carson*, 12–17.

106. A. Carson, *Reasons for Separating* (1806), 107; Acworth and Carson, *Two Sermons*, 55; *Works* 1:432.

107. Acworth and Carson, *Two Sermons*, 56; *Works* 1:433–34.

108. A. Carson, *Right and Duty*, 19; *Works* 2:23.

109. Acworth and Carson, *Two Sermons*, 65–66; *Works* 1:440–41.

110. Moore, *Life of Alexander Carson*, 144.

111. Acworth and Carson, *Two Sermons*, 63; *Works* 1:438–39.

112. Moore, *Life of Alexander Carson*, 71.

The Gospel-Centered Evangelicalism of Alexander Carson

every subject interesting. There was a great variety in all his addresses. His chief glory, however, was the gospel theme. Here he shone out in full luster—here all the powers of his mighty mind found ample scope—his manly eloquence was at home. His heart was riveted to the Cross."[113] He even viewed the church infrastructure through the filter of evangelism. The Tobermore church building, which was built in 1814, had galleries installed at each end of the building. When someone suggested the removal of the galleries, Carson apparently replied, "What! Remove or tear down those galleries, which enable so many perishing sinners to hear the gospel every Sabbath! No, never. I got the money which erected them from Mr. Haldane, so I will never consent to have them taken away."[114] While this story makes clear Carson's bond with the Haldanes, more importantly, it shows that Carson's desire for people to hear the gospel was more important than making the building more comfortable. For Carson, there was never a time when the church did not have to be concerned with sharing the gospel to unbelievers.

Beyond the boundaries of the local church, Carson's involvement in evangelism took various forms. His direct efforts for promoting the work of the Bible societies have already been discussed. Also, his work to equip members for evangelism was not simply linked to spreading the gospel in their communities. As previously mentioned, Carson's church members were also involved in the Dublin City Mission with David Nasmith. Looking at international endeavors, Carson noted in his sermon that the Baptist Missionary Society itself had served as encouragement for the founding of numerous other missionary societies.[115] As John Wolffe has noted:

> The publication of [William] Carey's *Enquiry* [*into the Obligations of Christians, to use Means for the Conversion of the Heathen*] was directly related to the formation of the Baptist Missionary Society in his own denomination in 1792, setting a trend that was followed by the London Missionary Society (1795), which was officially interdenominational but in practice became Congregational, the Edinburgh Missionary Society (1796, renamed the Scottish Missionary Society in 1819), the Glasgow Missionary Society (1796) and the Society for Missions to Africa and the East

---

113. Quoted in Moore, *Life of Alexander Carson*, 69.

114. Moore, *Life of Alexander Carson*, 21. See also Day and McWilliams, *Parishes of County Londonderry*, 66; Bleakly, "Fair Sheets for Memoir" (Public Records Office of Northern Ireland).

115. Acworth and Carson, *Two Sermons*, 78.

(1799), which became known as the Church Missionary Society (CMS) in 1812.[116]

Though Carson himself never served as a missionary in a foreign country, this did not keep him from having some influence outside of Ireland and Great Britain. A number of his works were republished in the United States, and he even wrote an evangelistic letter to the exiled Napoleon Bonaparte (1769–1821) in 1814.[117] Distance did not diminish his desire to share the gospel with others, and it seems that he did attempt to share the gospel when the opportunity presented itself.

While corporate missionary efforts were important, Carson refused to countenance Christians who were isolated and alone to shirk their evangelistic calling. Individual Christians should not feel useless in their efforts or give up in the face of indomitable persecution.[118] In one sense, as the pastor of his church, Carson stood alone. Therefore, his encouragement for Christians not to fear in their evangelistic efforts, even when alone, was not without empathy. His efforts towards Irish Catholics, both evangelistic and apologetic, were not always appreciated. At one point, some of the local Catholics were so furious at Carson that they attempted to burn down his home with the aim of murdering him and his family. Though this plot failed, concern for his safety led the local government to post a night watch at the Carson home. Moore even recounted an incident in which the guards were tardy in arriving one night, which almost led to a potentially deadly confrontation between Carson and a group of irate Catholics. These physical threats from local Catholics also extended to his church at times. Moore described one instance in which the deacons asked Carson to forgo preaching to avoid danger. In his typical dramatic fashion, Moore recounted Carson's reply, "'What!' exclaimed the intrepid soldier of the Cross, 'ask me through the fear of man to refrain from preaching the gospel! Entreat me not, I beseech you, for I would preach Christ though the wicked of all worlds were marshaled in hostile array before me.'"[119]

Carson also spoke on the various ways God equipped the church for the missions endeavor. The first equipping was a divinely-implanted one that determined, in a way, what roles the Christian could fill: "The duty of assisting in spreading the gospel must be viewed with reference to the

116. Wolffe, *Expansion of Evangelicalism*, 166.
117. *Works* 1.
118. Acworth and Carson, *Two Sermons*, 67–68; *Works* 1:441–42.
119. Moore, *Life of Alexander Carson*, 43–46.

different talents conferred on the people of God."[120] The talent of learning foreign languages, which was discussed previously, is an example of what Carson was referring to. Carson did not limit his classification here but included anything that a person has been given, including financial wealth. Carson encouraged his listeners, especially the wealthy, to "curtail other expenses, and deny themselves rather than the cause of Christ."[121] He also expressed admiration for how freely the Baptists had given for the spread of the gospel. Not only was the Baptist Missionary Society a model for others, but also the liberal giving of the Baptists was an example for others to imitate.[122]

Yet, Carson did not limit evangelistic service to the extraordinarily talented or the wealthy: "Every man, however weak and poor, may do great things, if he is thoroughly devoted to the Lord."[123] He believed that God had given every Christian a talent that could be used for God's glory. More important than the talent was the Christian's devotion to God. This did not mean that devotion was sufficient for any type of work, but Carson believed that God provided evangelistic opportunities for every Christian: "There is work which [the Christian] cannot do, but his Lord has provided work which he may do, and do greatly to the glory of God."[124]

CONCLUSION

The centrality of the gospel in Carson's theology was most apparent in the types of evangelistic endeavors on which he focused. The conviction that the Bible was God's revelation in which the main focus was the cross of Christ was made apparent by Carson's desire to put the Bible in the hands of people all over Ireland, along with giving them the ability to read the Bible. Carson, in his own words, showed how wide the gap was between the value of the gospel and the value of education. His efforts in fighting for the freedom to give Bibles to Catholics and even for the right to evangelize them show that Carson did not limit himself to one type of audience. Placing himself somewhat apart from the political aspects of Catholic Emancipation, he focused on the importance of religious freedom, which

---

120. Acworth and Carson, *Two Sermons*, 58; *Works* 1:435.
121. Acworth and Carson, *Two Sermons*, 59; *Works* 1:435.
122. Acworth and Carson, *Two Sermons*, 61; *Works* 1:437.
123. Acworth and Carson, *Two Sermons*, 81; *Works* 1:452.
124. Acworth and Carson, *Two Sermons*, 82; *Works* 1:453.

included the freedom to evangelize. Carson's theology of missions focused on God's role and the church's role, showing that his Calvinism did not absolve Christians of their active duty in spreading the gospel, but rather motivated them to it.

6

Conclusion

ALEXANDER CARSON'S VARIEGATED EVANGELICAL efforts reflect the centrality of the gospel in his theology. His enthusiasm for the spread of the gospel, through whatever means were available, was directly related to his understanding of the significance of the gospel for all people. It is clear that Carson believed the gospel to have the power to transform people's lives temporally and eternally. The primacy of the cross in Carson's understanding of the gospel is also evident, especially in Carson's defense of the divine person of Christ and the sufficiency of his atoning work on the cross. Finally, he believed that only a Bible that was completely inspired in all of its words could produce a confidence in the gospel that gave up all for Jesus.

Chapter two explored the response to David W. Bebbington's claim that Robert Haldane led the evangelical shift towards the plenary verbal inspiration of Scripture. Kenneth Stewart claimed that Haldane was simply one in a line of theologians who believed the Bible to be inspired in every word and not just in its thoughts.[1] Stewart pointed to Louis Gaussen's *Théopneustie; ou Pleine inspiration des Saintes Écritures* (1840) as an advancement of Haldane's own views.[2] One distinctive Stewart noted about Gaussen's work was the Frenchman's practice of naming those whose ideas he repudiated, such as the Englishmen John Dick, Daniel Wilson, and John

---

1. Bebbington, *Evangelicalism in Modern Britain*, 86–87; Stewart, "Evangelical Doctrine of Scripture," 410.

2. An unsigned English translation of Gaussen's work, *Theopneustia: The Plenary Inspiration of the Holy Scriptures*, was published the following year.

Conclusion

Pye Smith.[3] While Stewart's description implied that Gaussen's practice was novel, Carson had the audacity to censure the views of those same Englishmen on the topic of biblical inspiration a decade before Gaussen in *The Theories of Inspiration of the Rev. Daniel Wilson, Rev. Dr. Pye Smith, and the Rev. Dr. Dick, Proved to Be Erroneous* (1830). Stewart's omission of Carson's contribution that came before Gaussen's work is not surprising given the general disregard for Carson in contemporary church history. While Carson's ardent defense of plenary verbal inspiration might not have had the lasting effect that Gaussen's did, his work made an undeniable impact on his contemporaries. For example, Thomas Chalmers (1780–1847), the Scottish theologian and professor of theology at the University of Edinburgh, referred positively to Carson's views on the divine authorship of Scripture in his *On the Miraculous and Internal Evidences of the Christian Revelation, and the Authority of Its Records* (1836).[4] Presbyterians in Ireland also "heartily" agreed with the Baptist minister's views on biblical inspiration.[5]

Carson's zeal for the Scriptures was primarily seen through his defense of the plenary inspiration of Scripture, but it was also evidenced in his principles for proper Bible translation and in how he believed the Bible was divinely preserved throughout history. Concerning Bible translation, the two primary examples discussed dealt with his general principles in the controversy over Ali Bey's Turkish New Testament and the controversy in the British and Foreign Bible Society over the translation of $\beta\alpha\pi\tau i\zeta\omega$. One of Carson's principles of translation that surfaced in these controversies was his commitment to the proper translation of every word in the original Scriptures, which matched his conviction that every word of Scripture was divinely inspired. Therefore, the translator's duty was to translate the existing text faithfully rather than judge the text or infuse his or her own ideas.[6] Carson was also an advocate for literal translations, because to translate the mere sense of Scripture failed to take verbal inspiration into account. Yet, he was also sensitive to the challenges of translating to another language and spoke against rigid literalism that resulted in losing the sense of the

---

3. Stewart, "Evangelical Doctrine of Scripture," 411.

4. Chalmers, *Miraculous and Internal Evidences*, 4:377; *Orthodox Presbyterian*, "Dr. Chalmers," 375.

5. *Orthodox Presbyterian*, Unsigned review of *Theories*.

6. A. Carson, *Incompetency of Rev. Professor Lee*, 5.

biblical text.⁷ Ultimately, Carson believed Scripture to be a divine message that was both divinely delivered and divinely preserved for humanity.

The third chapter explored Carson's views of the cross, or the nature of Christ's atoning work, as the central theme of divine revelation. His theology of the cross was shown to be based on his understanding of humanity's sinful condition, in which he upheld the standard evangelical views of universal sin, total depravity, and the eternal punishment of hell that sin deserved. Carson's works also reflected traditional evangelical views on the substitutionary atonement, with the harmonization of divine justice and mercy being a major theme. Carson's distinction between contradiction and incomprehension was especially evident in his discussion on how the atonement perfectly preserved both God's justice and mercy. Carson's Calvinism was also evident in how he believed the atonement revealed God's sovereignty, in how it was specifically applied to the elect. Finally, Carson's understanding of Christ's work as a finished work was examined within the context of his anti-Catholic works, specifically against the Roman Catholic Eucharist. While Bebbington might have characterized Carson's view of plenary verbal inspiration as part of a new movement within Evangelicalism, the Tobermore minister's understanding of the cross was clearly in line with the common position held by earlier Evangelicals.⁸ Carson's own words are an excellent example of Bebbington's assertion that the cross was the focal point of any evangelical system: "The atonement by his death is the centre of revelation, in which all its numerous lines meet."⁹ The various aspects of Carson's views on the atonement mentioned above are evidence of his inclusion within the mainstream of evangelical thought.

Carson believed that the way in which Christ's atonement was applied to a person's life was through faith in the gospel and not by works. The fourth chapter explored a number of aspects dealing with how the Christian was converted, focusing primarily on Carson's definition of faith, but also included his views on the role of works and the conversion experience. While his conviction that justification was only through faith and not by works aligned with mainstream Evangelicalism, his definition of faith was characteristically Sandemanian. Though not a Sandemanian, his belief that faith was an unsentimental belief in the gospel and his personal ties with the Scotch Baptists placed him, at least in this area, within a more

7 A. Carson, *Theories of Inspiration*, 139; *Works* 3:198.
8. Bebbington, *Evangelicalism in Modern Britain*, 14.
9. *Works* 1:284. Bebbington, *Evangelicalism in Modern Britain*, 15.

Conclusion

peripheral stream of evangelical thought. Yet, it was also shown that despite sharing this view of saving faith and church order with Scotch Baptists, he was very independent in his thought and not to be considered as a part of the Scotch Baptists. Unlike Archibald McLean, let alone the Sandemanians, Carson's convictions in this area did not seem to result in an inability to cooperate with other Evangelicals, especially in evangelistic endeavors. As his particular views on church order were discussed, it is also appropriate to raise the issue of baptism and the extent of its impact on Carson's Evangelicalism.

Carson was a biblicist, and he placed himself under the authority of Scripture. This submission to divine revelation was not confined to primary doctrines, but it also applied to biblical doctrines not essential to one's salvation. One of the clearest examples of this is seen in his work on the ordinance of baptism. While he did not wish to promote sectarianism, neither did Carson wish to sacrifice what he believed to be the biblical understanding of baptism at the altar of interdenominational relations: "While I gladly admit, that many who differ from me with respect to baptism, are among the excellent of the earth, I cannot, out of compliment to them, abstain from vindicating this ordinance of Christ. This would show greater deference to man than to God."[10] Though not essential to one's salvation, Carson did not believe the biblical testimony delegated baptism to "a thing of small moment."[11] That "nothing that Christ has appointed, can be innocently neglected" was adequate grounds for writing on the topic.[12] This desire to be faithful to all Scripture was reflected in his support for the proper translation of βαπτίζω. Also, the importance of the ordinance to Carson is further supported by the considerable effort evidenced in the second addition of his work, which was made more accessible to a popular readership and included numerous responses to his critics.[13]

Yet, the import Carson placed on this ordinance did not contradict the subordinate position he gave it in comparison to the gospel. This subordinate position was evidenced in both his works and church order. John Young pointed out that Carson was "ever more ready to hold fellowship even with those Pedo-baptists, who otherwise taught a pure gospel, than with such Baptists as he might conceive have departed from genuine

---

10. A. Carson, *Baptism in Its Mode* (1844), v.
11. A. Carson, *Baptism in Its Mode* (1844), vi.
12. A. Carson, *Baptism in Its Mode* (1844), vi.
13. See *Baptist Magazine*, Unsigned review of *Baptism*.

orthodoxy."[14] While Young attributed Carson's practice of not requiring baptism for church membership to liberality and kindness, George Moore denied "liberality of sentiment" as a motivation for Carson's practice.[15] The Tobermore pastor's rationale was theological rather than sentimental: "My recognition of all Christians I ground on authority of Jesus. . . . To disown those whom Christ acknowledges, is antichristian disobedience to Christ."[16] He did not believe that agreement over baptism could act as a foundation for unity between Christians. Only agreement on the gospel of Christ could unite people.[17]

Joshua Thompson placed Carson's views in the context of the communion controversy that has periodically arisen in Baptist denominations. While Carson's views on the role of baptism in the local church, specifically in the relationship between baptism and communion, were never clearly expressed in his lifetime, the examples given above, in conjunction with the evidence of how he admitted members into his Tobermore congregation, sufficiently show that Carson's devotion to believer's baptism by immersion did not play a role in how he viewed church membership. Thompson pointed out that Carson's Tobermore church was "both 'open' as to membership and communion," which was against the grain of how it had been practiced in Irish Baptist churches in the seventeenth and eighteenth centuries.[18] Proper baptism was obedience to Christ, but it did not play an effective role in one's justification or, therefore, in one's admittance into the local body of Christ.[19]

The last chapter showed that the centrality of the gospel in Carson's theology was most apparent in the types of evangelistic endeavors on which he focused. While the activism of Evangelicals took many forms, Carson's own efforts were almost exclusively evangelistic.[20] Carson's activism was examined in four categories. The first looked at Carson's efforts focusing on the Scripture as an effective tool for evangelism, primarily through

14. Young, "Memoir of Alexander Carson," xxxvii.
15. Moore, *Life of Alexander Carson*, 84–85. A. Carson, *Baptism in Its Mode* (1844), v.
16. A. Carson, *Baptism in Its Mode* (1844), v.
17. A. Carson, *Baptism in Its Mode* (1844), xi–xii.
18. Thompson, "Communion Controversy," 32–33.
19. Interestingly, Carson's son Robert Haldane Carson led the Tobermore church to have close membership, allowing only those baptized as believers to become members, though he did not seem to require membership for participation in the Lord's Supper. Thompson, "Communion Controversy," 33–34.
20. Bebbington, *Evangelicalism in Modern Britain*, 12.

Conclusion

Sabbath schools and Bible societies. His efforts in promoting Bible reading stemmed from the conviction that the Bible was God's revelation in which the main focus was the cross of Christ. Education per se had no eternal value, and the eternal was what Carson was most concerned about. The second category examined Carson's evangelistic efforts within the political sphere, which resulted from his efforts in fighting for the freedom to give Bibles to Catholics and for the religious freedom to evangelize the Catholics in Ireland. The third category was an examination of God's providence in the evangelistic efforts of Christians in Carson's thought. The final category showed that Carson believed evangelism to be the duty of all Christians, as individuals, churches, and societies. Carson's views were examined through his sermon given at the Baptist Missionary Society's jubilee and through how he carried out these views in his church and his own personal evangelistic efforts. On the whole, Carson's evangelistic efforts incorporated numerous methods and avenues.

Three conclusions flow out of this study. First, Carson's theological and ministerial convictions were rooted in his utter commitment to the plenary verbal inspiration of Scripture. The Bible was not simply a book containing divine revelation as his more liberally minded opponents believed, but the Bible itself was the very word of God. Second, it was on the firm foundation of this fully-inspired source of divine revelation that Carson built all the aspects of his theology with great confidence, without worrying about how he would be perceived by either Christians or non-Christians around him. This was evident in his explanations for departing from the General Synod of Ulster and his later departure from Congregationalism. This unshakable zeal was clearly apparent in his resolute defense of the gospel, whether dealing with the necessity of substitutionary atonement, the tension between divine justice and mercy, the exclusive role given to faith for justifying sinners, or the absolute duty of all Christians for being active in the spread of the gospel. Third, Carson's views on the gospel clearly place him within the wider stream of nineteenth-century Evangelicalism. If one accepts Bebbington's quadrilateral as standard characteristics of nineteenth-century Evangelicalism, Carson is an excellent example. While Carson clearly had other major theological convictions outside of these four characteristics, such as church order and baptism, these were clearly subordinate to the gospel, a conviction he made quite clear. All the theological controversies he was involved in over church order and baptism, which were outside the focus of this study, and over the Bible, which was included in this study, were not central enough for him to condemn those who truly believed in the gospel. Not only does Bebbington's quadrilateral serve as an effective framework for engaging with Carson's core theological views, but Carson serves as proof that Bebbington's quadrilateral does, in fact, include the primary theological convictions of nineteenth-century Evangelicals. While Bebbington did make a reference to Carson's involvement in the evangelical controversy over the inspiration of Scripture, the former's groundbreaking work purposely did not include a detailed study of Evangelicalism in Ireland.[21] Therefore, there is much significance in showing that Bebbington's characterization of Evangelicalism accurately describes an important, if somewhat forgotten, figure in Irish church history such as Alexander Carson.[22]

---

21. Bebbington, *Evangelicalism in Modern Britain*, ix–x.

22. While these conclusions are not a plea to place Carson on the same level as the most influential figures in nineteenth-century Evangelicalism, it can be argued that Carson clearly deserves more attention than he has received, not simply as a Baptist but as an Evangelical. Just as he was highly regarded by and helpful to Evangelicals of other denominations of his day, attention given to the more interdenominational aspects of his theology may be of interest to church historians today, including those specializing in areas other than Baptist history. Another area of further study should focus on Carson's significance in Ireland. Even in contemporary studies on Irish Evangelicalism, Carson has received a mere mention or been completely ignored. For example, Hempton and Hill, *Evangelical Protestantism in Ulster Society*; Yates, *Religious Condition of Ireland*. While this is evidence that even within nineteenth-century Evangelicalism denominationalism was still firmly in place, it also shows that certain strains of Irish Evangelicalism have been virtually ignored in terms of in-depth studies.

Bibliography

PRIMARY SOURCES

Books

Acworth, James, and Alexander Carson. *Two Sermons Preached in London, October 11th and 12, 1842, Before the Baptist Missionary Society: At a Special General Meeting, Held to Celebrate the Completion of Its Fiftieth Year*. London: Baptist Missionary Society, 1842.

Adams, Charles Kendall, et al., eds. *Johnson's Universal Cyclopaedia*. 8 vols. New York: Johnson, 1895.

Addison, W. Innes, ed. *The Matriculation Albums of the University of Glasgow from 1728–1858*. Glasgow: MacLehose & Sons, 1913.

———. *A Roll of the Graduates of the University of Glasgow from 31st December, 1727 to 31st December, 1897*. Glasgow: MacLehose & Sons, 1898.

Aird, Andrew. *Glimpses of Old Glasgow*. Glasgow: Aird & Coghill, 1894.

Alexander, William L. *Memoirs of the Life and Writings of Ralph Wardlaw*. Edinburgh: Black, 1856.

Bagot, Daniel, and John Scott Porter. *Authentic Report of the Discussion on the Unitarian Controversy Between the Rev. John Scott Porter and the Rev. Daniel Bagot, M.A.: Held on April 14, 1834, and Three Following Days; in the Meeting-House of the First Presbyterian Congregation, Belfast*. Belfast: Simms & McIntyre, 1834.

Bateman, Josiah. *The Life of the Right Rev. Daniel Wilson, D.D.: Late Lord Bishop of Calcutta and Metropolitan of India*. 2 vols. London: Murray, 1860.

Beecher, Edward. *Baptism: The Import of Baptizo*. London: Gladding, 1840.

———. *Baptism, with Reference to Its Import and Modes*. New York: Wiley, 1849.

Bickersteth, Edward. *A Treatise on Baptism: Designed as a Help to the Due Improvement of that Holy Sacrament, as Administered in the Church of England*. London: Seeley and Burnside, 1840.

British and Foreign Bible Society. *Proceedings of the Committee of the British & Foreign Bible Society, Relative to a Memorial Presented to Them by the Committee of the Baptist Union: To Which Is Prefixed a Brief Statement of Facts in Explanation*. London: Clay, 1840.

———. *The Twenty-Second Report of the British and Foreign Bible Society: With an Appendix, and a List of Subscribers and Benefactors*. London: Moyes, 1826.

Bibliography

Brown, John. *The Law of Christ Respecting Civil Obedience, Especially in the Payment of Tribute, to Which Are Added Two Addresses on the Voluntary Church Controversy.* London: Ball, 1839.

———. *The Law of Christ Respecting Civil Obedience, Especially in the Payment of Tribute: With an Appendix of Notes and Documents.* Edinburgh: Patterson, 1837.

———. *Vindication of the Presbyterian Form of Church-Government, as Professed in the Standards of the Church of Scotland: In Reply to the Animadversions of Messrs. Innes, Ewing, Ballentine, Glass, &c. Among the Modern, and of Goodwin, Lockier, Cotton, &c. Among the Ancient Independents; In a Series of Letters, Addressed to Mr. Innes; With an Appendix, Containing Remarks on Mr. Haldane's View of Social Worship.* Edinburgh: Inglis, 1805.

Brown, William. *Baptism by Pouring and Sprinkling: Together with Infant Baptism, Vindicated.* Belfast: M'comb, 1833.

———. *A Refutation of Mr. Carson's Review of the Rev. Mr. Brown's Work on Baptism.* Belfast: Wilson, 1834.

———. *Remarks on Mr. Carson's Defence of His Review.* Belfast: M'Comb, 1835.

Browne, George. *The History of the British and Foreign Bible Society, from its Institution in 1804, to the Close of its Jubilee in 1854.* 2 vols. London: Bagster and Sons, 1859.

Campbell, John. *Memoirs of David Nasmith: His Labors and Travels in Great Britain, France, the United States, and Canada.* London: Snow, 1844.

Carey, William. *An Enquiry into the Obligations of Christians, to Use Means for the Conversion of the Heathens: In which the Religious State of the Different Nations of the World, the Success of Former Undertakings, and the Practicability of Further Undertakings, Are Considered.* Leicester: Ireland, 1792.

Carlow Bible Society, and P. Skelton. *The Speak-Out, of the Roman Catholic Priesthood of Ireland; or, Popery Unchangeably the Same, in Its Persecuting Spirit, and in Its Determined Hostility to the Circulation of the Scriptures, in a Report of the Proceedings at the Anniversary of the Carlow Bible Society, Held 18th and 19th November 1824, with a Preface Containing the Marks of Corruption in the Church of Rome.* London: Westley, 1824.

Carmichael, Andrew. *Disquisitions on the Theology and Metaphysics of Scripture: With Strictures on Various Current Opinions in Divinity and Philosophy, Connected with Their Subjects.* 2 vols. London: Mardon, 1840.

Carson, Alexander. *An Address to the Children of the Tubbermore Sabbath School, No. 2.* Coleraine, UK: Hart, ca. 1837.

———. *An Answer to Mr. Ewing's Attempt Towards a Statement of the Doctrine of Scripture on Some Disputed Points Respecting the Constitution, Government, Worship, and Discipline of the Church of Christ.* Edinburgh: Ritchie, 1809.

———. *Answer to the Article in the* Edinburgh Presbyterian Review: *On Mr Carson's Refutation of Mr Ewing and Dr Wardlaw on Baptism; Shewing the Incompetency and Ignorance of the Reviewer.* Edinburgh: Whyte and Co., 1832.

———. *Answer to the Letter of the Rev. Professor Lee, in Reply to the Proof and Illustration of His Incompetency: For Translating, or Correcting Translations of the Holy Scriptures.* Edinburgh: Whyte & Co., 1830.

———. *Baptism in Its Mode and Subjects.* Philadelphia: American Baptist Publications Society, 1850.

———. *Baptism in Its Mode and Subjects Considered.* Edinburgh: Waugh & Innes, 1831.

Bibliography

———. *Baptism in Its Mode and Subjects Considered*. 2nd ed. London: Houlston & Stoneman, 1844.

———. *Baptism Not Purification: In Reply to President Beecher*. London: Simpkin and Marshall, 1841.

———. *Defence of the Review of Mr. Brown's Work on Baptism*. Edinburgh: Collie, 1835.

———. *The Doctrine of Transubstantiation: Subversive of the Foundations of Human Belief; Therefore Incapable of Being Proved by Any Evidence, or of Being Believed by Men Under the Influence of Common Sense*. Dublin: Tims, 1825.

———. *The Doctrine of Transubstantiation: Subversive of the Foundations of Human Belief; Therefore Incapable of Being Proved by Any Evidence, or of Being Believed by Men Under the Influence of Common Sense*. 3rd ed. Dublin: Carson, 1837.

———. *Examination of the Principles of Biblical Interpretation of Ernesti, Ammon, Stuart, and Other Philologists*. Edinburgh: Whyte, 1836.

———. *Existing Differences of Sentiment and Practice Among Christians, Injurious and Indefensible*. London: Dyer, 1842.

———. *The God of Providence the God of the Bible: or, The Truth of the Gospel Proved from the Peculiarities of Its Progress*. Edinburgh: Waugh & Innes, 1835.

———. *The God of Providence the God of the Bible: or, The Truth of the Gospel Proved from the Peculiarities of Its Progress*. Repr., Dublin: Carson, 1839.

———. *Grace Reigning Through Righteousness: Romans v. 21*. London: Dyer, 1842.

———. *History of Providence, as Manifested in Scripture; or Facts from Scripture Illustrative of the Government of God, with a Defence of the Doctrine of Providence and an Examination of the Philosophy of Dr. Thomas Brown on That Subject*. Edinburgh: Whyte & Co., 1840.

———. *History of Providence as Unfolded in the Book of Esther*. Edinburgh: Whyte & Co., 1833.

———. *History of Providence as Unfolded in the Book of Esther*. 3rd ed. Dublin: Carson, 1835.

———. *Incompetency of Dr. Henderson as an Umpire on the Philology of the Word Baptism: Proved from the Unsoundness and Extravagance of the Principles of Interpretation Implied in His Letter to Mr. Brandram, with Reference to That Question*. London: Simpkin and Marshall and Wightman, 1841.

———. *The Incompetency of the Rev. Professor Lee, of Cambridge, for Translating, or Correcting Translations of the Holy Scriptures, Proved and Illustrated, in a Criticism on His "Remarks on Dr. Henderson's Appeal to the Bible Society."* Edinburgh: Whyte, 1829.

———. *The Inspiration of the Scriptures: A Review of the Theories of the Rev. Daniel Wilson, Rev. Dr. Pye Smith, and the Rev. Dr. Dick, and Other Treatises*. New York: Fletcher, 1853.

———. *The Knowledge of Jesus the Most Excellent of the Sciences*. London: Hamilton, Adams & Co., 1839.

———. *A Letter to Mr. Greville Ewing: Occasioned by His "Attempt," &c*. Edinburgh: Ritchie, 1809.

———. *A Letter to the Emperor Napoleon on the Most Important of All Subjects*. London: Yapping and Hawkins, 1872.

———. *A Letter to the Rev. A. Maclay, M. A., of New York, on the Reply of the British and Foreign Bible Society to the Memorial of the Committee of the Baptist Union*. London: Wightman, 1840.

Bibliography

———. *A Letter to the Right Hon. William C. Plunket, His Majesty's Attorney General for Ireland: Containing Strictures on Some Parts of His Late Speech on the Roman Catholic Question in the House of Commons Touching the Cavan Reform*. Dublin: Curry, 1827.

———. *Letters to the Author of an Article in the* Edinburgh Review *on "Evangelical Preaching" in Which the Principles of That Writer Are Shown to Be in Direct Contradiction to the Word of God*. Edinburgh: Fraser & Co., 1837.

———. *Reasons for Separating from the General Synod of Ulster*. Belfast: Simms, 1805.

———. *Reasons for Separating from the General Synod of Ulster*. 2nd ed. Edinburgh: Ritchie, 1806.

———. *Refutation of Dr. Henderson's Doctrine in His Late Work on Divine Inspiration with a Critical Discussion on 2 Timothy iii. 16*. London: Hamilton, Adams, & Co., 1837.

———. *Refutation of the Review in the* Christian Guardian *for January 1832, of Mr. Carson's Work on the Inspiration of the Scriptures*. Edinburgh: Whyte and Co., 1832.

———. *Remarks on a Late Pastoral Address: From the Ministers of the Synod of Ulster, to the People Under Their Care*. Belfast: Simms, 1806.

———. *A Reply to Dr. Drummond's Essay on the Doctrine of the Trinity: In a Letter to the Author*. 2nd ed. Dublin: Carson and Knox, 1831.

———. *A Reply to Mr. Brown's Vindication of the Presbyterian Form of Church-Government: In Which the Order of the Apostolical Churches Is Defended; In a Series of Letters to the Author*. Edinburgh: Ritchie, 1807.

———. *Reply to Remarks on Mr. Carson's Treatise on Baptism, Contained in a Note in Mr. Bickersteth's Late Work on the Same Subject*. Ipswich, Eng.: Burton, 1840.

———. *Review of Dr. Brown "On the Law of Christ Respecting Civil Obedience, Especially in the Payment of Tribute: With an Appendix," Relative to Grammatical Accuracy, as It Bears on the Question of the Scriptures, in Reply to the Rev. M. Menzies, the Translator of Tholuck on the Epistle to the Romans*. London: Hamilton, Adams, & Co., 1838.

———. *Review of the Discussion on the Unitarian Controversy: Between the Rev. Scott Porter and the Rev. D. Bagot, M.A., Held in Belfast, on April 14th, 1834, and Three Following Days*. Belfast: Wilson, 1834.

———. *Review of the Rev. Dr. J. Pye Smith's Defence of Dr. Haffner's Preface to the Bible and of His Denial of the Divine Authority of Part of the Canon, and of the Full Inspiration of the Holy Scriptures*. Edinburgh: Lindsay & Co., 1827.

———. *Review of the Rev. Mr. Brown's Work on Baptism*. Edinburgh: Collie, 1834.

———. *The Right and Duty of All Men to Read the Scriptures: Being the Substance of a Speech Intended to Have Been Delivered at the Meeting of the Carlow Bible Society; Containing a Refutation of Several Parts of a Late Pamphlet by J. K. L*. Dublin: Tims, 1824.

———. *Strictures on the Letter of J. K. L. Entitled a Vindication of the Religious and Civil Principles of the Irish Catholics: Addressed to His Excellency the Marquis Wellesley, K. G. Lord Lieutenant General, and General Governor of Ireland, &c. &c. in a Letter to the Same Nobleman*. Dublin: Tims, 1823.

———. "The Style of Scripture as Evidential of its Inspiration." *Works* 3:1–90.

———. *The Theories of Inspiration of the Rev. Daniel Wilson, Rev. Dr. Pye Smith, and the Rev. Dr. Dick, Proved to Be Erroneous: With Remarks on the* Christian Observer *&* Eclectic Review. Edinburgh: Whyte, 1830.

———. *A Treatise on the Figures of Speech*. Dublin: Curry, 1827.

———. *The Truth of the Gospel Demonstrated from the Character of God Manifested in the Atonement: In a Letter to Mr. Richard Carlile*. Edinburgh: Waugh & Innes, 1820.

Bibliography

———. *The Truth of the Gospel Demonstrated from the Character of God Manifested in the Atonement: In a Letter to Mr. Richard Carlile*. 2nd ed. Dublin: Tims, 1826.

———. *The Truth of the Gospel Demonstrated from the Character of God Manifested in the Atonement: In a Letter to Mr. Richard Carlile*. Repr., Dublin: Carson, 1839.

———. *Unitarian Mystery: Or, Reply to Mr Carmichael's Strictures on Mr Carson's Views of Inspiration*. Belfast: Druitt et al., 1840.

———. *A View of the Day of Judgment: As Delineated in the Scriptures*. Belfast: Finlay, 1818.

Carson, George Ledlie, and Matilda Carson Hanna. *Memorials of the Family of Rev. Alexander Carson, LL.D.* Philadelphia: American Baptist Publication Society, 1853.

Carson, James C. L. *The Heresies of the Plymouth Brethren*. Coleraine, UK: M'Combie, 1862.

———. *The Heresies of the Plymouth Brethren*. 3rd ed. London: Houlston & Sons, 1870.

Carson, Robert Haldane. *The Brethren: Their Worship and the Word of God at Open Variance*. London: Stock, 1880.

———. *A Reply to the Late Work of the Rev. Thomas Witherow, on the Ecclesiastical Polity of the New Testament*. Dublin: Carson, 1856.

Castlereagh, Robert Stewart. *Memoirs and Correspondence of Viscount Castlereagh, Second Marquess of Londonderry*. Edited by Charles Vane. 12 vols. London: Colburn, 1848.

Chalmers, Thomas. *On the Miraculous and Internal Evidences of the Christian Revelation, and the Authority of Its Records*. Vols. 3–4 of *The Works of Thomas Chalmers, D.D. & LL.D.* Glasgow: Collins, 1836.

Committee of the Baptist Union. *The Baptists and the Bible Society: Memorial, Relating to the Bengali and Other Versions of the New Testament, Made by Baptist Missionaries in India*. London: Wightman, 1840.

Dick, John. *An Essay on the Inspiration of the Holy Scriptures of the Old and New Testament*. Edinburgh: Ritchie, 1800.

Douglas, John. *Biographical Sketch of the Late Dr. Alexander Carson*. London: Stock, 1884.

Doyle, James Warren. *A Defence by J. K. L. of His Vindication of the Religious and Civil Principles of the Irish Catholics*. Dublin: Coyne, 1824.

———. *Doyle's Letter to the Lord Farnham*. London: Andrews, 1827.

———. *Letters on the State of Education in Ireland: And on Bible Societies; Addressed to a Friend in England*. Dublin: Coyne, 1824.

———. *Miracle, Said to Have Been Wrought by Prince Hohenlohe, in Ireland, on Monday, the 9th of June, 1823*. London: Hatchard and Son, 1823.

———. *A Reply to the Charge of Dr. Elrington, Law Bishop of Leighlin and Ferns, by the Right Rev. Dr. Doyle, Catholic Bishop of Kildare and Leighlin, with His Remarks on the Second Reformation, as It Is Called*. London: Andrews, 1827.

———. *A Vindication of the Religious and Civil Principles of the Irish Catholics: In a Letter, Addressed to His Excellency the Marquis Wellesley*. Dublin: Coyne, 1823.

Drummond, William H. *The Battle of Trafalgar: A Heroic Poem*. Belfast: Smyth and Lyons, 1806.

———. *The Doctrine of the Trinity Founded Neither on Scripture, nor on Reason and Common Sense, but on Tradition and the Infallible Church: An Essay Occasioned by a Late Controversy Between the Rev. Richard T. P. Pope and the Rev. Thomas Maguire*. Belfast: Hodges, 1827.

———. *Doctrine of the Trinity, Founded Neither on Scripture, nor on Reason and Common Sense, but on Tradition and the Infallible Church: An Essay Occasioned by a Late*

Bibliography

———. *Controversy Between the Rev. Richard T. P. Pope and the Rev. Thomas Maguire*. 3rd ed. London: Hunter, 1831.
———. *The Giants' Causeway: A Poem*. Belfast: Smyth, 1811.
———. *The Life of Michael Servetus: The Spanish Physician, Who, for the Alleged Crime of Heresy, Was Entrapped, Imprisoned, and Burned by John Calvin the Reformer, in the City of Geneva, October 27, 1553*. London: Chapman, 1848.
Dudley, C. S. *An Analysis of the System of the Bible Society, Throughout Its Various Parts: Including a Sketch of the Origin and Results of Auxiliary and Branch Societies and Bible Associations; with Hints for Their Better Regulation*. London: Watts, 1821.
Edinburgh Bible Society. *Statement by the Committee of the Edinburgh Bible Society, Relative to the Circulation of the Apocrypha by the British and Foreign Bible Society*. London: Hamilton, Adams, & Co., 1825.
Ewing, Greville. *An Attempt Toward a Statement of the Doctrine of Scripture on Some Disputed Points Respecting the Constitution, Government, Worship, and Discipline of the Church of Christ*. Glasgow: Lang, 1807.
———. *An Essay on Baptism: Being an Inquiry into the Meaning, Form, and Extent of the Administration of that Ordination; With an Appendix*. Glasgow: University Press, 1824.
Fitzpatrick, William John. *The Life, Times, and Correspondence of the Right Rev. Dr. Doyle, Bishop of Kildare and Leighlin*. 2 vols. Dublin: Duffy, 1861.
Fuller, Andrew. *The Gospel Worthy of All Acceptation; or, The Duty of Sinners to Believe in Jesus Christ*. Philadelphia: Cist, 1805.
———. *The Works of the Rev. Andrew Fuller*. 8 vols. Philadelphia: Anderson and Meehan, 1820.
Gaussen, Louis. *Theopneustia: The Plenary Inspiration of the Holy Scriptures*. London: Bagster and Sons, 1841.
———. *Théopneustie; ou Pleine inspiration des Saintes Écritures*. Paris: Delay, 1840.
Glas, John. *The Testimony of the King of Martyrs, Concerning His Kingdom, Explained and Illustrated in Scripture Light*. Edinburgh: Lyon, 1729.
———. *The Testimony of the King of Martyrs*. Vol. 1 of *The Works of Mr. John Glas*. Edinburgh: Donaldson, 1761.
Haldane, Alexander. *Memoirs of the Lives of Robert Haldane of Airthrey, and of His Brother, James Alexander Haldane*. London: Hamilton, Adams, and Co., 1852.
Haldane, James. *Reasons for a Change of Sentiment & Practice on the Subject of Baptism: Containing a Plain View of the Signification of the Word, and of the Persons for Whom the Ordinance Is Appointed; Together with a Full Consideration of the Covenant Made with Abraham, and Its Supposed Connexion with Baptism*. Edinburgh: Ritchie, 1808.
———. *Refutation of the Heretical Doctrine Promulgated by the Rev. Edward Irving: Respecting the Person and Atonement of the Lord Jesus Christ*. Edinburgh: Oliphant, 1829.
———. *A View of the Social Worship and Ordinances Observed by the First Christians, Drawn from the Sacred Scriptures Alone: Being an Attempt to Enforce Their Divine Obligation; And to Represent the Guilt and Evil Consequences of Neglecting Them*. Edinburgh: Ritchie, 1805.
———. *A Vindication of the Proceedings of the Edinburgh Bible Society, Relative to the Apocrypha, Against the Aspersion of the Eclectic Review: In a Letter to the Members of the Committee of the Parent Institution*. London: Hamilton, Adams, and Co., 1825.

Bibliography

———. *The Voluntary Question: Political, Not Religious; A Letter to the Rev. Dr. John Brown, Occasioned by the Allusion in His Recent Work to the Author's Sentiments upon National Churches.* Edinburgh: Whyte, 1839.

Haldane, Robert. *The Authenticity and Inspiration of the Holy Scriptures Considered in Opposition to the Erroneous Opinions That Are Circulated on the Subject.* Edinburgh: Lindsay & Co., 1827.

———. *The Books of the Old and New Testaments, Canonical and Inspired: With Remarks on the Apocrypha.* Boston: American Doctrinal Tract Society, 1840.

———. *The Evidence and Authority of Divine Revelation: Being a View of the Testimony of the Law and the Prophets to the Messiah, with the Subsequent Testimonies.* 2 vols. Edinburgh: Balfour, 1816.

———. *Exposition of the Epistle to the Romans: With Remarks on the Commentaries of Dr. MacKnight, Professor Moses Stuart, and Professor Tholuck.* Enlarged ed. 3 vols. Edinburgh: Whyte & Co., 1842.

———. *Exposition of the Five First Chapters of the Epistle to the Romans: With Remarks on the Commentaries of Dr. MacKnight, Professor Tholuck, and Professor Moses Stuart.* 3 vols. London: Hamilton, Adams, and Co., 1835–39.

———. *Review of the Conduct of the Directors of the British and Foreign Bible Society: Relative to the Aprocrapha, and to Their Administration on the Continent; With an Answer to the Rev. C. Simeon, and Observations on the Cambridge Remarks.* Edinburgh: Allardice and Co., 1825.

Hall, Archibald. *A Treatise on the Faith and Influence of the Gospel.* Glasgow: Collins, 1831.

Hall, Edwin. *An Exposition of the Law of Baptism, as It Regards the Mode and the Subjects.* Norwalk, CT: Weed, 1840.

Henderson, Ebenezer. *An Appeal to the Members of the British and Foreign Bible Society, on the Subject of the Turkish New Testament, Printed at Paris, in 1819: Containing a View of Its History, an Exposure of Its Errors, and Palpable Proofs of the Necessity of Its Suppression.* London: Holdsworth, 1824.

———. *Divine Inspiration; or, The Supernatural Influence Exerted in the Communication of Divine Truth: And Its Special Bearing on the Composition of the Sacred Scriptures.* London: Jackson and Walford, 1836.

———. *A Letter to the Rev. A. Brandram, M. A. on the Meaning of the Word ΒΑΠΤΙΖΩ, and the Manner in Which It Has Been Rendered in Versions Sanctioned by the Bible Society.* London: Jackson and Walford, 1840.

———. *The Turkish New Testament Incapable of Defence, and the True Principles of Biblical Translation Vindicated: In Answer to Professor Lee's "Remarks on Dr. Henderson's Appeal to the Bible Society on the Subject of the Turkish Version of the New Testament, Printed at Paris in 1819."* London: Rivington, 1825.

Jones, William. *Autobiography of the Late William Jones, M.A.* London: Snow, 1846.

———. *An Essay on the Life and Writings of Mr. Abraham Booth.* Liverpool: Smith, 1808.

———. *History of the Waldenses, Connected with a Sketch of the Christian Church from the Time of Christ to the Eighteenth Century.* London: Haddon, 1812.

———. "A Memoir of His Life, Ministry, and Writings." In *Sermons on the Doctrines and Duties of the Christian Life*, by Archibald McLean, iv–cviii. London: N.p., 1817.

Lee, Samuel. *Remarks on Dr. Henderson's Appeal to the Bible Society, on the Subject of the Turkish Version of the New Testament Printed at Paris in 1819.* Cambridge: Smith, 1824.

Bibliography

———. *Some Additional Remarks on Dr. Henderson's Appeal to the Bible Society: In Reply to a Pamphlet Entitled "The Turkish New Testament Incapable of Defence, &c. by the Author of the Appeal."* Cambridge: Deighton & Sons, 1826.

MacKnight, James. *A New Literal Translation from the Original Greek, of All the Apostolical Epistles.* 3 vols. London: Bell & Bradfute et al., 1795.

Matheson, Jessy J. Ewing. *A Memoir of Greville Ewing, Minister of the Gospel, Glasgow.* London: Snow, 1843.

Maxwell-Barry, John [Earl of Farnham]. *Report of the Speeches Delivered at the Reformation Meeting Held at Cavan, on Friday, the 26th Day of January, 1827.* Dublin: Curry, 1827.

———. *A Statement of the Management of the Farnham Estates.* Dublin: Curry, 1830.

McLean, Archibald. *Letters Addressed to John Glas in Answer to His Dissertation on Infant-Baptism.* Glasgow: McLean Junior, 1767.

———. *Sermons on the Doctrines and Duties of the Christian Life.* London: N.p., 1817.

Medway, John. *Memoirs of the Life and Writings of John Pye Smith.* London: Jackson, 1853.

Miller, Samuel. *Infant Baptism Scriptural and Reasonable: And Baptism by Sprinkling or Affusion the Most Suitable and Edifying Mode; In Four Discourses.* Philadelphia: Whetham, 1835.

Moore, George C. *Bigotry Demolished: The Close Communion Baptists Refuted, Examples Exemplified and Christian Union Vindicated.* Toronto: Hunter, Rose & Company, 1880.

———. *The Life of Alexander Carson, LL.D.* New York: Fletcher, 1851.

Munro, John. *Modern Immersion Directly Opposed to Scriptural Baptism, in Reply to Alexander Carson, M.A.* London: Snow, 1842.

Parry, William. *An Inquiry into the Nature and Extent of the Inspiration of the Apostles, and Other Writers of the New Testament.* London: Conder, 1797.

Peel, Robert. *The Speeches of the Late Right Honourable Sir Robert Peel, Bart: Delivered in the House of Commons, with a General Explanatory Index, and a Brief Chronological Summary of the Various Subjects on Which the Speeches Were Delivered.* 4 vols. London: Routledge and Co., 1853.

Plunket, William C., and David Plunket. *The Life, Letters, and Speeches of Lord Plunket.* 2 vols. London: Smith, Elder & Co., 1867.

Protestant, A. *Animadversions on Carson's Reply to Dr. Drummond's Essay on the Trinity.* Dublin: Shaw, 1827.

Sandeman, Robert. *Letters on Theron and Aspasio.* New York: Taylor, 1838.

Schleiermacher, Friedrich. *A Critical Essay on the Gospel of St. Luke.* Translated by Connop Thirlwall. London: Taylor, 1825.

Scott, Thomas. *The Holy Bible: Containing the Old and New Testaments, According to the Authorized Version; With Explanatory Notes and Practical Observations.* 6 vols. Boston: Armstrong, 1823.

Smith, John Pye. *On the Principles of Interpretation As Applied to the Prophecies of Holy Scripture: A Discourse Delivered in the Meeting-House in Fetter Lane . . . with Notes.* London: Holdsworth, 1829.

———. *On the Relation Between the Holy Scriptures and Some Parts of Geological Science.* 2nd ed. London: Jackson and Walford, 1840.

———. *The Scripture Testimony to the Messiah: An Inquiry with a View to a Satisfactory Determination of the Doctrine Taught in the Holy Scriptures Concerning the Person of Christ.* 3 vols. London: Holdsworth and Ball, 1829.

Bibliography

Stevenson, Andrew. *Two Letters, Addressed to the Rev. Alexander Carson: Being an Attempt to Vindicate Presbyterianism from the Aspersions Cast Upon It*. Londonderry: Boyd, 1810.
Taylor, W. Cooke. *Life and Times of Sir Robert Peel*. 4 vols. London: Jackson, Late Fisher, Son, & Co., 1851.
Wardlaw, Ralph. *A Dissertation on the Scriptural Authority, Nature, and Uses of Infant Baptism*. Boston: Peirce and Parker, 1832.
Wesley, John. *A Sufficient Answer, to Letters to the Author of Theron and Aspasio: In a Letter to the Author*. Bristol: Farley, 1757.
Wilson, Daniel. *The Evidences of Christianity: Stated in a Popular and Practical Manner, in a Course of Lectures, on the Authenticity, Credibility, Divine Authority, and Inspiration of the New Testament, Delivered in the Parish Church of St. Mary, Islington*. 2 vols. Boston: Crocker and Brewster, 1829.
Witherow, Thomas. *A Defence of the Apostolic Church, Including an Examination of the Claims of Independency to Be a Scriptural System, in Answer to Rev. R. H. Carson. A Supplement to "The Apostolic Church." A Refutation of Carson's "Reply to the Late Work of the Rev. Thomas Witherow."* Belfast: Shepherd & Aitchison, 1857.
———. *Three Prophets of Our Own: A Lecture Delivered Before the Young Men's Christian Association, Maghera, on Wednesday Evening, January 3, 1855*. Belfast: Morgan, 1855.

Articles

Αληθεια [Alexander Haldane]. "State of Religion at Strasburgh." *Evangelical Magazine and Missionary Chronicle* 4 (1826) 437–38.
Baptist Magazine. "Irish Chronicle." *Baptist Magazine* 30 (1838) 41–47.
———. "List of Baptist Churches in Ireland." *Baptist Magazine* 28 (1836) 548.
———. "Ordinations." *Baptist Magazine* 39 (1847) 775–76.
———. Unsigned review of *Baptism in Its Mode and Subjects*, by Alexander Carson. *Baptist Magazine* 36 (1844) 185–91.
Basel Bible Society. "From the Committee of the Bible Society at Basel to the Committee of the British and Foreign Bible Society." In *The Twenty-Third Report of the British and Foreign Bible Society: With an Appendix, and a List of Subscribers and Benefactors*, 118–20. London: Moyes, 1827.
Beecher, Edward. "Baptism—the Import of βαπτιζω." *American Biblical Repository* 3 (1840) 40–66.
British Review and London Critical Journal. "Bible Society of Ireland." *British Review and London Critical Journal*. 23 (1825) 124–44.
———. Unsigned review of *A Vindication of the Religious and Civil Principles of the Irish Catholics*, by James Warren Doyle. *British Review and London Critical Journal*. 22 (1824) 419–20.
Carson, Alexander. "Character and Empire of Satan." *Works* 1:295–307.
———. "Characteristics of the Style of Scripture as Evidential of its Inspiration." *Works* 3:1–90.
———. "The Doctrine of the Atonement, Set Forth in an Address to the Public, on the Nature and Importance of the Gospel." *Works* 1:1–136.
———. "Faith the Foundation of the Greater Part of Human Knowledge." *Works* 1:401–4.
———. "On Human Certificates of the Excellency of the Scriptures." *Works* 1:386–91.

Bibliography

———. "A Letter to the Emperor Napoleon, Sovereign of Elba, on the Most Important of All Subjects." *Works* 1:279–94.

———. "The Mahometan Fast of Rhamazan." *Works* 1:422–24.

———. "Observations on the Incomprehensibility of God." *Works* 1:241–44.

———. "Remarks on the General Resurrection." *Works* 1:197–206.

———. "Remarks on the Late Miracle: In a Letter to the Rev. Doctor Doyle, Titular Bishop of Kildure and Leighlin." *Works* 2:129–49.

———. "Remarks on the Sanctification of the First Day of the Week." *Works* 1:369–85.

———. "Remarks on the Standard of Divine Truth." *Works* 1:397–400.

———. "The Scheme of Salvation by Law and Grace Irreconcilable with Itself." *Works* 1:418–21.

———. "Solution of the Great Paradox, Exodus xxxiv. 6, 7." *Works* 1:414–17.

———. "The Testimony of the Lord Makes Wise the Simple." *Works* 1:409–13.

———. "The World by Wisdom Knew Not God." *Works* 1:405–8.

Central Prussian Bible Society. "From the Committee of the Central Prussian Bible Society to the Committee of the British and Foreign Bible Society." In *The Twenty-Third Report of the British and Foreign Bible Society: With an Appendix, and a List of Subscribers and Benefactors*, 134–36. London: Moyes, 1827.

Christian Guardian and Church of England Magazine. Unsigned review of *Statement by the Committee of the Edinburgh Bible Society, Relative to the Circulation of the Apocrypha by the British and Foreign Bible Society*, by Edinburgh Bible Society. Unknown vol. (1825) 307–13.

Christian Messenger and Family Magazine. "Items of News." *Christian Messenger and Family Magazine* 3 (1847) 570–74.

Christian Observer. Unsigned review of *The Evidences of Christianity: Stated in a Popular and Practical Manner, in a Course of Lectures, on the Authenticity, Credibility, Divine Authority, and Inspiration of the New Testament, Delivered in the Parish Church of St. Mary, Islington*, by Daniel Wilson. *Christian Observer* 29 (1829) 613–25.

Eclectic Review. Unsigned review of *A Critical Essay on the Gospel of St. Luke*, by Frederick Schleiermacher. *Eclectic Review* 1 (1829) 413–31.

———. Unsigned review of *A Vindication of the Proceedings of the Edinburgh Bible Society, Relative to the Apocrypha, Against the Aspersions of the Eclectic Review: In a Letter to the Members of the Committee of the Parent Institution*, by Alexander Haldane. *Eclectic Review* 24 (1825) 377–406.

Edinburgh Review. Unsigned review of *The Mysteries of Providence, and the Triumphs of Grace*, by unknown author. *Edinburgh Review* 64 (1837) 428–52.

Evangelical Christendom, Christian Work, and the News of the Churches: Also a Monthly Record of the Transactions of the Evangelical Alliance. "New Members." *Evangelical Christendom* 35 (1881) 253.

Frankfort Bible Society. "From the Committee of the Frankfort Bible Society to the Committee of the British and Foreign Bible Society." In *The Twenty-Third Report of the British and Foreign Bible Society: With an Appendix, and a List of Subscribers and Benefactors*, 122. London: Moyes, 1827.

Haldane, Alexander, and John Pye Smith. "Correspondence Between Dr. Smith, and A. Haldane, Esq. in Reference to Professor Haffner, of Strasburgh." *Evangelical Magazine and Missionary Chronicle* 4 (1826) 521–28.

Hanna, William T. C. "Alexander Carson." *Baptist Quarterly Review* 9 (1887) 193–202.

Bibliography

Henshall, J. "Letter from J. Henshall." *Christian Messenger and Family Magazine* 3 (1847) 470–72.
Jones, William. "On Rash and Unguarded Expressions." *New Evangelical Magazine and Theological Review* 3 (1817) 107–8.
———. "Views of the Late Dr. Carson on Church Order." *Primitive Church Magazine* 1 (1844) 562–64.
Krafft. "From the Rev. Mr. Krafft, Secretary of the Cologne Bible Society." In *The Twenty-Third Report of the British and Foreign Bible Society: With an Appendix, and a List of Subscribers and Benefactors*, 121. London: Moyes, 1827.
Macleod, Alexander. "Dr. Carson's Views of Church Order." *Primitive Church Magazine* 2 (1845) 12–13.
Monthly Repository and Review of Theology and General Literature. "Dr. J. P. Smith and Mr. Haldane on the German Rationalists." *Monthly Repository and Review of Theology and General Literature* 1 (1827) 128–33.
———. "Dr. J. P. Smith's Vindication of Dr. Haffner, of Strasburgh." *Monthly Repository and Review of Theology and General Literature* 21 (1826) 749–52.
———. Unsigned review of *A Reply to Dr. Drummond's Essay on the Doctrine of the Trinity, in a Letter to the Author*, by Alexander Carson. *Monthly Repository and Review of Theology and General Literature* 2 (1828) 335–36.
Orthodox Presbyterian. "Dr. Chalmers and the Divinity Class in the University of Edinburgh." *Orthodox Presbyterian* 1 (1830) 334–38, 374–77.
———. Unsigned review of *The Theories of Inspiration of the Rev. Daniel Wilson, Rev. Dr. Pye Smith, and the Rev. Dr. Dick, Proved to Be Erroneous: With Remarks on the Christian Observer & Eclectic Review*, by Alexander Carson. *Orthodox Presbyterian* 2 (1831) 68–71.
Presbyterian Review and Religious Journal. Unsigned review of *Baptism in Its Mode and Subjects Considered, and the Arguments of Mr. Ewing and Dr. Wardlaw Refuted*, by Alexander Carson. *Presbyterian Review and Religious Journal* 1 (1832) 516–37.
Primitive Church Magazine. "Announcement." *Primitive Church Magazine* 2 (1845) 224.
Smith, John Pye. "Extracts and Hints, Illustrating the State of Religion on the Continent." Pt. 6. *Evangelical Magazine and Missionary Chronicle* 4 (1826) 574–76.
———. "Extracts and Hints on the State of Religion on the Continent." Pt. 4. *Evangelical Magazine and Missionary Chronicle* 4 (1826) 391–92.
———. "Extracts and Hints on the State of Religion on the Continent." Pt. 5. *Evangelical Magazine and Missionary Chronicle* 4 (1826) 480–82.
———. "Reply to Alethia: On Dr. Haffner's Introduction to the Reading of the Bible." *Evangelical Magazine and Missionary Chronicle* 4 (1826) 475–78.
———. "State of Religion on the Continent. No. I. To the Editor." *Evangelical Magazine and Missionary Chronicle* 4 (1826) 25–27.
———. "State of Religion on the Continent. No. II. Facts and Observations Relative to the Circulation and Right Use of the Scriptures." *Evangelical Magazine and Missionary Chronicle* 4 (1826) 65–67.
———. "State of Religion on the Continent. No. III. On the Circulation and Right Use of the Scriptures." *Evangelical Magazine and Missionary Chronicle* 4 (1826) 199–200.
T. K. "On the Inspiration of Scripture." *Christian Examiner, and Church of Ireland Magazine* 11 (1831) 501–3.

[Young, John?]. "Memoir of Alexander Carson, LL.D. Minister of the Gospel, in Tubbermore, Ireland." In *Baptism in its Mode and Subjects*, by Alexander Carson, xxiii–xlvii. 5th ed. Philadelphia: American Baptist Publication Society, 1850.

Manuscripts in Public Records Office of Northern Ireland

Bleakly, J. "Fair Sheets for Memoir." MIC 6C/13, Box 42/I/4.
District Registry of Londonderry. "Ireland Probate, from the District Registry of Londonderry, for James Spencer Knox." D1118/14/K/18.
Fagan, Thomas. "Fair Sheets by Thomas Fagan." MIC 6C/13, Box 42/I/3.
Stokes, J. "Memoir of J. Stokes." MIC 6C/13, Box 42/I/2.
"School Statistics." MIC 6C/13, Box 42/I/5.

SECONDARY SOURCES
Books

Bebbington, D. W. *Evangelicalism in Modern Britain: A History from the 1730s to the 1980s*. Repr., London: Routledge, 2002.
Boase, Frederic. *Modern English Biography Containing Many Thousand Concise Memoirs of Persons Who Have Died During the Years 1851–1900, with an Index of the Most Interesting Matter*. 6 vols. Truro, UK: Netherton and Worth, 1908.
Bowen, Desmond. *The Protestant Crusade in Ireland, 1800–70: A Study of Protestant-Catholic Relations Between the Act of Union and Disestablishment*. Dublin: Gill and Macmillan, 1978.
Brown, A. L., and Michael Moss. *The University of Glasgow: 1451–1996*. Edinburgh: Edinburgh University Press, 1996.
Brown, Stewart J. *The National Churches of England, Ireland, and Scotland, 1801–1846*. Oxford: Oxford University Press, 2001.
Claydon, Tony, and Ian McBride, eds. *Protestantism and National Identity: Britain and Ireland, c. 1650–c. 1850*. Cambridge: Cambridge University Press, 1998.
Day, Angélique, and Patrick McWilliams, eds. *Parishes of County Londonderry XI 1821, 1833, 1836–7, South Londonderry*. Vol. 31 of *Ordnance Survey Memoirs of Ireland*. Belfast: Institute of Irish Studies in association with the Royal Irish Academy, 1995.
Elliott, L. R., and Harlan Julius Matthews. *Centennial Story of Texas Baptists*. Dallas: Executive Board of the Baptist General Convention of Texas, 1936.
Ganiel, Gladys. *Evangelicalism and Conflict in Northern Ireland: Contemporary Anthropology of Religion*. New York: Palgrave Macmillan, 2008.
Gordon, James M. *Evangelical Spirituality*. London: SPCK, 1991.
Greaves, Richard L. *God's Other Children: Protestant Nonconformists and the Emergence of Denominational Churches in Ireland, 1660–1700*. Stanford, CA: Stanford University Press, 1997.
Gribben, Crawford, and Andrew R. Holmes. *Protestant Millennialism, Evangelicalism, and Irish Society, 1790–2005*. Basingstoke, UK: Palgrave Macmillan, 2006.

Bibliography

Haldane, Alexander. *Memoirs of the Lives of Robert Haldane of Airthrey, and of His Brother, James Alexander Haldane.* London: Hamilton, Adams, and Co., 1852.

Harris, Harriet A. *Fundamentalism and Evangelicals.* Oxford Theological Monographs. Oxford: Clarendon, 1998.

Haykin, Michael A. G., ed. *The British Particular Baptists, 1638–1910.* 5 vols. Springfield, MO: Particular Baptist, 2003.

Haykin, Michael A. G., and Kenneth J. Stewart, eds. *The Emergence of Evangelicalism: Exploring Historical Continuities.* Nottingham: Inter-Varsity, 2008.

Hempton, David, and Myrtle Hill. *Evangelical Protestantism in Ulster Society 1740–1890.* London: Routledge, 1992.

Holmes, Andrew R. *The Shaping of Ulster Presbyterian Belief and Practice, 1770–1840.* Oxford: Oxford University Press, 2006.

Holmes, Finlay G. *Our Irish Presbyterian Heritage.* Belfast: Publ. Committee of the Presbyterian Church in Ireland, 1985.

Kentucky University. *Catalogue of Kentucky University, Lexington, Kentucky, 1891–92.* Lexington: Marshall, 1891.

Nettles, Tom J. *The Modern Era.* Vol. 3 of *The Baptists: Key People in Forming a Baptist Identity.* Fearn, UK: Mentor, 2007.

Nockles, Peter Benedict. *The Oxford Movement in Context: Anglican High Churchmanship, 1760–1857.* Cambridge: Cambridge University Press, 1994.

Presbyterian Historical Society of Ireland. *A History of Congregations in the Presbyterian Church in Ireland, 1610–1982.* Belfast: Presbyterian Historical Society of Ireland, 1982.

Public Records Office of Northern Ireland. *An Irish Genealogical Source: A Guide to Church Records.* Belfast: Crown, 2010.

Reid, James Seaton. *History of the Presbyterian Church in Ireland: Comprising the Civil History of the Province of Ulster, from the Accession of James the First: With a Preliminary Sketch of the Progress of the Reformed Religion in Ireland During the Sixteenth Century, and an Appendix, Consisting of Original Papers.* Edited by W. D. Killen. 3 vols. Belfast: Mullan, 1867.

Rice, Edwin Wilbur. *The Sunday-School Movement, 1780–1917, and the American Sunday-School Movement, 1817–1917.* Philadelphia: American Sunday-School Union, 1917.

Sell, Alan P. F., et al., eds. *Protestant Nonconformist Texts.* Vol. 2 of *The Eighteenth Century.* Aldershot, UK: Ashgate, 2006.

Smith, John Howard. *The Perfect Rule of the Christian Religion: A History of Sandemanianism in the Eighteenth Century.* Albany: State University of New York Press, 2008.

Starr, Edward, ed. *A Baptist Bibliography: Being a Register of Printed Material by and About Baptists; Including Works Written Against Baptists.* 25 vols. Rochester, NY: American Baptist Historical Society, 1959.

Stowe, Lyman Beecher. *Saints, Sinners and Beechers.* Indianapolis: Bobbs, 1934.

Talbot, Brian R. *The Search for a Common Identity: The Origins of the Baptist Union of Scotland 1800–1870.* Studies in Baptist History and Thought 9. Carlisle, UK: Paternoster, 2003.

Torbet, Robert G. *A History of the Baptists.* Valley Forge, PA: Judson, 2000.

Wiles, Maurice F. *Archetypal Heresy: Arianism Through the Centuries.* Oxford: Clarendon, 1996.

Wolffe, John. *The Expansion of Evangelicalism: The Age of Wilberforce, More, Chalmers and Finney.* History of Evangelicalism 2. Downers Grove, IL: IVP Academic, 2007.

Bibliography

Yates, Nigel. *The Religious Condition of Ireland, 1770–1850*. Oxford: Oxford University Press, 2006.

Articles

Acheson, Alan. "The Evangelical Revival in Ireland: A Study in Christology." *Churchman* 108 (1994) 143–53.
Atherstone, Andrew. Review of *The Emergence of Evangelicalism: Exploring Historical Continuities*, edited by Michael A. G. Haykin and Kenneth J. Stewart. *Churchman* 123 (2009) 89–92.
Briggs, Robert. "Alexander Carson." In *The British Particular Baptists, 1638–1910*, edited by Michael A. G. Haykin, 3:150–69. Springfield, MO: Particular Baptist, 2003.
Clouse, Robert G. Review of *Evangelicalism in Modern Britain: A History from the 1730s to the 1980s*, by David W. Bebbington. *American Historical Review* 96 (1991) 165–66.
Hanna, William T. C. "Alexander Carson." *Baptist Quarterly Review* 9 (1887) 193–202.
Kingdon, D. P. "The Theology of Alexander Carson." *Irish Baptist Historical Society* 2 (1970) 51–61.
Larson, Timothy. "The Reception Given *Evangelicalism in Modern Britain* Since Its Publication in 1989." In *The Emergence of Evangelicalism: Exploring Historical Continuities*, edited by Michael A. G. Haykin and Kenneth J. Stewart, 21–36. Nottingham: Inter-Varsity, 2008.
Neudecker, Hannah. "From Istanbul to London? Albertus Bobovius' Appeal to Isaac Basire." In *The Republic of Letters and the Levant*, edited by Alastair Hamilton et al., 173–96. Intersections 5. Leiden: Brill, 2005.
———. "Wojciech Bobowski and His Turkish Grammar (1666)." *Dutch Studies in Near Eastern Languages and Literatures* 2 (1996) 169–92.
Stewart, Kenneth J. "The Evangelical Doctrine of Scripture, 1650–1850: A Re-Examination of David Bebbington's Theory." In *The Emergence of Evangelicalism: Exploring Historical Continuities*, edited by Michael A. G. Haykin and Kenneth J. Stewart, 394–413. Nottingham: Inter-Varsity, 2008.
Thompson, Joshua. "The Communion Controversy and Irish Baptists." *Irish Baptist Historical Society Journal* 20 (1987–88) 26–35.
Wolffe, John. Review of *Evangelicalism in Modern Britain: A History from the 1730s to the 1980s*, by David W. Bebbington. *History* 75 (1990) 346–47.

Dissertations and Theses

Noonan, John A. "Baptists in Ireland: A Historical Study with Particular Reference to Their Involvement in Educational Endeavours 1649–1798." MEd thesis, University College Cork, National University of Ireland, 1974.
Van Bemmelen, Peter Maarten. "Issues in Biblical Inspiration: Sanday and Warfield." ThD thesis, Andrews University, Seventh-Day Adventist Theological Seminary, 1987.

www.ingramcontent.com/pod-product-compliance
Lightning Source LLC
Chambersburg PA
CBHW071456150426
43191CB00008B/1370